THE RISING

THE RISING

MURDER, HEARTBREAK, AND THE
POWER OF HUMAN RESILIENCE
IN AN AMERICAN TOWN

RYAN D'AGOSTINO

CROWN PUBLISHERS

NEW YORK

All rights reserved.
Published in the United States by Crown Publishers,
an imprint of the Crown Publishing Group,
a division of Penguin Random House LLC, New York.
www.crownpublishing.com

CROWN is a registered trademark and the Crown colophon
is a trademark of Penguin Random House LLC.

Parts of this book were adapted from pieces that originally appeared in
Esquire, and selected photographs were previously published in *Esquire.*

The publisher and author are grateful to the Petit family
for the use of their personal photographs, which appear
on pages 28, 33, 34, 36, 39, 43, 54, 58, 62, and 199.

Photographs on pages 113, 122, 226, and 239 by João Canziani.

Photograph on page 22 by John Woike Photography.

Library of Congress Cataloging-in-Publication Data
D'Agostino, Ryan.
The rising / Ryan D'Agostino.
pages cm
1. Murder—Connecticut—Cheshire. 2. Petit, William
Arthur. 3. Loss (Psychology). 4. Grief. I. Title.
HV6534.C44D34 2015
364.152'3092—dc23
[B]
2015009403

ISBN 978-0-8041-4016-4
eBook ISBN 978-0-8041-4017-1

Printed in the United States of America

Jacket photograph by Keith Hayes

2 4 6 8 10 9 7 5 3 1

First Edition

FOR MY PARENTS,

JOHN AND SHEILA D'AGOSTINO

CONTENTS

THE RISING

What is your life?
It is even a vapor that appears for a little time
and then vanishes away.

—James 4:14, tweeted by Bill Petit, 2013

J UST LOOK at this garden. Bill Petit raised these vibrant plants from when they were seedlings. Raised them with help from his daughters, Hayley and Michaela. The kids actually did pull a weed now and then.

The base of the memorial garden is behind the sunporch at the old brick mansion where Bill's parents live, Barbara and Bill Sr. They're in their eighties now, but they keep the big house clean and orderly, and they encouraged Bill to plant this garden while he was living here in those years after the tragedy. He designed it so the flowers, bushes, and small trees would form the rough shape of a heart—they curve up and around symmetrically before meeting at the center of the heart, where Bill built a . . . what's the word?

"I wanna say trellis," Bill says, and shakes his head. "Not called a trellis. What's it called?"

Bill is walking through the garden with his new wife, Christine, a woman as vibrant as an acre of flowers. She's a photographer, and that's how they met. Well, kind of. They first met at the country club—she worked there, he played golf there. Christine was the club's marketing director and, to earn extra money, also tended bar in the Founders Room, a cellar hangout where portraits of past club presidents lined the dark walls. She didn't know who Bill Petit was when he would come in, which is to say that she didn't know he was "Bill Petit." She didn't know that his wife and two daughters had been murdered in their home after being tortured for hours while Bill, who'd been bludgeoned in the head, was tied up in the basement. Christine was living out of the country when it happened and had missed the headlines and the incessant local news coverage on television. She knew only that this guy Bill was a member of the country club, and she knew she thought he was handsome.

He would come in with his friend Ron after a round of golf, and they would talk a little at the bar. Bill would order a Diet Coke with three cherries. He and Christine might have flirted, the best he knew how after all these years. Some of the other women who worked at the club, Christine's friends, noticed and smiled, but they didn't say anything to Christine.

Ron noticed, too.

"How about her?" Ron said to Bill one Sunday afternoon after eighteen holes, with a little smile. "The girl behind the bar."

Bill shrugged. He and Ron had known each other for forty years. A lot went unsaid.

"Not called a trellis. What's it called?"

"Arbor?" offers Christine.

They are arm in arm. Bill is still searching for the word.

"*Arch*," he says at last. "The heart meets at an arch. Oh, and there are some big lights up on that tree. There were big lights on those trees over there, too, but they came down in the last storm. And over there, that's a—I was gonna say ambrosia, but it's not that."

Christine says, "Rhododendron?"

"No, no. Mountain laurels? No." Bill is scratching his chin, staring at the plants. He doesn't like not being able to call up the name. He likes knowing every name. In Latin. It's not that he has any lingering head injuries from the attack, he just can't think of the name.

"That's a mountain laurel or a rhodie, isn't it?" says Christine, ever helpful.

"No, you're 0 for 2," Bill ribs her. "It's a . . . crap. It's not crap, it's—well, anyway, those are *Scabiosa* over there. Button flowers."

"It's *not* a mountain laurel?"

"No, not even close, dear."

"Get a book out."

This is their banter. It's old-married-couple talk. They poke each other playfully, constantly trying to make the other one laugh or at least to tease out a smile. Around her, Bill's own laughter surprises him. He had thought that all of that—quick jokes, laughter, happiness itself—was lost to him for good.

"Artemisia? No. Arte . . . *andromeda.*"

Christine was nervous that day a few years ago when she came over to take pictures of this garden. It was her first assignment as volunteer photographer for the Petit Family Foundation, the charity Bill established in memory of his wife and daughters. She liked Bill, but she didn't know he liked her, too. She thought *maybe,* but . . . then, as they were walking through the garden the day she photographed it—Bill pointing out the different species, Christine taking pictures—he stopped at one point, looked at her, and reached up and touched her earring. Her heart jumped. She walked away, started taking pictures again.

"I was like, *whoa!* I gotta go!" she says today.

Bill rolls his eyes and smiles when he hears her retell the story.

"I just asked you where you got 'em or something," he says.

"I know," she says. "But—you were closer than normal."

"Okay."

"It was one of my favorite moments."

He looks right at her, smiles, says softly, "Okay."

They get in the car after their stroll and Bill scans the radio, nixing songs, playing deejay. "Nope . . . nope . . . nope!" The road follows the meanderings of the Farmington River, and he's on a stretch with no stoplights, speed limit fifty, cruising along. "Colin Hay!" Bill has a near-photographic memory and knows Hay was the lead singer of Men at Work, and the car fills with his acoustic rendition of "Who Can It Be Now?" Bill lets it play. Dense, leafless trees fan out in triangles from either side of the road like a bow tie. Thin horizontal white and gray clouds lash the baby-blue midwinter sky.

"Nice blue," says Bill.

"Look at the layers," says Christine.

They drive on for a minute without talking.

Then Bill says, "Farmington tiramisu."

Down Unionville Avenue, getting closer to Plainville, roads he could drive blindfolded.

"My dad and my uncle Charlie used to run this package store here," he says. "And that's where I used to work when I was sixteen, that shop. Making sandwiches for the workers at Atlantic Pipe."

Christine smiles and says he sure doesn't make sandwiches anymore.

"I got paid for it," he replies. "You pay me, I'll make you a sandwich."

"I'll keep washing your socks."

"I'll just buy new socks."

This joking around with his new wife, the everyday back and forth, is often what helps Bill get through the day. Talking to the radio, saying whatever comes to mind, trading quips. It's so normal, banal even, and yet it's essential. He never thought he would get this part back.

Unionville turns into North Washington, and there's a cemetery on the left, across from a gas station.

"This is the cemetery the girls are buried in," Christine says, a note of sweet helpfulness in her voice. "We could probably drive by there on the way back."

Bill is impassive and doesn't say anything at first.

He is often silent. In fact, silence is the thing you notice first about Bill Petit, because for him silence is almost a character trait. His ability to keep his feelings silent is the hardest thing to understand about him, and it is the source of his great strength. Five years ago, two strangers broke into his home and destroyed everything that mattered to him. Raped and strangled his wife, Jennifer. Set a fire that took the lives of both his children and engulfed his home, to which he never returned. They beat him almost to death. Today, it is the very depth of his silence that has sustained him, that has helped him to go on living. That and the people around him, the people in this community, the people who have known him for the whole of his fifty-six years and who would do just about anything for him.

He drives on, the cemetery disappearing in the rearview mirror.

Look at his face: unchanged, showing nothing. His head, held together by scars gone pale, faces straight ahead at the road, always straight ahead.

"If it's still light out," Christine says. Bill slows down for a light, flicks his eyes up into the mirror at the traffic behind him, at the graveyard.

"Yeah," he says, in almost a whisper.

IT'S ALMOST ten o'clock in the morning, but the sun has never quite come out. A warm rain falls, soaking the midsummer-green grass and bobbing the heads of the orange flowers in the front yard.

Bill is tied to the steel support pole in the basement of his home. Plastic zip ties slice into his wrists, which are bound behind his back, around the pole. He has been trying for hours to free himself, sliding up and down. Blood flows steadily from the gashes in his head, pooling on the concrete floor around him, and he is hoping the up-and-down motion will keep the blood pressure steady throughout his body. He is a doctor, so he knows that he is losing a dangerous amount of blood.

His body feels like it weighs a thousand pounds. His ankles are bound together tight, first with plastic zip ties and then clothesline. There is some kind of cloth over his head, fuzzing his view of his own basement so that it hovers around him as a nightmarish otherworld. In a strange gesture he can't make sense of, the two men who have broken into his home shoved a couple of pillows under him on the hard floor. The cushions are now stained a deep red.

He works his tired legs underneath him so he's in a squat position, then he pushes, pushes, pushes until his six-foot-four, fifty-year-old frame begins to slide slowly up the pole, sweat and blood stinging his eyes, his head throbbing. The plastic ties cut into his ankles until the flesh is raw. He contorts his wrists in an attempt to leverage the weight of the pushing motion to loosen the bindings so that he might free himself. If he can break free, he might be able to save the girls.

Then he hears the thumping.

Coming from upstairs—the living room, as best he can tell. He decides it must be the men ransacking the house, gathering the things they plan to steal. But then . . . did he just hear someone moan? He thinks he did. The wounds and the fatigue have left him unsure of anything, anything at all. He might even be dead—being pounded in the head with a bat has left him without much blood and no clear thoughts. But he desperately tries to hold it together. He sits, opens his eyes wide, trying to summon cognition.

He hears it again.

"Hey!" he yells. Something like "hey"—he has so little strength, it comes out as a garbled cry, something other than language.

A man's voice responds from upstairs.

"Don't worry," the voice says. "It's all going to be over in a couple of minutes."

Bill is working furiously now. He knows this is the moment. These men are going to shoot him and his family—or something. It's going to end badly, he knows that. He knows he is too weak to take on two men who have at least one gun and a baseball bat. He can barely see through the blood clouding his eyes. His body doesn't feel like his own. There's no way he can break the ankle ties—the more he twists and tries to free himself, the more they constrict. But if he can break the rope and the ties around his hands, he will be off the pole and he could go next door for help. Dave Simcik's house. He'll somehow get over to Dave's and call the police.

He rubs his wrists together. The ties dig deeper into the skin, but still he rubs, desperately twisting his hands to try to pull the clothesline off while trying to bend and weaken the plastic.

Finally the plastic breaks and the ties burst off. He is free.

He climbs up out of the basement bulkhead door into the yard and rolls his body across the grass to his neighbor's driveway, fifty feet that feel like a mile right now. His ankles are still bound, but his hands are free, and when he reaches the driveway, he bangs on the garage door with all the force of his whole life. After a minute, the door opens and Dave appears. *Thank God.* But Dave, his neighbor for eighteen years, looks down at Bill, a beaten, soaking-wet man lying in his driveway covered with blood, and doesn't recognize him. Asks, "Can I help you, sir?"

Bill says, "Dave! It's Bill. Call 911! Quick. *Quick.*"

It seems like only a few seconds before a cop appears out of the rain and is standing over Bill, ordering him to stay down. Then another.

The first one, his gun still drawn, his arms bolt stiff, his eyes pivoting between Bill and Bill's home, shouts, "Who's in the house?"

"The girls," Bill gasps through the rain.

The officer repeats himself, as if needing more information, or as if he had expected a different answer. His voice is urgent and impatient, the voice of an officer in an emergency: *"Who's in the house?"*

Bill yells up at him, "The girls! The girls are in the house!"

WHAT A LIFE MEANS

THREE YEARS later, in the summer of 2010, a couple of the morning radio shows in Hartford aired brief interviews with a special guest, Dr. William Petit. He talked about how his life was going, talked about his beloved family, and talked about the upcoming 5K road race that would benefit the Petit Family Foundation, which he and others had established in their memory.

If you lived in the state, you remembered Dr. Petit. That summer of 2007, the headlines had dominated the local news for weeks. The details were too frightening for some people to follow in the newspapers and on the evening news. But everyone knew that what happened to the Petit family was about the worst thing that could happen to a family. And for the father to have survived was astonishing and, at first, confusing. As is characteristic of the Internet—all high velocity and few facts—some people wondered whether Petit himself had somehow played a role in the attack. But the newspapers added more and more facts to the story each day. The fact, for example, that the two perpetrators were small-time criminals who met at a halfway house. That one of them had seen the mother and younger daughter at a supermarket and followed them home. That the father was beaten in the head repeatedly with a bat, the eleven-year-old raped, she and her sister tied to their beds to suffocate and burn to death, their mother—the man's wife—strangled on the living-room floor.

And pretty soon the conspiracy theories quieted and the fever dreams went back to their dark corners of the Internet, and the dawning realization of what had happened that Sunday night in

Cheshire was perhaps even more frightening: This monstrous crime was a random act. It could have happened to any family. But of all the families in all the houses on all the quiet streets in all the towns in every state across the whole of this country and in the entire world, on that night, it happened to the Petits of Sorghum Mill Drive.

And now here was Bill Petit, sounding pretty upbeat on the radio, spreading the word about the road race for the foundation he had established in his family's memory, to support the kind of good works they had done.

But how?

How was he not living under a rock somewhere, shut off from the world? ("I did live under a rock, for a long time," he would say.) How was he not only alive but, apparently, attempting to live a life? From where had he found the strength to drive to the radio studio and talk to the world, in a voice that was as strong as he could make it, about the third annual Petit Family Foundation 5K road race?

How does a man come to be like Bill Petit?

William Arthur Petit Jr. is not a particularly easy man to get to know. He does not emote, and isn't interested in offering elaborate explanations of his psychological state or his emotional makeup. Or perhaps he doesn't know exactly how to do those things. But to get to know his character and the circumstances that produced him is to understand something of the nature of human fortitude, that quality that enables us, or some of us, to endure the very worst of what's possible on earth, and to go on living. To understand Bill Petit is, in part, to understand how it is possible to rise up from the deepest reaches of depression and hopelessness under one's own strength.

Petit is not conversant in the language of emotional recovery, and in fact it is his emotional reticence that saw him through this ordeal. Silence was a habit, in a way, a habit he kept up because it seemed to help him get through anything. On the surface he might appear to embody many features of the American male stereotype: silent, stoic, hardworking, uncomplaining, emotionally limited. But these qualities were evident in his boyhood, when he could be left to manage in his father's corner grocery store even before he could drive; in high school, when he worked hard enough to get accepted to an Ivy League college; and years later, when he established his own medical practice with his name over the door, working eighteen hours a day to build it and build his own career as an endocrinologist whose reputation was known well beyond his small town.

Before the tragedy, he was a stressed-out doctor with little time for friends or hobbies but was lucky enough to have a family life that restored him. And even now, in their absence, they restore him still. The memories of his daughters and his wife, and his confidence in what they would want him to do, proved to be a mighty and essential source of clarity and strength. He leaned on their memories, asked them questions in his mind, and knew their answers with absolute certainty.

To witness the resurrection of Bill Petit is also to understand the power of community, especially in small-town America. "You've got to understand this place. It was a good place," his friend Ron Bucchi says of Plainville, Connecticut, the town they grew up in together in the early 1960s, which is only about fifteen minutes from Cheshire. "It was a safe place. Ride your bike to the park. Play. You just had a sense of community." In some ways, that place and those people saved Petit. His parents had always been involved in their town, teaching Bill and his siblings that it was important to volunteer. Later, when he established the Petit Family Foundation, hundreds of volunteers gave thousands of hours to the early work of setting it up, and then the even more demanding work of sustaining it.

"People are kind," Petit says. It has become a pattern in Petit's life, this simple belief that if you give, people will give back. It was an article of faith with him and his wife, Jennifer. They instilled it in their daughters, and he speaks about it today when he makes appearances as the public face of his foundation. His reflex to help, and the townspeople's reflex to help him, is rooted deeply in the community that raised him.

People who know what happened to Petit often seem awestruck when they see him in person. If they have the courage to go up to him in public, strangers sometimes shake his hand. Or they just stare or they whisper to the person next to them, filled with wonder about what it's like to be him. Petit used to live what was in many ways an ordinary life: demanding job, devoted family, three-bedroom house in the suburbs, golf on Saturdays, church on Sundays. Nice. Well-off, but not rich and not extravagant. Many people who heard about the murders look for themselves in the lives of Bill and Jennifer. They wonder what they would have done that night, God forbid, and what they would have done if, like Bill, they had emerged from those horrors alive.

And yet, for Bill Petit, life was not ruined. Instead, Petit rather miraculously looked depravity in the face and came away from the experience with an essential piece of wisdom: that people are basically good.

What kind of man survives what he survived and believes *that*? Where did he come from?

EDUCATION

1957–1980

WHEN BILLY Petit was still in diapers, he went missing one morning. He couldn't have been more than two years old. His brother Glenn, just a baby, lay sleeping in his crib. His mother, Barbara, looked all over the house, calling Billy's name as calmly as she could, trying not to let the panic rise in her voice. Barbara is as even-keeled as they come, gets everything done without a fuss. And organized. She keeps her linen tablecloths pressed and hanging in a closet like vestments.

Oh Lord, Billy. Where the heck was he? Barbara pushed through the screen door out into the yard, saying her boy's name again and again. He couldn't have got far, and anyway someone would have seen him toddling along. Billy's uncle Charlie—his dad's brother— lived down the street. Barbara's aunt and uncle were across the street. Everybody had a lot of kids, everybody knew everybody, and *everybody* knew the Petits. This was around 1959, when there was a comforting sameness to everyday life in Plainville, the small-town assurance that each day would be pretty much like the day before, even if the day before wasn't anything special. There was gossip, like anywhere, but it was a hardworking town, a tough little place, proud that the rest of Connecticut seemed indifferent to its very existence.

Finally, Barbara found her son. He was next door. The neighbors grew strawberries behind their house, and little Billy had somehow crawled out of the house and was sitting on the grass, easy as you please, eating the berries, his tiny hands covered in sticky, sweet juice.

Bill Sr., Billy's dad, grew up on Broad Street, too, during the Depression. His family didn't have much money, and a few of the neighborhood boys used to work at the corner store, near where Main Street cut across the railroad tracks, sacking potatoes for a nickel a bag—their candy money. One day years later, after he graduated from Plainville High School, and after he served in the Marines, and after he worked, saved, planned, and worked some more, Bill Petit Sr. would own that corner store where he used to sack potatoes as a boy. He would work so hard that he'd own a lot of other businesses around Plainville, too. After he rose from a life of nothing to become a prominent local businessman, people would joke that the Petits owned the whole damn town.

When Billy got older, he and his three brothers and a sister who came along later roamed the Broad Street neighborhood with baseball bats and Whiffle balls and basketballs, collecting other kids for epic games on Hemingway Street—there was no traffic on Hemingway then, and hardly any on Broad Street even—until everyone's mothers called them all home for dinner. Or they would run through the woods to Norton Park. In the winter they ice-skated there, and in the summer they took swimming lessons. The park had once been the backyard of a wealthy local man named Charles Norton. The sprawling field sloped down from the mighty Georgian brick house he built in 1923, the biggest house in town.

One day, after Billy grew up and had a family of his own, Bill Petit Sr. would own that, too, and his grandchildren would run through its halls and across its lawn.

People had lived in Plainville straight through since the 1650s, and you got the feeling that the folks here now—there were twelve thousand or so around the time Billy was born—were not all that different from the first few souls who settled the place. When you talk to people who lived there when Bill was growing up, they talk about helping one another out. That, they say, is how everyone gets by. Hanna, Bill's sister, says the times seemed different then.

Everyone wasn't so caught up in their own separate lives, and the mere fact that you came from the same town as someone else mattered. Neighbors lent and borrowed and swapped and came over to watch the kids if you needed it. Billy observed all of this—the grown-ups counting on one another, coming and going from one another's houses. Plainville people knew right from wrong, put God and country first, didn't spit into the wind, and all the rest. When locals talk about the way the place used to be around 1960, they use words like *wholesome*.

Bill Sr. loved the town. He served it in one way or another for the better part of forty years—town council, board of education, chamber of commerce, Downtown Merchants Association. Barbara, too. She helped found the Plainville Historical Society and served on the library board, the Republican Town Committee, the Plainville Art League, the Athletic Backers Club, the Ladies Guild at Our Lady of Mercy, Little League, the Visiting Nurses. They both did a lot for the community, and the community would return the favor one day. There always seemed to be people at the Petit house, dropping something off, holding meetings, chatting about this issue or that. Local politics was a big thing. Hanna remembers being upstairs as a kid, listening to the grown-ups as they talked downstairs. "It was always about community," she says. "I think people fight more now. It's more left versus right, and back then it was, What can we do to make this a better place to live?"

Barbara Petit wasn't strict, but she ran an orderly house. The days were stitched together with routine. She always posted a chore chart on the refrigerator. With five kids, you had to. She liked structure, organization, predictability—Billy would end up like her in those ways. Bill Sr. went into business with his brother Charlie, starting with that corner grocery store. They bought a flower shop, a liquor store, a video store, and a chain of convenience stores. When Billy was fourteen, his father used to leave him in the grocery by himself—the one where the older Petit had sacked potatoes as a boy—to run the store. He's so *mature,* Barbara's friends would tell her. He was trustworthy, but it was more than that. He watched his father at work, and he used to try to be like him. Bill Sr.'s voice was deep as a gravel pit and he never raised it. He was pragmatic and equable and friendly, and his son tried to be the same way. By that time Billy was at least six foot two. A rawboned teenager, he already had the presence of a man, not only because of his height but also because he was quiet and respectful and could crack a dry joke, and if there was some problem, he tried to solve it. Standing at the till, selling milk to the ladies running their errands and cigarettes to the men after their lunches at the Main Street Diner, Billy never flinched. He had wisdom, which seemed impossible for a fourteen-year-old kid from Plainville, and yet there it was, in the set of his eyes.

Even at ten or eleven, Billy'd had a way about him—smarts, the old-timers called it. Bill Sr. says it was nothing he and Barbara taught him, or any of their other kids. But, for example, when they went on family vacations, the seven of them jammed into the car up to Vermont or someplace, they wouldn't always have reservations for a place to stay. So they winged it. Bill Sr. would pull into the parking lot of whatever decent-looking motel they could find when the sun was starting to set, and it was Billy he would send in to the office to ask about the rooms and what kind of price they could work out. Billy would stride inside and negotiate a good rate while Pops kept the car idling.

From the adults in his life, Billy picked up the value of keeping your feelings inside and just doing. Later this would make him seem opaque, almost unknowable, to some people, but as a boy and a young man it translated into a work ethic that surprised even his parents. "Definitely a self-starter," Big Bill says. "And I don't know where that came from. People see how well he does and they say, 'Well, you raised him right, you must have done this and that.' And

I say, 'We raised him, sure—you know, he lived in our house.' But I didn't go to college and didn't have that education. I didn't say to him, 'Bill, you've got to do this, that, and that.'" Bill and Barbara were plenty proud of all of their children, and they were all pretty smart, but Billy just went after his goals with a cool ferocity that his father didn't recognize even in himself. And when Billy got what he wanted, he would spread his mouth into a handsome, thin-lipped grin—not smug, but pleased, a grin that said, "Nothin' to it."

Once—that's how many times Hanna recalls Billy getting in trouble at home: "Mom says the only time was when he decided to light matches—he went behind the hutch in the dining room. My mother was pretty in tune with everything that went on in the house. She had the ears, she had the eyes, and she never would have suspected it was Billy. But she caught him, and he confessed, and that was the end of that."

There was mischief here and there as he got older. He and Glenn, his brother a year younger, shared a room, and Billy figured out how to lock Glenn out. Sometimes he would even lock the younger kids *in* the room.

Billy liked all of this—liked being the best. He didn't show that he liked it, but he liked it. Liked doing well, liked winning. It wasn't that he was competitive, exactly—there's a difference between being competitive and wanting to win. A competitive man craves competition for its own sake, relishes looking down on whoever came in second. Billy's desire to win had nothing to do with that. He never looked down on a kid left in his dust. That wasn't kind, gave him no satisfaction. No, Billy liked to win because winning wasn't easy, even for a big, smart, good-looking kid like him. If you won, it meant you had worked hard. And if you worked hard and you won, then the world made sense.

One day, years later, after his world had fallen apart, winning would take on a different meaning. The victories he would work for would have nothing to do with studying or basketball or being a doctor. A few minutes' peace, an hour's rest without a nightmare—these would become his small but essential aspirations.

Billy met Ron Bucchi when he was ten and Ron was eleven. Ron was another Plainville kid, tall like Billy, Catholic like Billy, a good kid like Billy. They played Little League—Billy was on the Owls, who were managed by his friend Mike Chambrello's dad. Mike played for the Cubs, and Ron and his twin brother, Rick, were on the Seals. Billy would play sports all day long if you let him. There was scarcely a blade of grass in the Petits' backyard on Broad Street because of all the ball that was played back there—the bare feet and worn-smooth soles of sneakers pounding the dirt every day after school, the basketballs and hardballs and footballs bouncing around the yard where the lawn had once been.

Billy was not only the oldest Petit child but one of the oldest kids in the neighborhood, so he had a built-in authority that made kids follow him. He was a leader in these games. He had a quick smile that told any kid he was welcome to play, but he liked to have his way, too. Billy was afflicted with the bursts of impatience that you sometimes see in precocious kids. He wasn't cruel. He was intense.

His little sister, Johanna—everyone called her Hanna—loved gymnastics in elementary school. But Billy had other ideas for her. He figured she would be tall, like her four older brothers, so he took to having sit-downs with her, the way a father might do with his daughter. Drill some common sense into her. *You've got to give up the gymnastics,* he'd tell her. *You're not going to be a dancer. You should be playing more ball.* He was methodical, pragmatic. "Goal-oriented," Hanna says today. "Always make a list, set your goals, and if you don't achieve them, reset your list and aim for things that you can achieve. Yeah, we followed him."

In junior high, Billy and Ron Bucchi played on a local basketball team sponsored by the Columbian Squires, the youth arm of the Knights of Columbus. Billy lived for basketball. Just as he loved to spend hours behind his house dribbling in the grass until it was dirt, he loved being out on a gym floor. He was a pure shooter. Used to shoot the lights out, Big Bill says. On the basketball court, Billy's competitive drive showed itself more than anywhere else, even with his own teammates. "Oh, we used to get on each other's ass all the time," Ron says. They were regional champs for a couple of years, went to the tournament in Glens Falls, New York, up past Saratoga Springs, a good three-hour drive from Plainville. Ron and Bill would ride up with their families, watching the towns slip past out the windows.

At Plainville High, Billy was the same quiet leader he was in the neighborhood growing up. Maybe he was too much the boss sometimes, maybe too quick with a sardonic remark, but when he went too far, he knew how to laugh it off in a way that told you he didn't mean it. He didn't have trouble making friends. He looked serious one minute but might throw his arm around your shoulders the next. It had a charming effect, this odd mix of introversion and playfulness, and after college and medical school, it would morph into a uniquely comforting bedside manner. Dozens of his patients would say he was a doctor any patient would want.

"He had a real fun-loving personality, an outgoing personality. Playful," Ron says. "It's just pretty amazing. And this is coming from a guy who's known him since I was eleven. Think about the kids you've known since you were eleven years old. A bunch of them might be doing well, but you wouldn't sit back and say, 'He's amazing.' And he's the only one of them I could say that about."

Billy had a steady girlfriend for at least a couple of years, a pretty girl named Wendy—the children in her family were named for the siblings in the Darling family in *Peter Pan*. Billy lettered in cross-country, basketball, and track. As captain of the basketball team, he led the Blue Devils to the CIAC tournament his senior year, 1974. He was class president. National Honor Society. Won the Boys' State Award and the D.A.R. History Award—the day they took pictures for that one, he wore a pair of loud, Mad Hatter checkered pants, held a five-inch-thick book as a prop, and grinned his grin, a grin that told you life was fun.

Not that Billy talked much about these accomplishments. In a reserved, New England family like the Petits, you didn't brag. It was, Go about your business, don't cause a fuss. When you want something, work for it.

His senior year, his dad drove him around the Northeast to look at colleges. At one place in upstate New York, some tiny school, the basketball coach said to the tall, affable high-school senior, "You can start for me." On the long car ride back to Plainville, Bill Sr. could tell that his son was excited. But beneath the thrill was a pronounced agitation—common sense fighting for air. Behind the wheel of the family car, Bill Sr. asked, matter-of-fact, in that deep drawl that seemed to rise from somewhere down under the floorboards, whether Billy thought basketball was going to be his future. He was good, sure. He made Plainville proud, made his father proud. But what, did he think he was going to be in the NBA? Play for the Celtics? Was that really in the cards?

Billy listened. He already knew the answer. He ended up turning down the coach who promised him he would be a starter. He turned down Yale University, too—he didn't want to go to college in a city. Instead he chose Dartmouth College, the Ivy League school in the woods of Hanover, New Hampshire, a dot on a straight stretch of the Connecticut River.

The basketball court was still a place where Billy felt he belonged, and he made the varsity team his freshman year at Dartmouth. But

right away, it felt different from Plainville High. Even at a small
liberal-arts school like Dartmouth, *everybody* had been the captain
of his high-school team. Bill could have hung in, but he didn't want
to give it less than his best, and between his schoolwork and the
jobs he took to help pay his tuition, the commitment to basketball
proved too much. He had also been granted a partial track scholarship, and the money helped. Bill Sr. did well for himself running his
small businesses back in Plainville, but he hadn't yet bought the big
house on the hill, and for now the Petits were still like most families
in the town: They had what they needed but not much more. To
supplement the track scholarship, Billy landed a work-study job in
the Dartmouth cafeteria. And every week he would stop into Mc-
Nutt Hall, a three-story building of brick and New England granite
on the edge of the college green that housed administrative offices,
including student financial services. He'd ask the administrators
whether they knew of any other scholarships or grants he had over-
looked, or that no one had claimed. Any other jobs? Any more dollars? Bill popped in so frequently that the administrators who sat
behind their desks in McNutt, away from the classrooms and the
dorms, knew him by name. Once, his father recalls, Billy did un-
earth a scholarship no one knew much about, given by a graduate
down in Texas or someplace. All Bill Sr. could do was shake his
head and admire the way this kid figured out how to *better* himself.
How to make it work.

"Some of us back then were accused of acting thirty when we
were seventeen or eighteen," Ron Bucchi says. "That's kinda the
way Billy was. Most of us were first-generation college boys. Big
Pops [Bill Sr.] joined the Marines at seventeen or eighteen and came
back and started working in the family business. They grew up on
hard work. So for us I think there was a sense of maturity by senior
year of high school."

At Plainville High, each graduating senior wrote a quotation under his or her photo in the yearbook, *The Beacon*. Under his picture, Billy wrote this: "I never quit and I never lose and when the going gets tough I get going."

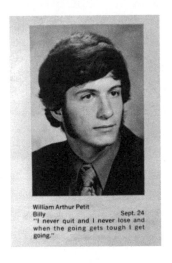

William Arthur Petit
Billy   Sept. 24
"I never quit and I never lose and
when the going gets tough I get
going."

Billy thought he wanted to be a teacher, and maybe a coach, too. He loved sports, and he had inherited from his parents an inclination to help people. Teachers helped a lot of people, he figured.

The courses offered by the undergraduate department of education at Dartmouth College in the 1974–75 academic year included freshman seminars, supervised field work in schools, and a class called Principles of Teaching that consisted of "a consideration of the several theories regarding the functions of the teacher and the art of teaching." Students majoring in education would focus their studies not only on education itself but on attaining a "broad liberal arts background," and were required to take several classes in other disciplines, like philosophy (Philosophy of Education), sociology (Sociology of Education), and psychology (a class simply called Learning). When you got to be an upperclassman, there was copious "independent study."

To Bill, the course of study he would apparently have to follow to become a teacher seemed a little . . . soft. He revered teachers, but maybe his brain didn't work that way after all. He had a computational mind, a tendency to tally and multiply and add and subtract and to note the exact date and time of things, almost by reflex. Since they were kids, Ron has suspected that Bill possesses a photographic memory, or something like it. You want to know what Bob McAdoo's best season was during the three years he played for the Knicks in the mid-'70s? The final records of the University of Connecticut women's basketball teams of the last ten years? Jim Rice's batting average the year he took over for Yaz in left field for the Red Sox? Bill could tell you. Harmon Killebrew stats. The starting line-ups for the Minnesota Twins, a team for some reason he once loved, from any era. All those courses about the art and theory of teaching didn't match up with the empiricism his brain craved. Numbers were important. Statistics showed which team had hustled the most. Grades showed which students had studied hardest.

Numbers could prove things.

He fell easily into the sciences. Dartmouth didn't have a pre-med program, so Bill joined the Nathan Smith Society, a group for students interested in medicine and health. After graduation he left New Hampshire for the medical school at the University of Pittsburgh, one of the most competitive in the country. He had chosen to be a doctor. And just as the ladies in McNutt Hall knew Billy by his first name because he used to drop by so often, in 1979 the ladies in the financial-aid office at the University of Pittsburgh School of Medicine came to know him, too, for the same reason. Once, during his first year there, Barbara was trying to reach her son on the phone. She eventually called the main office and said, "You probably don't know my son, but I need to get a message to him: William Petit." And the woman on the phone said, "Oh, Bill! We know Bill."

JENNIFER

1981

ONE DAY in 1981, Bill met his wife.

He was a third-year medical student making his rounds at Children's Hospital in Pittsburgh, walking the halls with the same half-serious swagger he showed growing up as the leader of street games with the neighborhood kids. He zipped past the nurses' station and into a corner room to check on a young girl named Becky. She had post-streptococcal glomerulonephritis, a rare, painful kidney disorder that can last for months. There, standing by Becky's bed, was a pretty blond nurse.

Bill could feel his heart beat, and his head felt light.

Acting cool as could be, he walked up next to the nurse and saw that she was about to check Becky's blood pressure. His nerves sent him into know-it-all med-student mode, and he proceeded to try to show the nurse the proper way to take a patient's blood pressure. The nurse watched, smiled, and when the tall med student was finished, she proceeded to do it again, the correct way.

The nurse was Jennifer Hawke, a local Pennsylvania girl a couple of years younger than Bill. She was slight and a little shy, and he flirted with her—he could be goofy when he wanted to be. Eventually, he asked her out.

Jennifer's father was a preacher, and the family had always lived in the parsonage of whatever church he was posted to. She didn't go out much—her younger sister, Cindy, sometimes had to coax Jenny into having what most people think of as fun. Pittsburgh, where Jen lived during nursing school, was a workingman's city, and people blew off steam at night. Neon-lit bars with pool tables, bowling alleys with beer by the pitcher, dance halls, hockey games. Even some nice places where you could get a glass of wine. But after flying around the hospital all day, Jen rarely had much energy for the bar scene. She worked twelve-hour shifts and usually all she had the energy to do was sleep. She had a good time when she went out, though, even if she wasn't meeting any dreamboats. She was thin and sweet and still had the innocent, playful eyes of a young girl. Men would ask her to dance, and when she'd tell them she was a nurse, sometimes they'd try to turn it into a pickup line. She had told one guy she was a pediatric nurse, and the dope whispered in her ear that in that case, she could probably give him a great foot rub.

For their first date, Bill took Jennifer to a restaurant in Pittsburgh called Tramp's. And the best part for Bill was, his parents had driven down from Plainville for a visit. Bill didn't think twice about asking them to come along, too. Why wouldn't this girl want to have dinner with his folks?

"It was a great night," Bill Sr. said many years later. "Jennifer, as it turned out, became our daughter-in-law, but she could have been our daughter. That's the way Bill is. 'Mom and Dad, come along on our date.'"

Plus, Bill Sr. paid.

On their next date, his parents weren't there. There were more dates, and it wasn't long before Bill Petit and Jen Hawke were a couple.

Jen had dated the same boy through most of high school back in Greenville, ninety minutes north of Pittsburgh. He had become like another member of the family, and Cindy thought of the guy as a kind of older brother. He and Jen had been broken up for years, and he'd gone off to Harvard and lived in Boston. One weekend, after Bill and Jen had been dating for a while, Bill was over at the

Hawkes' house. Cindy was about to leave on a trip to Boston to interview for jobs, and she was planning to crash at Jen's old boyfriend's place. Bill heard this and bristled. Cindy was sitting on the counter in the kitchen and remembers Bill putting his hands on the counter on either side of her, looking her in the eye, and asking her what exactly she was up to. Why was she staying at this guy's apartment? Was Cindy trying to get Jen and him back together?

It wasn't like that, Cindy told him. This guy was a pal. In that moment, she felt awkward. But to Bill, Jennifer Hawke wasn't just any girl. He was falling in love with her, and he wasn't taking any chances.

The little charge that lit him up in that moment—he could be like that sometimes. "He's a tough one, no doubt about it," Hanna says of her brother. "He demanded the best from himself, and he demanded the best from everybody around him. It's hard." Silly things could be hurtful. Once, he and Jen were on a long car trip and Cindy was in the backseat. They were chatting away, and Cindy couldn't remember some innocuous piece of trivia—Marilyn Monroe's real name or something. Bill snorted, said she must've been living under a rock.

It came out of nowhere and sounded meaner than he meant it. But it was an oddly derisive little swipe. Why did Bill bite someone's head off sometimes if they said something he thought was wrong or that he disagreed with, or even some silly mistaken fact? It was as if, once in a while, he let his own intelligence get the best of him, wielding it like a weapon instead of keeping that old quiet confidence quiet. The fact was, according to his friends and family, that he was right a lot of the time. Most of the time, really. And sometimes he couldn't help telling you how right he was.

Cindy knew Bill by this point, knew it was just a dumb thing and that he didn't mean to hurt her feelings. But he had.

. . .

On April 13, 1985, two years into Bill's internship at Strong Memorial Hospital in Rochester, New York, Jennifer's father, Rev. Richard Hawke, married Bill and Jen at Stone United Methodist Church in Meadville, the small Pennsylvania town where he was pastor. Old Stone Church, as it was known, sat on the edge of Diamond Park, a grassy oval in the center of Meadville. When the light hit the church's towering stained-glass windows just right, it refracted down onto the south end of the park like a kaleidoscope.

Dick Hawke barely came up to about Bill's chest, and he spoke softly, his voice smooth and pliable, like worn copper. But deep in his eyes lived staunch goodness, a firm command of right and wrong. People listened when he spoke. Bill liked him a lot, liked hearing him talk.

April 13 was not the sunniest day of the year, but other than that, everything was perfect. Bill had been raised Roman Catholic. Altar boy, catechism, Catholic school, guilt, fear, love, Easter dinner, heaven, hell, all of it. Jen was Methodist, and a preacher's kid. All the same, for the wedding Jen agreed to have a Catholic priest join her father and bear witness.

Bill and Jen had each grown up in a version of small-town America, so they understood that part of each other. But there's your hometown, and there's your family. When Jen walked into her first Petit-family gathering back in Connecticut, she was like a freshman stepping into the college dining hall for the first time, seeing a thousand people but no place to sit.

"Oh, we'd have fifty, fifty-five people up at Grandpa's house at holidays," Bill Sr. says. "She would tell us privately, 'I'm not used to this. I've never seen this, and I don't really understand it—but it's nice. It's nice.' She went with the flow. She had a way of fitting in."

Hanna was probably more excited than anyone about the arrival of Jennifer in Plainville: finally, an older sister. "I had a lot of friends, but I never had a sister, and Jen was beautiful and she was sweet, and she very much came into our family," Hanna says. "I think it was overwhelming at first. She comes from a much smaller family, and we all live right around the corner from each other's business."

As the relationship between Bill and Jennifer deepened, people noticed something different about Bill. He seemed mellower. Oh, he was still the same charge-ahead Billy Petit—when the going got tough, he got going. He still worked harder than anyone he knew, and he still liked things the way he liked them. He could still bite your head off if you didn't agree with his way of doing something, Hanna says. A perfectionist. But Jennifer knew how to handle him when he got frustrated or was being perhaps a little narrow-minded about something. When she took his hand in hers, even without a word, it could settle his bones and calm his head. And she knew how to remind him, in the gentle way she learned from the preacher who raised her, that while something might be very, very important to him right this second—might seem worth losing his cool over—in the context of the whole wide world, it wasn't important. *People do the best they can,* she would tell him. *People are good, and you're good, and this just isn't worth getting upset over.*

And he would look at her. Jennifer, right again.

But Jennifer Hawke-Petit—her new name—was not just the doctor's wife. True, she was certainly quiet and always she tried not to say a bad word about anybody. (Hanna used to tease her that the worst thing she would ever say about a person was that they were a "baddie." "Oh, he's such a baddie!" And Hanna would say, "I can think of a few other words.") It wasn't that Jen saw only the goodness in people—she was not blind to the human capacity for cruelty—it was that she gave people the opportunity to show that they were *capable* of goodness. But she was canny and clever and funny and could debate her husband on any topic. "She was strong and intelligent in her own right," Hanna says. "It wasn't like Jen couldn't figure stuff out."

At first, the way Jen and Bill behaved toward each other seemed strange to Jen's little sister, Cindy. "I used to tell her that sometimes it seemed like the way they got along was not to," Cindy says. "Everything was always a debate." But Jen would tell Cindy, No, you've got it all wrong—that's just the way Billy's mind works. Jen actually enjoyed tossing ideas back and forth, enjoyed the intellectual challenge of it. "And she was not one to back down," Cindy says. "She was very good for him in that way, because a lot of women wouldn't do that or weren't intelligent enough to do that. But she would give him a run for his money in their little debates."

After medical school Bill got the internship in internal medicine in Rochester. Frigid, remote Rochester, New York, a hard little city on the shore of Lake Ontario, farther north than Buffalo, average low temperature in January of 18 degrees Fahrenheit. And, as Bill and Jen would come to learn was true in a lot of cities, there weren't many jobs for pediatric nurses. So, in support of her husband—whose specialty was endocrinology, a branch of internal medicine dealing with the glands that deliver hormones to the bloodstream (his particular expertise was treating diabetes and thyroid problems), and who had been accepted into a great American hospital—she took a job as a nurse for adults. She brought to it the same gentle, easy way she had with children. It wasn't her plan, but she made herself part of Bill's.

Jen dreamed of sunshine. A sun worshipper, Bill called her. Her need for warmth was almost a craving. If it were up to her, they would have moved to Florida. And here she was in this boreal tundra, across the lake from *Canada*, living in an apartment that looked like every other apartment around it (Cindy called their neighborhood "Clone Village"), scraping ice off the windshield before work. She was feeling tired a lot, more than she ever had. Jen had always had the busy energy of a bird building a nest, the kind of person who couldn't sit for long if there was work to be done. But she would call Cindy and tell her that's all she felt the strength to do sometimes—just sink into the couch cushions like an old man on Thanksgiving.

The residency led to a fellowship for Bill at Yale's endocrinology-metabolism and diabetes program at Yale–New Haven Hospital and the West Haven VA Medical Center. *Yale.* It was an achievement. First an Ivy League college, then a top medical school, now an elite fellowship. It was also Connecticut. New Haven's winters were about as cold as Rochester's, so Jen felt no closer to the sun. Plus, as in Rochester, there were no openings on Yale's pediatric unit. Not at first, anyway. But not long after they moved, a position opened up on the pediatric/adolescent unit. Jennifer applied for and got the job, and she would not be just a nurse on the unit. She was hired to run it.

This is what Jen used to tell her sister Cindy about her husband: She said Bill made her the best person she could possibly be.

HOME

1987–2007

THE HOUSE was on a corner quarter-acre lot that gently sloped down to the sidewalk. The aesthetic was early-1980s American suburb: vaguely colonial design, cement foundation sticking up out of the dirt, too-small windows sometimes awkwardly placed. Some were close to the roof, or wedged against a corner. One whole face of the house had almost no windows at all. Aluminum siding in a shade of pearl sheathed the exterior. There was a patio in the backyard next to a sunroom that extended off the back of the house. Two-car garage. The building was angled on the lot such that the front door faced a short horseshoe of a street called Hotchkiss Ridge, but the driveway came in off Sorghum Mill Drive, so that's where the house had been assigned a postal address: 300 Sorghum Mill Drive, Cheshire, Connecticut.

As big a selling point as the house itself was the quiet that surrounded it. Sorghum Mill was a street that not many people drove down unless they lived on it or on one of the short loops or stubby dead-end streets that jutted off of it. The street was so quiet that early on Sunday mornings, or on summer afternoons or snowbound winter days, and especially at night, the world around it seemed to fall away.

Of course, a lot of people in Bill's extended family couldn't believe it. *Cheshire?* they would say. *Why not Plainville? Everybody lived in Plainville. Cheshire was twenty minutes away!* But Bill and Jennifer had found their home. Cheshire was a sweet town of old trees and good schools. It was hilly, laced with curvy roads that occasionally brought you to a small farm or past a red barn, survivors of the steady shift away from agriculture in central Connecticut, a shift that had begun before Bill was born.

He had finished his fellowship at Yale and established a private practice in Plainville, downtown on Whiting Street, a few doors from Petit's General Store. (The fact that his office was in Plainville made the family feel a little better about him living so far away.) His practice was affiliated with New Britain General Hospital, which was almost a half hour from the house on Sorghum Mill Drive, farther than his new office in Plainville. Bill was going to be doing a lot of commuting.

Jennifer was still working at Yale as the head of the pediatric unit. But there was another change coming. On October 15, 1989, a brilliant sunny autumn day, Jennifer gave birth to a baby girl, whom they named Hayley Elizabeth.

When Hayley was barely tall enough to see over a hospital bed, Bill started taking his daughter on his rounds. He worked so much, and it was one way he could spend a little time with her. But it was also his way of showing her the world—showing her how adults act. He had learned this at his father's grocery, and she learned it at the hospitals and medical centers of central Connecticut. They would hold hands, and she would mostly watch and listen. And everything she learned made her more curious.

Hayley was just two when her aunt Hanna gave birth to her first child, Hayley's cousin Abby. One evening, at Hanna's house, Hayley followed her aunt into the bedroom when she went to breast-feed Abby. Hayley wanted always to know what was going on and to see what people were doing. As Hanna sat on the bed with Abby in her arms covered with a blanket, Hayley stood at the window, looking up at the sky. "Auntie Hanna," she said, "where do all those stars come from? How did they get made?"

A well-worn story in the Petit family is that when Hayley turned four, Bill gave her a toy doctor bag with a toy stethoscope. At the hospital, the walls in most of the patients' rooms were papered with finger paintings and Magic Markered get-well cards from the grandchildren and nieces and nephews and sons and daughters of the people in the beds. But in some rooms, the walls were bare. Bill used to tell Hayley that it would be nice if she wanted to draw a picture for anyone who looked lonely, or even if she just went in to say hello. That would brighten their day, he told her. And so she did.

Bill and Hayley, three, on a family vacation in 1993. "She always seemed older than her years," he would say many years later.

Bill wanted Hayley to know everything. In the backyard, he would tell her the names of each species of tree. *That's a maple, you can tell by the shape of the leaves. Here's a birch.* The Latin names, which he also knew, could come later. He taught her the names of bird species, sometimes identifying them by their calls. Day after day and season after season, these became the moments that made up a childhood.

What Bill couldn't tell Hayley, he showed her. Once, when she was still just a toddler, he gently took her tiny hand in his and held it a few inches over a candle's flame so she could feel the heat on her skin. "Hot, hot," he said, as Hayley pulled her hand away from the fire.

A year after Hayley was born, when Bill was thirty-four years old, he joined the Country Club of Farmington so he could play golf. He and Ron Bucchi joined at the same time, because they had both taken up the sport and they planned to play together when they could. There had been a string of years when Bill and Ron didn't see each other much, and they weren't the kind of guys to have long chats on the phone. Life was happening. Bill had been in med school in Pittsburgh, then doing his residency in Rochester, then the fellowship at Yale. He was busy becoming a doctor and getting married. Ron, meanwhile, found an amazing girl himself. Susan Houlihan was funny and smart; Ron met her at a beer festival in the ROTC Hall at the University of Connecticut in January of 1974. They got married three years later.

Ron stayed local, building a life close to the community where he grew up. After Plainville High he went to college at Central Connecticut State University in New Britain, the next town over, earned an accounting degree, then got a job with an accountant in Plainville. Pretty soon he was doing taxes for Bill Petit Sr. and

Ron Bucchi, *left*, presents his old Plainville friend Bill with a fundraising award. Both were young fathers, golfing on the weekends when they could.

all his businesses, then for Big Bill's brothers, too. Mr. Petit even helped Ron land a seat on the board of the local YMCA. The Petits did what they could to pass down their sense of duty to their children's generation.

Ron was tall, like Bill, and lean, with dark Italian eyes, olive skin, and combed-back hair that didn't move. They would catch each other quickly on the phone during the week to talk about tee times for the weekend. They'd pull into the club's driveway early most Saturdays, around 6:30 in the morning, grab a coffee and a bagel or something, and walk out onto the course.

It wasn't a ritzy club, Farmington. Nice, but not stuffy. Bill liked the history of the place. The clubhouse looked like a big white mansion. It was built in 1901 after the original, which dated to 1767, burned down. The entrance was open and airy, with a formal sitting room off to one side and a hostess station at the foot of a grand staircase. The ballroom had a drop ceiling, putty-colored walls, and heavy drapes. Out back was a sprawling terrace overlooking the first tee. If Bill and Ron played an afternoon round, they'd usually end up going for a beer in the Founders Room.

The country club became part of Bill's world: house, yard, Whiting Street office, hospital, club. They knew him there. The club—its creaky floors, dark wood railings with the varnish wearing thin in spots, uniformed college kids rushing around serving food and clearing glasses, the way the sky over the course looked bluer and deeper on September mornings, when you could feel the first chill of fall if you breathed in through your nose—came to seem like a kind of home to him.

The golf relieved some of the pressure of the work that was keeping Bill away from Sorghum Mill Drive more and more. And while the golf kept him away, too, he and Ron played so early in the morning that he felt he didn't miss much quality time at home. He kept at it, working on his swing, honing his short game, almost always playing with his dad or with Ron or both of them. His medical practice was growing, and he was earning a reputation as one of the most respected diabetes specialists in the state. But at home, whenever possible, he tried to turn all that off—the beeper, the worries about patients and paperwork, the nagging thoughts about a hook or a slice—and focus only on his daughter. In 1993 a new show came on television, *Dr. Quinn, Medicine Woman.* It starred Jane Seymour as Dr. Michaela Quinn, a strong, plucky physician who moves to Colorado in the 1860s, bucking the male-dominated customs of the Wild West. Bill and Hayley liked to watch the show on the couch in the family room with a bowl of popcorn between them.

When he was at home with his wife and daughter, in the quiet house on the quiet street in the quiet town, he had everything he wanted.

Jennifer, pregnant with Michaela; Bill; and Hanna's husband, Dennis Chapman, 1995.

In 1995, Jennifer became pregnant again, and on November 17, a month after Hayley's sixth birthday, Jennifer gave birth to another daughter. Bill and Jen asked Hayley if she had any ideas for a name for her baby sister. She suggested naming her after Dr. Quinn. They called her Michaela Rose.

· · ·

For years, Jennifer had sometimes felt more tired than she thought she should. Cindy had noticed first, way back when Jen was in nursing school in Pittsburgh. After Hayley was born, it got worse, but that seemed normal for a new mom. After Michaela was born, she left her job in pediatric care, but she still had two small kids, a busy husband, a three-bedroom house to take care of, and the family's schedule to coordinate. She was still a preacher's kid (a PK, if you're in the club) and was active in the Cheshire United Methodist Church. She was charming and could crack a joke, and she was good at making friends around town—she met people through church and through the girls' schools, and those relationships kept her busy, too. With Bill's schedule, Jennifer was the reason they had any friends at all outside the Petits' Plainville circle, wide and welcoming though it was. Jen was exhausted, but it seemed explainable.

Then, in 1998, she started feeling more acute symptoms. Parts of her felt strange, hard to move sometimes. Anesthetized. But like a lot of doctors and nurses, her first instinct was to tell herself it was either something imminently catastrophic or nothing at all—and not to seek medical attention. She joked to Bill that it was probably brain cancer. To Hanna, she would say, *Oh, it's nothing, probably a little Bell's palsy*. Still, Hanna said, even if that's all it was, Jen should get it checked out. The symptoms were getting in the way of her daily life. The fatigue was relentless, and the numbness pronounced. Finally, she went to a doctor.

Jennifer was diagnosed with multiple sclerosis. After her secret fears of some terminal nightmare, a part of her was relieved. You could treat MS. Research into the disease had accelerated in the 1950s and '60s after the discovery of DNA, and by the '80s progress was steady. Doctors now understood more about how the disease slowly attacked a person's autoimmune system. There were different kinds of MS, and every case was different, but with the better understanding came more accurate diagnoses and more effective treatments. Still, Jen's first thoughts were not about research or treatment or DNA but about Bill and the girls. She worried over how long she would be able to take care of them, to be a good mother and wife. Would she keep losing strength? Would she become a burden?

The day she and Bill sat down and told Hayley, who was nine years old, that her mother had an illness, Hayley didn't cry. Her response was to ask what she could do. They did some research and found that in Connecticut, the National MS Society held an annual MS Walk. You could walk by yourself or form a team, and the more walkers on your team and the more people who sponsored you, the more money you could raise.

Hayley found a pad of lined paper and started writing letters to everyone she knew. Her grandparents, Aunt Cindy and Uncle Bill, Aunt Hanna and Uncle Dennis, Mr. and Mrs. Bucchi—lots of people started receiving Hayley's notes in the mail, asking for their support. She had formed a team, she wrote. She had named the team Hayley's Hope. If they would sponsor her team in the MS Walk, she could help raise money to find a cure for multiple sclerosis.

Hayley sealed the envelopes, mailed them off, and waited.

Within days, envelopes started appearing in the mail, addressed to her, with checks inside. In April 1999, she walked in the Connecticut MS Walk. The next year, she sent out the letters again, and again the checks came in. By her senior year of high school, in seven years, Hayley had raised $55,000 to try to save her mother.

Michaela Rose Petit became "KK" to her family early in life, shorthand for her name, which was pronounced Mih-*kay*-la. Bill took to calling her KK Rosebud. She had long honey-colored hair and eyes that could trick you—they looked almost sleepy sometimes, but the second she smiled, they sparkled. Michaela was often shy to the point of not talking, but she could be feisty, too, a side Jennifer and Bill had never seen in Hayley. A "stubborn streak," Hanna would call it. "She was smart like her sister, but she fought back and spoke her mind—to them. To everybody else she was quiet, quiet, quiet. But to her parents she let her feelings be known."

Martha's Vineyard, 1999.

As she got older, Michaela grew to be a picky eater—another difference between her and Hayley—and eventually became a vegetarian. But she loved to cook, loved to be around the making of food. Hanna was a professional chef, and she used to try to teach all the cousins how to make simple dishes like fresh pasta. But Hanna always felt Michaela was the only one who truly wanted to learn. Jen used to take the girls over to their great-grandmother Triano's house on Friday nights—Bill's grandmother, Barbara's mother. When she was old enough, Michaela would help Gram Triano cook. Pizza became the thing. A few photos of pizza night still survive today, and the stories persist: The girls would watch their Gram stretch the dough, then KK would add the sauce and grated cheese. When it got close to the time Bill was scheduled to pull into the driveway after work, KK would call him on his cell phone and tell him what was for dinner. When he arrived, she ran to him, yelling "Da-da's home!" And when he sat down to eat, Michaela made sure she was the one to serve him, special.

Michaela watched the Food Network, especially the shows hosted by anyone with what Bill later called "pizzazz." Rachael Ray, Emeril—chefs who always seemed to be having a great time. Sometimes when Jennifer took Hayley to the mall for new basketball shoes or a pair of jeans, KK would stay behind with her Gram. She didn't like shopping. Her mother's car was barely out of the driveway before Michaela was grabbing a bottle of root beer from the fridge and a tub of vanilla ice cream from the freezer while her Gram got down the tall glasses from the cupboard. Michaela made the root beer floats herself, copying the cooks she saw on TV. She seemed to love the theater of cooking, and for the grown-ups, it was fun to watch *her* having so much fun. But when the spotlight was on her, she recoiled. Once, at a family party, she was serving a dish she had cooked, and the person holding a video camera asked her what she made for everybody. She blushed. "I made . . . this," she managed, with a shy giggle.

They had that in common, Hayley and Michaela: shyness. But they were very different girls. Hayley was content to sit in her small room, decorated all in blue, pictures taped to the walls at meticulous angles, and read. Michaela somehow scored the bigger bedroom down the hall, and it was pink and girly. She couldn't fall asleep without a movie on, so Bill and Jen let her have one of those tiny TVs in her room that you had to get really close to in order to see anything. She loved it. Whenever Hanna's son, her cousin Andrew, slept over, the two of them would finally give in to exhaustion at what seemed to eight- and nine-year-olds like an ungodly hour, after watching movie after movie.

Michaela revered her older sister. She also looked up to her cousin Abby, who called her Cakes. Abby was more girly than Hayley, and KK loved that. Michaela was curious about makeup and nail polish and clothes and bathing suits, things Hayley showed little interest in. Abby would try to wrestle Hayley to the floor and pin her down so she could apply mascara to her eyes, but Hayley would fling her away, laughing.

Michaela and the cousins looked up to Hayley much the same way kids used to look up to Billy. Once, when Hayley was about fifteen, Jen and Hanna took their children to Lake Compounce, an old-timey amusement park in Bristol, another hardworking central-Connecticut town. Andrew was about nine. Everyone was taking rides on the Wildcat, a rickety-looking roller coaster built in 1927. But Andrew was scared. He asked his older sister if it was scary. He asked his mom. But he really wanted to find Hayley. When he did, he asked *her* if the ride was scary. She told him it might be a little scary but that it would be okay. So Andrew took a deep, serious nine-year-old's breath and decided to ride the Wildcat—with Hayley. He would only ride it with her. He knew Hayley wouldn't lie.

Abby used to tell Hayley, *You're stuck with me as your best friend for the rest of your life.* Looking back, Abby feels they were drawn to each other because they were so different. Abby would come up with crazy ideas, and Hayley would tell her why they were impossible. Abby would carry on hollering about one thing or another, and Hayley would smile at her like she was nuts and tell her to calm down. Michaela observed both of them, missing nothing.

Bill was a University of Connecticut basketball fan. He started bringing Hayley and Abby to games when they were little, and they would wear decals of the Huskies' mascot on their cheeks. The girls would sit in the backseat and giggle the whole way there and the whole way back about who knows what. Incomprehensible, silly girl stuff. Bill would tilt his rearview mirror so he could see them and ask with mock seriousness, "What's so funny back there?"

They would have sleepovers and watch *Father of the Bride*, the Steve Martin version, and *Father of the Bride II,* over and over and over again. They would laugh so hard they'd cry, and they would write down all the best lines in little notebooks until they could recite the movies from memory. Hayley and Abby developed a whole language between them—not jokes, but things that made them laugh, things no one else could ever understand, things they swore would stay just between them forever. They never went a day without talking. When Hayley enrolled at Miss Porter's, an elite, private all-girls school nearby, Abby had never even thought about private school. But two years later she applied and got in, too, so she could be with Hayley. Abby even went out for the crew team, despite a fear of open water and boats. Crew is a cultish sport. You have to make it your life, and Bill joked that for dedicated rowers a good day was when you worked out so hard you threw up. This was not Abby's style. But Hayley rowed crew, so Abby rowed crew.

At Porter's, everyone called Abby Hayley's shadow, but she also knew when to keep her distance. School was different from hanging out at home. Hayley's friends were smart and popular. Abby was younger, so despite their closeness she would never be so bold as to barge in on Hayley and her friends in the lunchroom. She'd wait until Hayley got up to get some more salad or a new fork, and then she'd skip over to her and ask for a ride home from school or for advice about a certain teacher—anything to get a public minute with her cousin. Sometimes she'd plead for Hayley to drive them off campus for lunch, just this once. But that was against the rules, and Hayley was not a rule-breaker. She would just smile and shoot Abby a look that said, Not a chance, kiddo.

When Abby was at her Uncle Billy and Auntie Jen's house, Bill was always imploring them to go outside. When he wasn't working, nighttime was for popcorn in front of a movie or a ball game, but the days were for gardening and basketball and keeping his lawn green and lush. He was constantly trying to get the girls to pull weeds. They would play epic basketball games in the driveway, Bill and Hayley and Abby and Hanna and whoever else was there, and when the score hit 21 or whatever the game was, Bill would yell, "Okay, twenty minutes, pull all the weeds you can. Go!"

Hayley used to say to Abby, "You know, when I get married, KK has to be my maid of honor. It has to be the sister." And Abby would say, "What do you mean? She's so young! If you're gonna be mine—which you are—don't I have to be yours?" And Hayley would smile, shrug, and say, "No, it has to be KK."

Friday nights were for pizza at Gram Triano's, but the Petits spent endless afternoons at the house Bill's parents had bought on Red Stone Hill in Plainville. Bill Sr. had built his network of local businesses into a small empire, and he now lived in the proud old Georgian mansion perched above Norton Park, the biggest house in town, in whose shadow Bill and his friends used to play as kids. In every direction, the lawn unfurled in great green fields, which was unusual for Plainville, where many of the houses were lined up in tidy suburban rows on identical lots, a sidewalk out front, narrow yard in back.

At Barbara and Big Bill's, the rooms always seemed to be filled with people. Barbara made sure the wood floors always gleamed, and the fourteen-foot ceilings made the rooms look like great halls. The kitchen was just to the left of the front door, and when you walked in, the warm smell of whatever was on the stove engulfed you. Jennifer fell into the routine, but it was a lot—the parties, the food, every birthday, every recital, every holiday. So different from her house growing up. In Plainville, there seemed to be something to celebrate every weekend, and everyone showed up to everything. Bill had eight aunts and uncles on one side and three on the other and about forty-two first cousins. It seemed like as soon as the dishes were dry from the last party, they were being set out for the next. Even if Cindy was visiting from North Carolina, or Jen's parents were over from Pennsylvania (in the summer) or up from Florida (in the winter), if there was a party at the Petits', off they all went.

Family was family. Jen rolled with it. And, truth be told, it was hard not to have fun with the Petits.

For Cindy, it was a chance to see what her older sister's life was like. Jen could always handle anything, and Cindy marveled at how Jen joined the Petit family carnival with such apparent ease. She loved when Jen could make it down to North Carolina to visit her with the girls between Christmas and New Year's Day so Cindy could see her big sister and Hayley and Michaela could spend time with Cindy's kids, Lydia and Evan. Jen had a "striking beauty," Cindy says. "When she would come downstairs dressed, you couldn't wait to see her because you couldn't wait to see what she was going to be wearing, and how she was going to have fixed her hair. It was always amazing and fun to look at, and fun to watch, and to have someone like her as your role model."

Bill's diabetes and endocrinology practice grew, and his register of patients seemed to continually expand. Doctors knew him to be a dedicated physician, "a man cut from the old cloth—a doctor's doctor," says his friend Steve Hanks, who would become the chief medical officer at two different hospitals in Connecticut. Bill treated all his patients equally, Hanks says. He was even known among the transgender community as an endocrinologist who would treat transgender patients without hesitation or prejudice, noteworthy in itself but perhaps especially because Bill was conservative politically. But in his office, everyone mattered, and everyone received the care they needed.

Around the time Jennifer was diagnosed with MS, Bill was named the director of the Joslin Diabetes Center, a well-known and respected treatment and research facility affiliated with the Hospital of Central Connecticut. He started seeing patients four and a half days a week there. While he made his rounds, there was always a resident or fellow from the endocrinology program at the UConn Medical School with him. "Every day was a teaching day," he says. "Every interaction was a potential teaching moment." He liked this new role, and he tried to pass along every bit of information he knew. But he was working even longer hours, seeing his family even less. Still, he stayed silent about the stresses that were building in his life, because for him, silence was useful in getting through just about anything.

In 1996 Jennifer started working again, too, taking a position as codirector of the student health center at Cheshire Academy, a private high school in town, just a few minutes from Sorghum Mill Drive. The way she engineered it, she and another woman would split the responsibilities, each running the center two and a half days a week. That way, Jen felt, she could be totally present wherever she was, at home or at the school. For the mother of two young girls who wanted part-time work that fulfilled a need to help people, the job was perfect.

Cheshire Academy had been around since 1794, and its campus

covered more than a hundred manicured acres. The brick buildings were handsome and well-maintained, the athletic fields of higher quality than those at some colleges. Some of the faculty lived on campus in charming colonial houses. The school kept classes small. Students who lived in Cheshire and the surrounding towns could attend as day students, while others from all over the country, and from other countries, too, lived on campus as boarders. Jennifer, the nurse whom Bill had first seen standing calmly at the bedside of a sick girl in a Pittsburgh hospital, had entered a whole world of children who would come to rely on the serenity that seemed to surround her. They were children who needed a nurse who knew what it meant to be a mother. They were children who sometimes just needed a hand getting through the day. When a student walked in and stood at the Dutch door to the office, Jen would slide her glasses off and let them hang from the chain around her neck, look up, and say, in her routine singsong way, "What's the matter?"

Running a health center at a high school was about more than handing out Band-Aids and Tylenol. At any boarding school, there are kids with everything from depression to ADHD to life-threatening allergies, and that was true at Cheshire. Jennifer wanted the school's health center to be the best it could be—"state of the art," she used to say. She and the other director, Deb Bond, were there to work. There was a third nurse who worked with them, Patty Poisson, whose husband was an art teacher at the school. The three women created an environment in which, first and foremost, students could feel comfortable. For all the medical emergencies they faced over the years—broken bones, midnight trips to the ER, the occasional sprint across campus with an EpiPen to help a girl who was in anaphylactic shock—the nurses most often provided comfort. And when a child whose parents lived across the country was feeling concussed by the pressures of academics or friends or sports or just being in high school, very often that child went to find Mrs. Petit. Once, when Jen's nephew Andrew was sleeping over at the Petits' house with Michaela, Jen got a call on her beeper about a student who was feeling the worst kind of homesick. So Jen packed up Michaela and Andrew and drove over to the campus so she could comfort the child.

Jen dressed up for work every day, a quirk that didn't seem to align with her quiet, unshowy way and that amused Patty. She wore stylish skirts and matching sweaters and high-heeled shoes. And always her pearls—a simple string of small pearls that was something of a signature for Jen, whether she had on jeans or a party dress. She wasn't showing off, and the clothes weren't all that expensive. She just liked to look put-together. But sometimes by the middle of the morning she'd groan to Patty, "What's the matter with me? Why did I wear these awful shoes? They're killing me." And Patty would laugh.

It was Jen's confidence and her ability as a nurse that most inspired Patty, her new friend. At night Jen would tell Bill about the kids who had come into the health center that day, and ask his opinion about how she had handled this situation or that. Jen liked when they disagreed, because it forced each of them to make their case, and she could then be sure that whatever conclusion they reached was the right one. She constantly read up on current practices in her field and knew every protocol. But her deeper, more essential knowledge was of when to ignore protocols. Patty never saw Jen reach for pharmaceuticals as a first response.

Jennifer believed in chicken soup. There was a kitchenette at the health center, and there were always cans of Campbell's in the cupboard. She believed in pulling up a chair so that she and a student were sitting almost knee to knee, taking the kid's hand in hers, and asking what was wrong. She believed in the restorative power of letting a child lie on the bed while she made tea or rubbed her shoulders or sat back and said nothing. She could see when a kid just needed someone to help her slow down.

Her work was demanding, and sometimes Jen and Bill would

pick a weekend and seal themselves off from the world. They would turn off their cell phones, shut down the computer, leave the car in the garage, and just be. The house on Sorghum Mill Drive had become, to them, home. They had made it theirs. Not that they poured a lot of money into it. Every time Cindy came up to Connecticut to visit, she couldn't believe Jen had no curtains on the windows. When Cindy mentioned that she had to get her floors redone or that she had ordered granite countertops for her kitchen, Jen looked at her funny. Their priorities were different. As fashionable and put-together as she always looked, Jen was a shrewd shopper who saw no shame in finding a good deal at Marshalls. Toward the end of her life, she had hemmed and hawed about an Oriental carpet for the house, a real extravagance. She must've kept it on loan for a year while she decided whether to go ahead and buy it. Easy assumptions about a doctor's wife in Connecticut didn't fit Jennifer Hawke-Petit.

It wasn't that Bill and Jen were cheap. Their generosity could stun you. Once, when Cindy's two children were young, she wanted to sign them up for a local swimming league. They both loved to swim, but Cindy and her husband had been able to afford lessons and leagues only occasionally, for a few weeks or a month at a time, paying as they went. She was going on about this to Jen, just talking, and Jen told her she wanted Cindy to be able to say yes to the summer swimming league all at once without having to worry. And Jennifer mailed her sister a check for the entire fee for both kids, $500.

Bill had gotten serious about his gardening on the weekends. He knew all the spots in his yard where the sun shined brightest before disappearing behind a ridge to the west. He would kneel in the grass, his fingers digging into the cool soil until it stained his hands. Out in the freshness of his yard, away from the sterilized, climate-controlled hospital air, he could actually work up a satisfying sweat. He mostly planted flowers so that in the summer he could cut little bouquets and bring them inside for the girls. But he landscaped the rest of the yard, too. When Hayley was about three years old, he planted a small Japanese maple, maybe two feet tall when he got it, next to the driveway near the house. Across the driveway was a chamaecyparis, a bush in the cyprus family that had soft evergreen leaves that felt just like yarn against your skin. As he had with Hayley, he taught Michaela the names of every plant, sometimes in Latin. (Ron Bucchi's two sons used to caddy for him and Bill at the club, and Bill could add a good twenty minutes to a round of golf because he'd stop at every pond and instruct the boys on what kinds of fish swam in it. "It'd be like golfing with Euell Gibbons," Ron says. "Billy's going through the flowers around the tee box, telling the kids what kind they were.")

In every corner of the garden, Bill worked with efficiency to encourage growth and support life. He set the timer on the underground sprinkler system so that his grass and all his flowers would be watered at 5:30 each morning. On the north side of the house, he and Jen used to cut off the wilted blooms on a row of rhododendrons to encourage new flowers to grow, a process called deadheading, which helped maximize the number of flowers each bush could produce during the summer. He did the same thing to the flowers on the tee boxes at the golf course. Deadheaded them while Ron and his two sons stood watching.

Out in front of the house was a huge viburnum, which had spectacular white flowers in the springtime and little berries in the summer and fall. That bush was the exception to Bill's obsessive care. He barely touched the thing and it grew like mad. People used to stop and take pictures.

The best times outside were when Michaela gardened with him. Together they would wander the yard, looking for new places to grow flowers, mostly four-o'clocks, her favorite. They planted a large bed of them behind a rock wall at the end of the driveway.

Four-o'clocks are showy flowers, red and white and pink and yellow, trumpet-shaped, bushy. Michaela liked them because they had pizzazz. Bill liked them because they were easy to plant—pop the seed in the soil about a quarter inch down, cover it up, boom. Done.

Bill and Jennifer had settled into the life they wanted. They had two beautiful daughters, different from each other, each wonderful in her own way. They had a kitchen with a table by the window looking out into the backyard. Bill's practice was thriving, and Jen felt fulfilled in her job at Cheshire Academy. They went to church on Sundays. For vacations, they walked the beaches of Sanibel Island, Florida, collecting shells. At least once a year they drove to see Jen's parents, the girls' Popup and Meemaw, in Slippery Rock, Pennsylvania, where they would kayak in the creek and go to country fairs and working farms. Their families were close on every side.

But life isn't easy for anybody.

Jennifer, for one thing, was coping with a disease that sapped her energy and was causing frightening degeneration in her body. One of the worst parts was that she was deprived of her precious sunshine. Heat exacerbated the exhaustion that was part of MS, so one of the things she loved doing best—sitting outside all afternoon, soaking in the warmth that had always made her feel so good and so alive—often made her feel her worst. Plus, she had to give herself shots all the time. From most people, Jennifer hid her disease well. Not because she felt embarrassed, but because she didn't want anyone to feel pity for her. She didn't want to be a burden. Around her family, however, it was sometimes the opposite. She would keep her medication right in the refrigerator, visible. When it was time to give herself a shot, she lifted her shirt a little and poked the needle into her stomach, or she did it in her thigh, just above the hem of her shorts. Never in front of Hayley and Michaela, but Cindy frequently saw Jen administer the shots. Her parents, too. At first,

Cindy thought this was odd. She wondered why Jen couldn't just go into the bathroom. Cindy asked their mother about it. Marybelle Hawke had been a nurse herself. She told Cindy her thoughts: Part of the reason Jen doesn't hide it from us is that she doesn't want us to forget that she has this disease. Maybe she doesn't want us to forget that she's dealing with it. Maybe deep down, she doesn't want to sound like she's complaining about having a low energy level, or not being able to travel, or needing to lie down. MS is not something you can see. But a shot is something we can see. Maybe she wants us to remember.

And Cindy thought that made sense.

Bill had begun to accept speaking engagements, sometimes in faraway cities—driving around, flying all over, talking to rooms full of people about endocrinology and diabetes. It wore him down, and Hanna, for one, used to talk to him about slowing down the juggernaut that his medical career was becoming. But Bill explained: At these speaking engagements, he could make a couple thousand dollars in a single night, and it went straight into the girls' college funds. It may have been exhausting, and the travel could be miserable, but it was money in the bank. Hanna would frown when she saw the McDonald's wrappers on the floor of his car after one of his trips. But he'd look at her as if to say, What am I supposed to do?

He had also been asked to write a book, a text on diabetes. He already had almost no free time to himself, and now whatever time he did have, at least for a while, would be devoted to writing. As it was, he woke up at six in the morning. Around seven he'd be on his way to the hospital and talking on his cell phone with the office. He wouldn't get home until seven or eight at night, when he would spend a couple of hours with Jen and the girls. So that left a few hours: From ten at night until two in the morning, he would work on the book. Then he was up at six to start over again. It went on this way for a couple of years. Jen held the family together.

In 2004, Bill was playing golf with Ron one day when Bill passed out with atrial fibrillation. He came to, but Ron drove him to New Britain General Hospital, where the doctors discovered that his heart had slowed to between fifteen and thirty beats per minute. A normal heart rate for an adult is between sixty and a hundred. Fifteen to thirty is dangerously slow. He was hospitalized for a week, and the doctors installed a pacemaker. This put Jennifer into a quiet panic. She was worried about losing Bill while her own health was deteriorating, and about leaving the girls parentless. Bill's instinct was not to talk about his ordeal, and he never learned how afraid she was until years later. Her friends told him. At the time, Jennifer never said a word.

In the wintertime: basketball. Bill now had season tickets to both the UConn men's and women's teams. For years, in the 1970s and '80s, the UConn men's team was a humble program, playing most of its home games in a rundown field house that felt more like a high-school gym. Then, in 1990, the team shocked the world of college basketball, playing deep into the NCAA tournament, coming within a single possession of advancing to the Final Four, the pinnacle of the sport, for the first time in the school's history. That team captured the hearts of the state, and since then the men's team had been a perennial national powerhouse. The women's team was even more dominant, winning five national championships in nine years, including 2004, when the men won, too. For a basketball-loving family like the Petits, it was a fun time to be a UConn fan.

The core was Bill, Hayley, Bill Sr., and Hanna. Hanna would pick up her dad and Hayley, then they'd stop by and get Bill at his office on Whiting Street. As they motored east on I-84, sometimes in the snow, Bill would sit in the backseat making calls on his cell phone and eating a tinfoil-wrapped plate of food that Barbara had sent for his supper. Jennifer came to two or three games a year—that was plenty for her—and Michaela sometimes, too. But Hayley truly loved it. For her and her dad, it was their thing. When she got to high school, she was always busy, rowing crew, serving as cocaptain of the basketball team, doing her homework until after midnight alongside Bill up in the second-floor room they used as an office. She pushed herself hard. At the UConn games, though—at the UConn games, it was glorious. Father and daughter, standing and cheering from the minute the Huskies ran onto the court. They knew every player and all the statistics. They screamed and whooped and clapped and jumped, losing themselves for part of an afternoon or an evening. It was the perfect activity for this father and this daughter. Just so much . . . *fun.*

There was a boy they used to invite along sometimes. Jen was getting to be good friends with Patty Poisson, from the health center, and her son Otis was a sweet kid who liked basketball, too. He was only a year older than Hayley. Bill liked Otis because Otis liked basketball. He started inviting Otis to UConn games, and the three of them would ride to Hartford together—Bill driving, Otis and Hayley in the back, a tall, good-looking boy and a tall, pretty girl at the awkward age of thirteen or fourteen, not talking.

Patty and her husband lived on the campus of Cheshire Academy, and they also had a daughter, Mairi, who was two years older than Michaela. In the afternoons, when Michaela finished school, she would come to the health center to wait for Jen. Her homework at that age took only a half hour at the most, and when she was done, she would plead to Jen, "Mom, when can we go home?" Mairi's routine was the same as Michaela's: zip through her homework and then wait for her mom to finish work. So the two girls started playing together. Michaela was not only tall for her age but mature—all that time spent watching Hayley and Abby—and the two girls got along as if they were the same age. At first they would play in the health center itself so Jen and Patty could keep an eye on them. Once, they turned a linen closet into their office, with a little desk and a step stool for a chair, a bell outside (for when they had the door closed), and a mailbox taped to the wall. They complained whenever there was no mail waiting for them, so Jen and Patty would deposit little notes in the mailbox while the girls were in school.

On the days when Patty's husband, Fran, wasn't coaching sports or tending to faculty business, he would be at their house on campus after school, and the girls would go there and play for hours. They played outside in the rain, they played dress-up, they concocted elaborate snacks in the kitchen. KK was quiet around Fran, but around Mairi she could be hilarious. She was even freer at her own house. Michaela had a box full of earrings before she even got her ears pierced. She had a trundle bed in her room, and when Mairi came for sleepovers they would watch *Spice World,* the Spice Girls movie, or the Lizzy McGuire movies, over and over. Or *Legally Blonde.* She and Mairi, and even Jen and Patty, could recite that one from memory.

Michaela, Christmas morning, 2006.

Michaela had already discovered that she loved cooking by the time she and Mairi found themselves with glorious long afternoons to fill, and they staged make-believe cooking competitions in the Poisson kitchen. Mairi gawked at the stuff Michaela came up with, hunched over the kitchen island. The best day was when Michaela made hot chocolate that was spicy. Spicy hot chocolate! She was probably not even nine years old. She wrote down the recipe on blue-lined paper in big bubbly handwriting with a red Magic Marker and left it for Mairi:

> *Michaela's Chocolate Chili*
> 1) *cinnamon   sprinkle*
> 2) *chocolate chips   handful*
> 3) *chili powder   sprinkle*
> 4) *½ cup milk*
> 5) *tablespoon ovaltine*
> 6) *whipped cream*
> 7) *melt chocolate, add all other ingredients,*
>   *then put whipped cream on top*

Otis Poisson was tall for his age, like Hayley, with a long, muscular frame. He was boyish and handsome, with sandy hair and blue eyes, and was not shy so much as hesitant to give himself over to the world. That could make him seem quiet, but Otis was smart and friendly, and happiest when he was running around on a basketball court. From even the first few times he was around Hayley, usually with their moms, at some school event or family thing, Otis felt that she *got* him, and that he got her.

Fran and Patty Poisson hosted a party every Christmas Eve for anyone who was on campus. Neither of them had a big extended clan to fly off and visit, so they made their home a place where people could come and feel like family. It was an open house, friends and coworkers and students and neighbors coming and going all night. The Petits always had so much to do on Christmas Eve. There was church, of course. And then it was the crowd of Bill's family, a huge gathering at his parents' house in Plainville, with two Christmas trees and acres of food, kids running everywhere. But every year, on the way home, they would stop in at the Poissons' party. Even if it was ten or eleven o'clock. And they wouldn't just pop in. They'd take their coats off, eat some food, and have something to drink. They would visit. Mairi and Michaela would squirrel off somewhere and be little girls, and the grown-ups would talk about grown-up things. Otis and Hayley, all elbows and knees and flashing eyes, would talk quietly, the shyest of flirting. Otis loved that the Petits were always the last ones at the party, because they were the people he really wanted to see. He wanted to see Hayley.

By their junior year, Hayley and Otis were close friends. She was the person he wanted to talk to first when something great happened, or something bad, or sometimes when nothing was happening at all. More than anyone else in his life, he loved to make her laugh. She was so smart, and so funny herself, so to get a good laugh out of her was an accomplishment. She would do this wonderful thing with her eyebrows, inverting them while she laughed at his jokes, like this boy was too much.

Otis played varsity basketball for Cheshire Academy, and Hayley for Miss Porter's. They both loved to practice—gym rats, Bill called them. Because his parents worked at the school, Otis could get into the gym anytime he wanted. The summer between junior and senior year, he used to call or text Hayley at night to see if she wanted to come over and shoot around. She always dropped whatever she was doing, jumped into her sweats, and drove over. In the gym, she and Otis would put their sneakers on and start shooting. They'd joke around a little, which was easy. After a while, they'd start a game of one-on-one. Hayley was over six feet, and strong. Bigger than plenty of high-school boys. She could compete against Otis. But the games were just fun. Both of them knew they weren't there only to practice driving the lane or boxing out. They were there because of the other one.

Once, when school was out for vacation, they went to the gym and saw a plastic sign next to the gym floor saying that it had been resurfaced, and no one could use it. Otis went back and checked the next day, and the sign was still there. Finally he called Hayley and told her to come over, because the floor had to be dry by then. But the sign was still there. They tapped the floor with their fingers, careful. It felt dry, not even tacky. Totally fine to play on. They looked at each other, smiled, hid the sign, laced up their sneakers, and started shooting around. After a few minutes, the maintenance man, who knew Otis, walked in, an unhappy look on his face.

Sign? Otis and Hayley said. No, we didn't see a sign.

The maintenance man looked both annoyed and confused as he left. As soon as he was out of earshot, they just laughed. It was about as much trouble as either of them had ever caused, and neither would have done it without the other.

They kept playing. In the gym—sneakers squeaking against the glossy floor, the lights bright even as dusk fell over the town around them, sweat in their hair, smiling when the other one made a good shot. They could have been anywhere.

When they finished playing that night, they put the sign back out on the floor and ran out laughing. That would really confuse the guy.

Hayley and Otis both applied to Dartmouth early-decision. They both wanted it badly, and they wanted it for each other just as badly.

Dartmouth is one of the best colleges in the country, founded in 1769. Nelson Rockefeller went to Dartmouth. Thaddeus Stevens. Robert Frost. Of course, to Hayley the most important alumnus was her father, William A. Petit Jr. Her entrance essay was called "My Dad." "My dad looked on as my four-year-old hands clasped the handle of the black medical bag he'd just given me for my fourth birthday," she wrote. "Looking inside I saw a child's stethoscope and various other instruments which mirrored his professional tools. From then on I had gone with my dad to the hospital on Saturdays. I loved trailing behind Dad's long, white coattails through the endless maze of hallways with shiny white floors. I was always fascinated when he strode confidently into a patient's room, talked to them for a few minutes, and recommended a treatment. I clearly remembered how he always made the patients laugh or smile before leaving. He possessed this amazing God-like power not only to heal people physically, but also to make them feel safe and brighten their days. His presence made the hospital seem a fortress and anyone within its walls safe."

Hayley was cocaptain of both the crew and basketball teams.

The college had recruited Hayley to row on the crew team. Otis wanted to play basketball there. He was good, really good, but the coach told him he couldn't intercede with the admissions office for him. Still, Patty drove Otis up to New Hampshire to visit the school. They walked around, and Otis bought a Dartmouth windbreaker. They ate at Lou's, a restaurant that had been serving pancakes to Dartmouth students since 1947. When Otis wasn't looking, Patty bought two coffee mugs that said "Meet Me at Lou's." One for Otis, one for Hayley. Gifts for when they got accepted. But when they arrived home that night, Patty was unpacking the car, and the mugs were nowhere. She looked under every seat, in every bag. Then she remembered that when they stopped for gas on the way home, she threw away a bunch of trash from their trip. She must have thrown away the mugs by mistake! Patty felt like kicking herself.

On the day in December when Dartmouth was scheduled to send notification e-mails to the students who had applied early, Hayley ducked into the library as often as she could to check her e-mail on the computers. Abby followed her, so excited for her cousin to find out good news. Abby wanted to be there partly because Hayley was so modest that if she got in, she probably wouldn't even tell anyone. When Hayley found out she had been accepted, Abby tackled her, screaming with laughter.

Hayley, of course, didn't go out of her way to tell anyone. She didn't even call her father. Instead, one of her friends called and told Dr. Petit herself.

Hayley didn't call her dad because, for one thing, he was working. Seeing patients was the most essential part of his job, the most important part of his day. Also, in a family like the Petits, you didn't talk too much about yourself, didn't run around looking for pats on the head. Hayley was what grown-ups call wise beyond her years, as Bill had been. Her friends had a saying, WWHD, for "What would Hayley do?" She knew she could just tell him that night when he got home. No point stopping the world.

Hayley did tell one person right away, though. She called Otis. She urged him to check his e-mail as soon as he could. But he had a basketball game after school that day, and this was before everyone had smartphones, so he would have to wait until he got home that night. When he did, his parents and Mairi stood behind him as he logged on to check his e-mail. There it was, a message from Dartmouth College: "After thoughtful consideration, the Admissions Committee has decided to defer final action on your early decision application for the Class of 2011." Instead of accepting him early, the admissions office would reconsider Otis's candidacy during the regular admission period. "To assist in your planning," the e-mail concluded, "you should be aware that in recent years a very small proportion of deferred candidates have ultimately been offered admission to the College."

Patty thought about those coffee mugs. "Meet Me at Lou's." Maybe it was good she threw them out accidentally. Otis gave his Dartmouth windbreaker to Hayley.

If anything, the Dartmouth thing—Hayley getting in, Otis not getting in—made them even better friends, it seemed to Patty. Hayley downplayed getting chosen, and Otis made her feel good about her acceptance. The very fact that it didn't cause any awkwardness between them seemed to prove the strength of the bond between them. Otis had a girlfriend at Cheshire Academy his senior year, and she grew jealous over Otis's friendship with this Miss Porter's girl, Hayley Petit. His girlfriend could sense that it was a special friendship, and she didn't much like it. Mairi and Michaela used to giggle about their older siblings. If Otis and Hayley get married, they thought, we'll be sisters! It was a grand scheme, and Mairi and Michaela signed up for a new Web site called Facebook for the express purpose of spying on Otis and Hayley, who were also on the social network. Michaela was only in fourth or fifth grade at this point, so she wasn't active on Facebook—Bill barely knew what Facebook was, didn't even know she had a page. But she and Mairi loved looking at Hayley's. Even Jen and Patty talked about how much fun it would be if Otis and Hayley found their way to each other.

To Otis and Hayley, it was something deeper than a crush. They were the same, in so many ways. Everyone thought Hayley was beautiful and Otis was handsome, and they were both athletic and intelligent and confident, but they were still teenagers, and being a teenager isn't easy. They had their own friends at school, of course—Hayley's group of eight girls, and Otis's circle of guys. Her friends knew she liked the boy from Cheshire Academy, but it was hard to explain that he was different. At their age, to find someone of the opposite sex who was so like you, who got every dumb joke you made and understood the constant daily collision of awkward moments and successes and disappointments that made up your high-school life—that was unusual. That was special.

Senior spring, Hayley was organizing her annual Hayley's Hope team for the MS Walk, collecting money to fight multiple sclerosis. In April she sent a Facebook message to Otis:

> *Hey!*
> *I got your check today . . . thanks so much, that was so nice of you! (and I'm kind of impressed you have your own checks haha) My mom said I should invite you to come to the walk on sunday . . . in case you need community service hours? haha i don't even know, but you can come if you want to walk 5 miles :) I also hear (from my mom obviously) that you're visiting Wesleyan this week sometime, so I hope it's fun!*
>
> *hayley*

Just a quick Facebook post, one of billions of messages flying around the world each minute by the spring of 2007. Airy and light, managing to not mean much and yet meaning everything all at once.

Bill tells the story of Hayley's graduation from Miss Porter's School as if he's retelling a legend. She had experienced lung problems, serious but not uncommon, and they were exacerbated during her final week of high school. "Hayley was and will always be my hero for her Senior Week," he will say years later. "She was at school Tuesday night of Senior Week and felt pain in her left shoulder and knew what it was. She knew because she had had a right-sided sponta-neous pneumothorax—a collapsed lung—during a cross-country meet. She called crying and we rushed to Farmington and took her to the hospital. The X-ray confirmed the diagnosis and a chest tube was placed between her chest wall and her lung. I had hoped the leak in her lung would seal so she could graduate with her friends. There was no progress. Further tests showed she needed surgery. I left briefly one night to accept her writing award at the ceremony she could not attend.

Hayley's graduation from Miss Porter's School, June 2007.

"Late Thursday we made a decision: She went into surgery at 10:00 p.m. and had a partial removal of the top part of her left lung. She still had a tube in place and got back to her room by about 2:00 a.m. At 8:00 a.m., the nurses helped us bandage her up so she would not bleed on her white dress, and we signed her out for grad-uation. The surgeon, a friend of mine, was not entirely happy, but she had the tube in place and a nurse and an M.D. with her. She got a standing ovation as she walked across the stage on her own power twelve hours after a major surgery. She barely made it through the ceremony, and by 12:30 we were taking her back to the hospital for her convalescence.

"She showed what a tough and brave kid she was that day. I had previously looked up to her, but now did so more than ever. She was a hard worker, honest, kind, and very brave. I often wished I could be as calm and tough as Hayley."

A few weeks later, Bill and Jen threw a graduation party for Hayley in the backyard. It was raining that day, but it was warm, so they put up a tent and everybody sat outside. Aunt Hanna, the professional caterer, cooked everything—she was in and out of the kitchen all day. There was beer and soda, stored in the basement fridge, and friends and family. Hayley's girls, the tightknit group of eight from Porter's, were there. Abby and Andrew were there. The Poissons were there, too, which meant Otis was there. Jen had invited Patty's family specially. She had written a card to Otis when he graduated from Cheshire Academy a couple of days before Hayley's graduation. In it she wrote, in her neat handwriting with the curlicue here and there: "Otis, We're very proud of you and think Dartmouth made a huge mistake! Wesleyan is lucky to have you and we are privileged to call you our friend. I'm counting on you to help Hayes get back into shape! Love, Petits."

Hayley's friends, of course, all wanted to meet the boy and took turns talking to him. This made Otis feel very much like "the boy," which was fine with him. Mairi and Michaela giggled about this all afternoon.

SUNDAY

July 22, 2007

THE CHESHIRE United Methodist Church is on Academy Road, down the street from Cheshire Academy. It's a hulking white building, built in 1970 and redolent of the often unfortunate architecture of the era—an overlapping series of featureless, cutout facades with white peaks. One Sunday morning, Bill, Jennifer, and Michaela attended the nine-thirty service—Hayley was away at a friend's house for the weekend or she would have been there, too. The Reverend Stephen Volpe, a buoyant, moon-faced man whom everyone calls Pastor Steve, led the worship, standing as he always did in front of the austere dark cross, backlit on a gleaming white slab behind the altar.

The three Petits stood for the opening prayer, a call-and-answer between Pastor Steve and the congregation, taken from *The Africana Worship Book*:

Invisible God, be visible through our faith today.
Praise God who empowers us with faith to see what others
*   miss.*
Will we stop our building a better future because of evil?
No! Our God will deliver us from evil.
Will we concede our dreams for our world, your Creation,
*   because of evil?*
No, God will judge all evildoers.

Pastor Steve didn't give a sermon that morning. Instead, some of the younger church members who had participated in the United

Methodist Action Reach-Out Mission by Youth, or U.M. ARMY, stood and spoke about their experiences on that year's weeklong mission. Bill and Jen felt a certain pride listening to this. A few years earlier, one of the very first members of Cheshire United Methodist to participate in U.M. ARMY was Hayley Petit.

This morning Hayley was in Ipswich, Massachusetts, a beach town north of Boston, where a bunch of her gang had gone up to hang out one more time before the summer wore thin and everybody scattered off to college. By the time Bill, Jen, and Michaela walked out of church around eleven-fifteen, Hayley was already on her way home, driving the old Mercedes clunker that her parents had bought used and felt was as safe as any car for a seventeen-year-old girl. Hayley called it the Tank.

Some Sundays, Bill and Michaela snuck up the road to the Notch Store for the homemade doughnuts they served only on Sundays. It was supposed to be their secret—Jen had been trying to encourage Bill to eat healthy, especially since his heart trouble—but somehow Michaela always let it slip. On that day, though, they returned straight to Sorghum Mill Drive for lunch. It was a July Sunday, with mercifully little to do. Bill's dad called and asked if he wanted to play golf. The sky over central Connecticut was as blue as it gets, and the temperature was already up over 80. Jen and Michaela told him to go ahead—they were thinking of heading to the beach anyway, and that wasn't Bill's thing. This was something of a routine during the summer months at home, or on vacation—girls in the sun (Jen shaded by an umbrella), Bill on the golf course. It worked for everybody.

On his way to the club, Bill called Ron to see if he wanted to join him and his dad for golf. Ron lived about halfway between Bill's house in Cheshire and the club in Farmington. But Ron hadn't shaved all weekend and was working in the yard and figured that by the time he showered and drove the fifteen minutes to the club . . . He told Bill to go ahead, he'd catch him next weekend.

Shortly after Bill left, Hayley showed up from her trip on schedule and the three Petit girls jumped in the family minivan and drove to Silver Sands State Park, on the shore of Long Island Sound, about a half hour away. It would be crowded, but it was a beautiful stretch of beach near a breeding ground for herons and egrets, and the girls would bring their books, maybe take a walk on the old boardwalk, and just sit. Jennifer would be careful not to get too much sun.

Bill finished up his golf game a little after six and checked in with Jen on his cell. She told him that she and Michaela bought some groceries at Stop & Shop for dinner, and that KK wanted to cook dinner for the family. Jen asked Bill to stop by a farm stand on his way home for some fresh corn or whatever looked good. He pulled in to a couple of places, but it was a Sunday evening and everyone had closed up for the weekend, so he drove home. By seven-fifteen, he had hugged Hayley and was hearing about her trip as he dug into the tomato bruschetta that Jennifer and Michaela had made. The sky was clouding up a little, but the air was still bright and warm, and Sorghum Mill Drive was quiet. Bill's daughter was home safe. There was food on the stove. He had played pretty decent golf with his dad. Life was good.

They decided to eat in the sunroom. Jen helped Michaela serve the pasta and sauce they had made with local tomatoes, which Bill made a fuss over, and after supper the girls sat around the table talking. Eventually Bill picked up the Sunday paper and sank into the living-room couch. After a while, he glanced up and noticed that it was going on ten. Ten o'clock Sunday night was when *Army Wives*, a new show the girls liked, came on TV. They switched places—the girls took over the living-room couch, and Bill went back out to the sunroom with the paper.

He was exhausted. He had gotten some sun out on the golf course, and he had just eaten a big plate of pasta. Not long after the girls' show started, he was out cold on the couch, a section of the newspaper on his chest. When *Army Wives* ended, at eleven, the girls locked up the house and went upstairs to bed, leaving a light on in the kitchen for the cats, as usual. With her dad asleep on the couch downstairs, Michaela curled up in her parents' bed, where she and Jennifer read the latest Harry Potter book together, and fell asleep.

This wasn't the first time Bill had zonked out on the couch for the night. He had never needed much sleep, but especially since Jennifer's MS diagnosis, she got tired early. He didn't like to wake her by climbing into bed, and anyway, he could function fine after a night on the couch, even on five or six hours of sleep.

He awoke from a dream to find himself in the darkened house, the lamp by the couch glowing just above his head. He reached up to turn it off, closed his eyes, and fell back asleep.

Be sober, be vigilant; because your adversary the devil
walks about like a roaring lion,
seeking whom he may devour.

—1 Peter 5:8, tweeted by Bill Petit, 2013

MONDAY

July 23, 2007

THE PAIN comes slowly, like a thought.
Ow. What the . . . ?

It is a shock, being awakened this way. You're pretty sure you are in your home, on your couch, but you can't see, and someone is hitting you, hard.

Aaaow!

By the time Bill feels the blows, they stop.

The pain racks every part of his head. There is blood in his eyes. He had been sleeping, a deep, thick sleep after a hot day, but now suddenly he isn't sure whether he is sleeping or dreaming, whether the pain is real, whether he is in the sunroom or some place that only looks like it. Everything is black. He feels his house around him, and yet what's happening is so incongruous and nonsensical as to seem impossible. Where are the girls?

Seconds pass before he determines that the pain is actual. That this is happening.

Two people—two men, black shapes in the blackness of the glass room—look down at him. His eyes throb feverishly, but he can see their figures floating in the gauzy darkness, and at the end of an arm he sees a handgun. Nine millimeter. Bill has treated plenty of cops over the years who come in wearing guns in their holsters, and he always asks what they're carrying. Plus, he watches *NCIS* sometimes. He knows a little about guns, and this one looks like a 9mm. But whose gun is it? Not his. He doesn't own weapons, unless you count the baseball bat the other guy is holding, the one the guy just used to beat Bill's head with. The bat was a giveaway from Ronrico Rum. Bill picked it up once at the liquor store his dad used to own.

The men bind his wrists with plastic zip ties, then they tie rope over the zip ties, tight, his palms pressed together as if in prayer. Then they tie his ankles together the same way, so tight that the medial malleolus on each ankle—the bony ball that sticks out at the base of the tibia—is pressed hard against the other and he can't even rub them together. Warmth spreads across his face, into his eyes— his blood. He has been taking a prescription blood thinner called Coumadin since he had the heart trouble a few years ago, so as he lies on the couch, he is bleeding out faster than most people would. His right eye throbs.

Only one of the men speaks. While Bill lies there stunned, a few feet from the table where only hours before he had sat with his wife and daughters eating dinner, the talker tells him they're just there for the money, and to stay calm. They ask him where the safe is, and Bill tells him there's no safe in the house. Now the talker seems to be leaving the room—Bill can't tell for sure, because his eyes are full of blood and the men have thrown some kind of cloth over his head, maybe a shirt. But that's what it sounds like from his voice and his footsteps—that he is leaving Bill here with the other guy. As the talker leaves, Bills hears him say, "If he moves, put two bullets in him."

What to do? This is bad. So what to do? What's the strategy? Yell? Be quiet? He decides to stay quiet. Try to attack this guy? Ridiculous. There's the gun, obviously. Bill can barely move. The pain is horrible. The plastic ties slice into the skin on his wrists and ankles. He feels like he is going blind. He goes over his options again and again, but right now, at this very moment, he does not seem to have any. There are two men in his home, one of them on the big side. The other one, who's probably off looking for a safe, might have a gun, too. Bill is a pretty big guy, but in this state he can't even stand up, let alone take on two men with guns and a bat and whatever else they want to use on him. At least Bill doesn't hear any sounds from the rest of the house—no sounds of violence, no screams from upstairs, where he assumes the girls are. The men said they only want money. It makes sense that they would incapacitate the man of the house, the only one who could hurt them. But that didn't mean they would hurt the girls, too. Why would they? Maybe they haven't even woken the girls.

He doesn't know how long he is left lying there, barely able to move, unable to see much of anything. He slides in and out of consciousness, his brain a slushy mess of fear, feverish pain, and the cloudiness of being awake when it should be sleeping.

But the men have woken the girls upstairs.

Michaela had fallen asleep in Bill and Jen's bed next to her mother. The talker yanks pillowcases over their heads and tells them not to worry, that he is only there for money. He brings Michaela to her bed across the hall. He covers Hayley's head, too, in her bed, in her room at the top of the stairs, and all three Petit females are tied by their wrists and ankles to the posts of their beds, their own panicked breaths amplified under the pillowcases, afraid to close their eyes but unable to see, listening to the unsettling quiet.

Bill's head is so thick with pain it feels as if something is inside trying to beat its way out. Eventually—suddenly—both men are once again standing over him as he lies on the couch. They rip him from his delirium. He feels them cut the zip ties and clothesline from around his ankles and his relief at being able to move his legs again is immense. They grab him by both arms and jerk him to his feet. When he is standing, he wobbles—he has lost so much blood already, and his legs are weak from being bound together so uncomfortably for . . . How long have they been tied together? He doesn't know. He tries to figure it out, his mind working to compute. He definitely fell asleep sometime between ten and eleven—that's when

Army Wives was on, and he knew he hadn't lasted long after the girls migrated to the living-room couch. He woke up once to turn off the light but doesn't know when that was. There isn't a hint of brightness that he can see now—even through the shirt covering his face, he probably would be able to see the dimmest membrane of sunlight to the east, because the sunroom has east-facing windows. But there is no light. His best guess is that the men broke in between 2:00 and 3:00 a.m., and that he has been incapacitated on the couch for two hours or so.

The men walk him up the step from the sunroom into the living room, up the other little step into the kitchen, and toward the basement door, which is off the kitchen. *They're bringing me downstairs,* he thinks. He listens for any sound that might suggest the girls' presence, but hears nothing. He again considers making a move, but what's he going to do, kick them? Start swinging his tied-together hands, only to have the guy with the gun shoot him in the leg? Then where would he be? But it's confounding, the silence. The not knowing. He hasn't heard anything from the girls. He doesn't know where they are. Even in his demolished state, the impulse to protect is elemental. He is a man who always believes he can do anything. But right now, there is nothing he can do but shuffle his aching feet across the kitchen floor he has walked across a million times before.

His hands are still bound palm to palm, and he can't see, but he reaches for the railing on the basement stairs, and the tips of his fingers read it like braille, guiding him down the steps he knows by heart but that now feel uneven under his bare feet. It is an indescribable feeling, being a prisoner in your own home, being beaten to the point where you can barely manage to walk from here to there in a house you've lived in for twenty-two years. For Bill right now, everything is familiar and grotesque at the same time, a fever dream of his own life.

The Petits had never bothered to convert the basement to living space. It's just a basement—concrete floors, a tangle of electrical wiring running out of the breaker box and along the ceiling joists, plastic storage boxes full of old stuff, a refrigerator. The men walk him to the steel support pole in the middle of the room and slide him down it so he's sitting on the floor with his back against the pole. He is a few feet from the two cats' litter boxes and an open bag of Fresh Step. Blurry scraps of memory and life whir in and out of his sight line—tiny rocking chairs, a miniature puppet theater, tiki torches leaning against the wall, a table of paint cans. One of the men jams a couple of cushions, taken from upstairs, under him. They retie his hands together tight, behind his back and around the pole. Once again they tie his ankles together with a plastic zip tie and then a few wraps of clothesline over that. He doesn't keep those zip tie things in the house, which means the men must have brought them. Same with the clothesline, which they tie around his waist and chest, bracing him hard against the metal pole.

Bill can barely move.

The shirt is no longer on his head, but now they throw a quilt over him. One of Hayley's elementary-school teachers, Mrs. Watkinson, made it for Hayley and gave it to her when she graduated from high school a few weeks ago.

Upstairs, the men search for money. They pull out drawers, empty cupboards, turn over boxes—they want a score, and they don't seem to understand that most suburban families, affluent though their clapboarded, landscaped homes may give them away to be, don't store cash in their credenzas. Eventually they figure out that there are no piles of money in the house. They find a few jars, one emblazoned with a Boston Red Sox logo, full of loose change, and one of them empties the coins into a bag, a pathetic little grab. They find wallets. Bill's is worn, the leather used up like an old football, the plastic window for photos held in place with Scotch tape. There's no cash inside, but there are four wallet-size photographs of Jennifer, two each of Hayley and Michaela, and three photo-booth snapshots of Bill and his daughters.

Inside Hayley's neat leather wallet with the pink trim: $103 cash and a bunch of gift cards, probably given to her on her graduation, to Bob's, a chain of clothing stores; Starbucks; Banana Republic; and the Dartmouth Co-op. And a new Bank of America ATM card that her parents had gotten for her to take to college.

The men have ripped the phone cord next to the bed in the master bedroom out of its jack. They continue to search the house and eventually find a bankbook showing a Bank of America account flush with nearly $30,000. Their plan changes. They'll wait until the bank opens, and then one of the men will drive the wife to the bank and wait in the car while she withdraws $15,000—that's the number they choose. The other one will keep watch at the house.

Bill knows none of this. He sits on the concrete basement floor in dark silence, trying to make his brain work for him, the way it always does. It feels swollen and bruised—he can feel his pulse in his skull. But he tries. His body feels unbearably heavy, and his mind is careening between half-sleep, desperation, fear, calculation, pain, and unconsciousness. His blood is soaking the couch cushions, Mrs. Watkinson's quilt, the basement floor. But there are a few things he knows, because he can still hear: He realizes that he heard the birds outside start singing when he was still upstairs—that would have been around 4:45. Then, down in the basement, he heard an electrical box click. That was the timer activating the sprinkler system: 5:30. He has lived here for two decades. The house's familiar noises become his clock.

One of the men rummages around in Bill's two-car garage and finds several empty windshield-washer-fluid containers in the recycling bin. Bill is no mechanic, so for him car maintenance consists primarily of making sure the Petits' three cars—Jennifer's Chrysler Pacifica minivan, Bill's used Mercedes, and Hayley's car, the Tank—always had washer fluid. The man throws the plastic jugs into the minivan.

Bill hears a car engine start. Are they leaving? No other noise suggested this. He redoubles his efforts trying to twist out of the ties.

The man drives the van to a Citgo station nearby and pumps ten dollars' worth of gas into the plastic containers but none into the car, walks into the minimart, and hands the cashier a twenty. He's wearing a gray T-shirt and jeans, just another guy buying gas on a Monday morning. The cashier, Selma Haddad, looks in his eyes, as she does with every customer, hands him his change, and thanks him. He walks back out to the hijacked minivan and drives away. He gets lost. He calls his friend back at the house. Calls him once, calls him again. Eventually, the man who went to buy gas finds his way back to 300 Sorghum Mill Drive, the plastic containers sloshing on the floor of Jennifer's minivan.

A sweet sound drifts down from upstairs into Bill's basement hell, a sound both familiar and incongruous. It is Jennifer's voice, distant, muffled, but kind. Bill hears her voice every day in this house, in other rooms, talking to the girls, talking to her parents on the phone—Jen's voice in this house has been the mood music of his existence for a long time. But now the sound has a different tenor. It is a sign that she is okay, a clue to what might be happening, a note of comfort after hours of terror. And yet there is also the unshakable truth that he is witnessing his wife, who must be petrified, having a conversation with two men who broke into their home and beat his skull with a bat. This must be what it feels like when the plane you're in starts suddenly dropping—you're still alive, holding your wife's hand, but your world appears to be hurtling toward disaster and there is nothing you can do.

They are probably in the kitchen, because the kitchen is just up the basement stairs and it sounds as if the door at the top is open. Jennifer is calmly saying that she will need to get her purse and her husband's checkbook before they go to the bank.

So they're taking her to the bank to get money because there's no cash in the house. Bank won't be open for a while. But maybe this is good news. Maybe this move by these guys—a fairly stupid move on their part, it would seem—will draw the police. Or maybe Jen will give them some money and they will actually leave. Good, sweet Jenna. Inclined against hatred, wanting to trust. But she's no pushover. She will have a clear head through this.

Bill knows his blood pressure must be dangerously low and tries to estimate his blood loss. It's a lot, so far, and the torrent of blood pouring out of him makes it harder and harder to move without feeling like he's going to faint. Eventually he figures out that if he stands up and then slides down the pole, the weight of his body moving down raises his blood pressure and makes him feel something resembling strength. Up and down he struggles, slowly building his strength while at the same time trying to free his hands and feet, the hard plastic ties still slicing into his skin.

Then, a little while later—it's hard to figure how long—he hears Jen's voice once more. This time she is leaving a message for Mona Huggard, the nurse who manages the office at Bill's medical practice, telling her that Bill is feeling sick today and asking her to cancel all his appointments for the morning, a full schedule of patients. That will be a surprising message for Mona to hear. She's worked for Bill for eighteen years. In all that time Bill has maybe called in sick once.

Things are happening.

All that matters for Bill right now is getting himself off this pole.

. . .

Thump, thump, thump.

The hell is that?

Thump.

Coming from the living room, it sounds like. Maybe the men are ransacking the house. Maybe they're piling up the TV and furniture and whatever else they're going to steal. Getting it ready to load into a car or something. He can't bring himself to imagine that what he hears is the sound of his wife being raped on their living-room floor. Can't make himself think about what has happened to his two girls, his beautiful Michaela and Hayley.

Then he hears what sounds like a moan.

"Hey!" he yells. It takes all the strength he has just to make a sound, and the word barely forms in the air.

A man's voice responds back down the basement stairs.

"Don't worry," the voice says. "It's all going to be over in a couple of minutes."

He can't stay tied to this pole anymore. He reaches deep, musters energy he doesn't seem to have, and presses his wrists against the plastic ties, doesn't care if they slice his damn hands off. Finally, all the scraping and rubbing against the pole and the twisting of his wrists has worn down the plastic ties, and they burst off. He contorts his hands out of the clothesline knots, unties the lines around his waist and chest, and he is free.

He has to get next door to Simcik's, his neighbor. Dave can call the police.

He tries for a couple of seconds to force the ties off his ankles, but they're too tight, and anyway he is mobile now. No need to unbind his feet, no seconds to waste. He drags himself to the stairs that lead up through the bulkhead door and into the backyard, then he pushes his body up the stairs themselves, propelling himself along on his hands and elbows. When he gets to the top, his heart feels like it's beating two hundred times per minute. Feels like it's going to explode right out of his chest. But he keeps going. His whole life, he has never given up on anything important, never given in, never relented. He has never not won. But right now, he knows one thing, and it might be the only thing he knows for sure: He needs help.

He falls. Just outside the bulkhead doors in the backyard, he tries to stand so that he can hop efficiently across the yard toward Dave's house, but he falls. He pushes himself back up onto his feet, but he falls again. His body can't do what he wants it to do. But he has to get to Dave's—it can't be much more than fifty feet, but it might as well be a mile if he can't walk, can't even hop. The grass is slick with the morning rain, which makes it even more difficult to keep his footing. He tries to crawl, but even that proves impossible, because he does not have the strength to support his body and his legs are tied together, so they have to move as one. He just keeps slipping, his arms sliding out from under his own weight like the legs of a newborn colt. He is getting nowhere.

So he rolls.

He lies prone on the grass and rolls across the backyard, through the copse of trees on the border of his yard and Simcik's, past some bushes, up toward Dave's driveway. When he gets close, he starts yelling, "Dave! Dave! Dave!"

He rolls right up to Dave's white garage door and starts pounding on it. His ankles are still tied together tight, but his hands are free and he is banging on the door with the force of his whole life. Finally, finally, the garage door opens and Dave appears. Thank God. But Dave, his neighbor for eighteen years, looks down at Bill, a beaten, soaking-wet man lying in his driveway covered with blood, and asks, "Can I help you, sir?"

Bill says, "Dave! It's Bill. Call 911! Quick. *Quick.*"

It seems like only a few seconds before a cop appears out of the rain and is standing over Bill, ordering him to stay down. Bill assumes it's a cop, anyway. His gun is drawn and he doesn't seem to know whether Bill is a suspect or a victim. Then another officer is there, who looks more like a SWAT team member—the black pants, the black vest. Bill is trying to tell them to cut the bindings from his ankles, but they won't.

The first one, his gun still drawn, his arms bolt stiff, his eyes pivoting between Bill and Bill's home, shouts, "Who's in the house?"

"The girls," Bill gasps through the rain.

The officer repeats himself, as if needing more information, or as if he had expected a different answer. His voice is urgent and impatient, the voice of an officer in an emergency: *"Who's in the house?"*

Bill yells up at him, "The girls! The girls are in the house!"

AFTERMATH

Monday, July 23–Friday, July 27, 2007

Barbara Petit calls her husband, Bill Sr., at 10:15 to tell him that the fire alarm at Billy and Jennifer's house is going off and that they aren't answering their cell phones. When the alarm company can't reach anyone in the home, they call Bill's parents as a backup, and Barbara is worried.

Bill Sr. is downtown in Plainville and decides to first check Bill's medical office on Whiting Street. Mona, Bill's nurse, tells Mr. Petit that Jennifer left a message early that morning saying that Bill was out sick. Bill Sr.'s first thought is his son's weak heart. He and Mona call around to the few area hospitals where it would make sense for Billy to go if he were having a cardiac emergency. None has admitted a William Petit.

It's not even a mile and a half from Bill's office to Big Bill's house on Red Stone Hill, so Bill Sr. drives up to his home to tell Barbara he's going to Billy's house in Cheshire to see what's going on. On the twenty-minute drive, he calls Bill and Jen's home number and everyone's cell phones. There's no answer on any of the numbers. The only response he gets is Michaela's sweet voicemail greeting on her cell.

Bill Sr. exits Interstate 84 and is driving down Mountain Road toward Sorghum Mill Drive when an ambulance speeds by going in the opposite direction. Then two Cheshire police cars race past him and turn left up Sorghum Mill, and his heart drops into his stomach. He puts his blinker on and takes the left turn, as he has countless times before.

The yellow police tape stretches clear across the road, visible through the steady rain, and Bill Sr. can't imagine what's going on. And then, just beyond the tape, he sees a car—a minivan. It's totaled. Just destroyed. It looks like Jen's Chrysler, but it couldn't possibly be. He stops his car, opens the door, and sees that, in fact, it is his daughter-in-law's car. And his body begins to weaken. The fire alarm, a car accident, no answer on the phone ... William A. Petit Sr., the patriarch of an American family that is both normal and extraordinary, stands in the rain, his face slack and his heart pounding and his knees shaking, and he can feel in his gut that something has happened that will be more than he can bear.

He tries to approach Jennifer's car, but a Cheshire police officer stops him. Bill Sr. tells the officer that the car belongs to his daughter-in-law. At this the cop freezes for a second. He tells Mr. Petit to wait there while he gets someone to talk to him.

Fifteen minutes pass. He is too far down the road to be able to see his son's house. He just stares at the mangled Chrysler Pacifica, unable to fathom what could have caused this. And what about the fire alarm in the house? How would that lead to this?

Finally, the chief of police, accompanied by two other officers, walks up to Big Bill and says, "Your son is on his way to the hospital, and there are three deceased in the house."

The ambulance that roared past Bill Sr. on Mountain Road carries the almost lifeless body of his son. The driver swerves onto 84 going west and blows by four quick exits in downtown Waterbury before screeching up to the emergency-room entrance at St. Mary's. In the emergency department doctors immediately begin suturing and stapling the pulsing lacerations on Bill's head. The Coumadin makes his blood almost as thin as water, and it seeps from the wounds in little rivers. His body, in shock from what he has endured over the last seven hours and from the loss of between five and seven pints of blood—almost beyond what a human being can stand—convulses, and he vomits. This happens a few times before the ER staff administers an anti-nausea drug to stop the retching.

Bill Sr. calls home to tell Barbara. Her sister Johanna answers and tells him that Barbara is already on her way to Cheshire. He tries to tell Johanna what happened, but he can barely get the words out of his throat. He is sobbing. Finally he forces himself to say, "They're all gone." Johanna doesn't understand. Big Bill can't respond at first—he can't talk, his voice a hostage of dread. After fifteen or twenty seconds, he finds the voice to tell her that Jennifer, Hayley, and Michaela are dead.

When Barbara pulls up to the police tape, the cops bring her over to her husband. Barbara is screaming. Hanna pulls up and leaps from her car, yelling, waving her arms. Andrew and Abby sit in Hanna's car, crying uncontrollably. The EMTs check Bill Sr.'s vital signs.

Bill's brothers Glenn and Brian arrive and drive their parents to St. Mary's, and Hanna follows them. Their other brother, Mike, his wife, and Hanna's husband, Dennis, meet them there. The family is shown to a waiting room, where a police detective tells them everything that's known about what happened at 300 Sorghum Mill Drive that morning, his words echoing around them like some faraway noise. The ten of them stand in the hospital waiting room, a place unfamiliar to them all, and try to comprehend what the detective is saying.

Eventually they are shown in to see Bill. Their darling Billy. Billy, their big brother. Uncle Billy. He is lying on a hospital bed, his clothes cut off, his body limp with exhaustion and blood loss, purple bruises and cuts around his wrists and ankles. He looks horrible, unrecognizable, like no version of Billy they have ever seen. The doctors are in the middle of sewing the wounds, but they pause for a moment because he lifts his head. He looks into the faces of his family, and he asks about the girls. His father just looks at him, his eyes clouding with tears, and shakes his head.

Ron Bucchi returns to his office around one o'clock after having lunch with a client. His phone rings, and it's one of Bill's cousins— not unusual, really. Ron has known Bill for forty years and done accounting work for half the family.

What number Sorghum is Billy?

Three hundred, says Ron.

Oh my God.

Ron finds the head of his firm and tells him he has to leave right away. "They killed my friend's family," he says, running out.

He speeds home. Ron lives on a quiet cul-de-sac in Kensington, another peaceful central-Connecticut town. Like Bill, he is a local boy done good, and he lives in a gorgeous home with an open kitchen looking out to woods in the backyard. Susan is there, and her mother has stopped by to visit. Ron tells them what happened, makes sure Susan is okay—thank goodness her mom is there—then runs back out to his car and races the twenty minutes to St. Mary's.

He hardly leaves the hospital for the rest of the week. He goes home at night to sleep, and to give the family time alone with Bill, but during the day he is there, using a hospital conference room on the same floor as Billy's room as a makeshift command center from which he handles all the tasks that are too much for the Petits to think about, the details that must be dealt with when a catastrophe falls out of the sky. First, on that Monday, there is the issue of Jen's parents. They're elderly. They live in Pennsylvania, at least six hours away by car when it's not raining. Ron speaks to them by phone, and they tell him they're going to get in the car. He says, No, wait, I'll call you back. Ron makes a couple of calls. At the country club, there are some guys with money. He calls a buddy, says, Do you know anybody who has a plane? A couple more calls and he reaches a guy who has an account with a private charter company. Ron tells the guy what's happened, his voice gravid with panic and pain and the urgent, shaking need to help. The guy orders a plane into the air and within an hour or two, Dick and Marybelle Hawke are flying up to Connecticut in a stranger's jet.

Ron helps the hospital staff deal with the reporters who are showing up wanting an interview with Bill, or with Ron, or with anybody. He is also charged with organizing a memorial service for Jennifer, Hayley, and Michaela, to be held this Saturday. He secures an auditorium at Central Connecticut State University. He sets up committees to oversee parking and sound systems. He works with the Petits' church, United Methodist, to get the choir to perform, with musicians from a music school in Hartford. Everyone is on edge. The church people want something elaborate ("a Busby Berkeley production," Ron says later), and Ron just wants a simple, relatively quick service that his friend Bill can survive without fainting, because it will be a miracle if he can show up at all. But eventually Ron and the church people figure things out, and everyone is reasonably satisfied with the plan.

It also falls mostly to Ron to arrange the funeral for the three Petit girls. He asks Bill, who is still hooked up to an IV, What do you want me to do?

White caskets, Bill says. I just want white caskets. You can figure out the rest.

At the burial on Friday in Plainville, in West Cemetery, there is no headstone on the graves. It will take Bill some time to decide what kind of stone he wants, and what he wants it to say. It will take him some time to get it perfect.

It will take some time to make himself set the stone, so heavy and final, into the earth.

It will take years.

REMEMBRANCE

July 28, 2007

O N THE morning of the memorial service, the staples are still in Bill's head, crusted with purple blood. They bind together the flaps of scalp that the baseball bat tore apart 130 hours earlier. A long gash cleaves the back left side of his head, and on the right side of his forehead, a crimson line tears through the skin like a zipper, straight down from his hairline before hooking in just above the eyebrow.

A tailor from Melluzzo's, a men's clothing store in the next town over, comes to his parents' house to make sure the new suit fits. The same man had appeared at St. Mary's Hospital a few days before to measure him, because William A. Petit Jr., fifty years old, father of two, successful endocrinologist, director of clinical research at the Hospital of Central Connecticut, medical director of the prestigious Joslin Diabetes Center, owner of a cream-colored three-bedroom colonial on a corner lot in a nice town, has no clothes. Everything he owned burned in the fire. So somebody had called Melluzzo's, and the man now shows up with a new charcoal suit, a crisp white shirt, and a gray striped tie. Bill puts on the clothes, ties the tie with unsteady hands, stands before the mirror, and gingerly combs his dark hair over the wound in the back.

A couple of limousines arrive—some friends of the Petits own Bailey Funeral Home in Plainville, and they sent the cars. The limos pull up the long lasso drive in front of the house on Red Stone Hill, and Billy climbs into the first one with his parents, Hanna, and Bill's friend Steve Hanks. Hanks is a buddy from the hospital—when Steve became chief medical officer in 2004, Bill was running the childhood

[88]

diabetes center. Tall and slim with a face all sturdy angles and dark features, Hanks slides into the seat next to Bill. He's a friend, but today he's at Bill's side as a physician. During the five days he spent at St. Mary's, Bill was receiving intravenous fluids. They tried to give him a blood transfusion on the first day, but he said no, let's wait and see if it replenishes on its own. Doctors always hate treating other doctors, he knows, because as a patient, a doctor will do things like refuse a blood transfusion if he thinks he knows better. Eventually, they did give Bill a transfusion that brought his hemoglobin count up to nine grams. The normal count for a male, according to Bill, is between fourteen and fifteen grams. So on this Saturday morning, Bill still feels dizzy sometimes, the head wounds are still tender and throbbing, and his ankles and wrists, where he was tied up, are still laced with bruises. Truth is, Bill Petit is a mess.

The day before, Friday, after the doctors at St. Mary's told him he could go, and after Bill watched the three white coffins disappear into the earth in the cemetery in Plainville, he had gone to the house on Red Stone Hill. His family has told him his own house was burned, uninhabitable, and he knows he can't go there, but he doesn't know just how bad it is—the smoke stains around the windows outside, and inside, devastation. A crime scene, detectives toiling in the darkened ash. So Bill spent the night at his folks' but didn't sleep much. It wasn't his bed, his new clothes felt odd, and when he reached over to turn off the lamp on the nightstand, his fingers didn't know how to find the switch without him looking, the way they could next to his own bed.

No one says much on the ride to Welte Hall, the auditorium at Central Connecticut State University that Ron arranged for the service. State troopers escort the limousines all the way from Plainville to New Britain, and by the time they get off Route 9, the Petits can see cars streaming onto the campus. It's a Saturday morning in July, so there isn't much else going on at CCSU. The cars pack the four-story garage next to the hall and spill over into the student-center lot out back. The sky is a matte gray, and the air is thick and hot and smells like rain. The people, hundreds and hundreds of them, and then thousands of them, converge purposefully and silently on the six double doors that lead into Welte. They've heard about the service on the news or read about it in the papers. There are close friends, family members, strangers. Most are dressed up, some aren't. They are old and young, from all over the state, must be. They come to offer hope, or in search of it, or both.

And there are the girls in black dresses. So many girls in black dresses—high-school girls, grade-school girls, clutching one another as they walk. Friends of the Petit girls. Reporters, notepads and recorders in hand or stuffed into breast pockets, nose around the sprawling patio out front, acting hesitant, approaching some of the girls in black dresses. *Excuse me, hi, I'm so sorry. Are you a friend of Hayley's?* Some of the girls stop to talk.

CCSU workers had prepared the day before, hauling folding tables, setting up chairs, and dragging a heavy red cloak across the stage as a backdrop. When the doors open at ten, the people file into the auditorium, taking only a few minutes to fill the 1,814 scratchy maroon seats. When the seats are all taken, the lobby, a good twenty feet deep, jams up, too—the school has set up TV screens out there to show the service, and more in overflow rooms. By the time the service is about to begin, four thousand people are watching the stage.

This is the community that produced Bill Petit, come to wrap itself around him. It's the community that Bill Sr. and Barbara have served their whole lives. Sometimes people wondered why they did all that, gave so much of their time to serving on boards and running committees. Maybe this is why, because when you help the place you're from, the place you're from helps you. In a strong community, this reaction is reflex. When someone needs help, there will be enough people—not everyone, but enough—to give their time to help. And Bill Petit needs help.

He sits in a room backstage, waiting for the service to begin. Ron is there, too. Thank God for Ron. He and Hanks and the hunched, worried inner circle in the backstage room just want to get Bill through this before he passes out.

Three easels stand behind the podium holding huge posterboard photographs of the girls, each one draped with white roses and curtained with lace. The Reverend Richard Hawke stands to speak. Jennifer's father. The man who, with his wife, Marybelle, raised Jen never to say a bad word about anyone, to believe that everyone is capable of good. He is a compact man, short and lean, but his voice resonates like the clang of iron, and when he crinkles his forehead in earnestness, it gives his words the unimpeachable authority that is the special province of small-town preachers. He begins by quoting John 11:25–26, in which Jesus tells the sister of his friend Lazarus, who is dying, "I am the resurrection and the life. Those who believe in me, though they die, shall live. And whosoever lives and believes in me shall never die."

The image of Hayley's smiling face, wreathed in the photograph by an ivy wall behind her, gazes over his right shoulder. Over his left shoulder is the poster of his own daughter, her face larger than it was in life, smiling in an evening dress. Next to her, beaming, is Michaela. Dick Hawke is assuming two roles here. He is Rev. Hawke, a clergyman trying to summon words from Scripture and a message of hope at an impossibly sad time. But he is also Dick, Daddy, Popup—a father mourning the loss of his firstborn child to a brutal rape and murder just six days ago, and a grandfather reckoning with the torture and asphyxiation of two of his grandchildren. Perhaps by the force of his own will, the role of clergyman pushes through to the fore—his voice is somber but clear and strong, and if you didn't know his name, you might assume he was a pastor brought in from the local church to offer spiritual wisdom to the proceedings of a devastated family, so steady and purposeful is his demeanor. He doesn't use the first person, never refers to "my daughter" or "my granddaughters." Under the circumstances, his reserve is astounding.

"Today we come together to celebrate the Petit family, the Hawkes and the Chapmans"—he pauses very slightly between the name of each family, careful to give each the same emphasis— "the Trianos, the Renns, and many others. We welcome you. We welcome you to this service. You who have come from far distances. We have people from Maine to Florida to Texas"—he speeds up, the list gaining momentum and power—"to New York, New Haven, Utah, Wyoming." He invokes the metaphor of Good Friday, when Christ died and was buried: "You have come from everywhere because that dark Friday covered your light as well, and you come to support us to the beginning of a new life in Christ. We come today to celebrate—and I use that word in the greatest and highest sense of its meaning. It's a religious term: We come to celebrate the lives of"—and here he draws out each syllable of the girls' names, perhaps the first time since the murders that many of the four thousand people have heard the full names, which is why Rev. Hawke pronounces them with purpose and deliberation—"Jennifer . . . Lynn . . . Hawke . . . Petit. Hayley . . . Elizabeth . . . Petit. Michaela . . . Rose . . . Petit." He looks out at the crowd. "You have come to strengthen us in our resurrection and hope. And perhaps we can covenant together with each other today to strive to build a new world. To have a new hope. And a place of peace. We hope that being together will not be in vain, but will bring about a strength to all of us as we make this new beginning. It is with heartfelt thanks and gratitude we welcome you. All of you." He looks down at the podium. His volume drops, and for the first time, he allows into his magisterial voice a faint note of sadness, of despair—even of defeat. "Whoever you may be. Wherever you're from. Whoever you are."

He doesn't look up as he collects his papers. The piano starts in from somewhere off to his right. On the stage, there's a harp, about sixty singers and musicians—Ron tried to keep the bursts of music to a minimum, lovely though they are. Bill sits in the front row, lower right corner of the auditorium, just in front of the steps that lead to the podium. You can see the back of his head from almost any seat, and the staples look black against the paleness of his scalp.

No one thinks Billy is going to speak today. Sure, last night, when Ron left Red Stone Hill around eight-thirty, Billy had told him that yeah, he was going to stay up and work on some remarks, and that he was going to stand up and speak. Absolutely. That was Bill: No way he could be kept down, no way some cuts on his head were going to keep him from speaking at a memorial for his own wife and daughters. And Hanna had read a draft—last night, or this morning, it was a blur. But privately everyone thought: Not a chance. They didn't even list him in the program. The wounds on his head are hideous, his vision is blurry on and off, he gets dizzy— the thought of him rising, walking up the steps, and standing before the four thousand people . . . Billy is mortal, and there are some things even he can't do.

Another hymn ends. Two high-school girls wait for the last note to fade before one of them, tall and athletic in a black dress, sun- glasses nested in her blond hair, lets out a short, I-can't-believe-this sigh, and says, "We're Bill's nieces." She is Hanna's daughter, Abby, best friend to Hayley, devotee of her Uncle Billy. Her composure is astonishing as she reads from John 14. "And where I am going, you know the way. I will not leave you as orphans. I will come back to you. Just a little while now, and the world will not see me anymore. But you will see me. Because I live, you will live also."

Her cousin Brook, by her side, a full head shorter in a white headband, a heart-shaped locket, and a gray blouse, says, "Per my uncle's request, we'd now like to invite all the children to come for- ward to the front of the stage."

Maybe a dozen children, mostly from the family, walk from their seats to the stage. Abby and Brook hand each child a white or a pink flower. Ron is up there supervising, waving the kids along, patting a child on the shoulder here and there. Dick Hawke walks up to the lip of the stage and gently waves over his grandson, Evan— Cindy's boy—and whispers something to him. The boy squats and listens to his grandfather, nods, then steps to the microphone and says, "Can we have *all* the children come forward please." This was meant as a clarification: Bill didn't want only the children in his family up there. He wants to see a parade of children, a mass, a celebration of kids standing side by side, holding flowers, looking beautiful in their dresses and their too-big suits perhaps bought for this very occasion. The reality of the loss of his own children has not yet fully set in, and right now he wants to see every child in the building up there. His head darts from side to side, a sudden jolt of life in him, as the children, so many beautiful children, walk quietly down the aisles around him, some of them stealing glances at him, others head-down, little boys holding their big sisters' hands, none of them knowing where to look. Bill reaches out to give a high-five to a few of them as they pass by his seat, and one girl's mother motions for her to give him a hug. The children line up on the steps, Abby and Brook pressing flowers in their hands, and before long there's a line—a *line* of children spilling down the steps and onto the auditorium floor, so many of them are there, come to see the man whose own were taken from him. Come to pay respects. They crowd onto the stage in front of the three posters, looking nervous in the unexpected spotlight, pursing their lips with solemnity. Ron looks like a teacher lining up students for a recital, pointing, scooting a kid a few inches to the right, waving them up the stairs, making sure every kid has a flower.

At the podium in front of all the kids now stands a handsome teenage boy in a charcoal suit, his hair combed forward. He looks over to Ron for his cue, and then says, "Hello, my name is Evan, this is my sister, Lydia." These are Cindy's kids—Jen and Bill's niece and nephew. Evan looks up at the crowd for a second and lets out an audible, nervous exhale. He shuffles a page on the lectern and says in his deepening teenage voice, "I found these papers at the house, um, where the Petits lived. These are quotes from a book we found . . . of Hayley's. I'll read a couple of them."

The house.

This poor boy—has he been in the house? On this morning of flowers and new dresses, those words—the house—are an unintended reminder of not just why everyone is here but how it happened.

"The first one's by the Beatles," Evan says to the crowd in a low monotone, allowing the beginning of a smile at the pleasing image of Hayley listening to the Beatles. He looks down and reads: "There are places I'll remember all my life, though some have changed. Some forever, not for better, some have gone and some remain. All these places have their moments, with lovers and friends, I still can recall. Some are dead and some are living. In my life, I've loved them all."

The final quote Hayley had written down in her book, salvaged by her cousin from her burned-out room and read now by him into a microphone to people she loved and people she will never meet, is both earnest and chilling. "This last one I believe is by Nike— that's who Hayley had [writing] it: 'Somebody may beat me, but they're going to have to bleed to do it. If you can't win, make the guy ahead of you break the record. Tough times don't last, but tough people do.'"

It was only last Sunday, six short days ago, that Bill, Jennifer, and Michaela sat in Cheshire United Methodist and heard Pastor Steve speak about the U.M. ARMY, but to Bill it feels as if that brilliant July morning happened in another life. Pastor Steve stands now before a different congregation, wearing his black suit and clerical collar, a silver cross the size of a paperback hanging from a long chain around his neck. Jennifer was an active member of his church, so he knew her pretty well. He allows some pain into his voice today, some anger, some consternation as he tries to convince the mass of people before him that Bill's wife and daughters are in a better place. He elongates the last words of some sentences, ending almost in a whisper. "Remember this: That Jennifer, Hayley, and Michaela are no longer suffering," he says. "They are free of all earthly terrors and pain. They are with God. They are *with God.* They are resting in God's peace, living in the home of God, where Jesus tells us there are many dwelling places. They are there now. They are making it home. They are *making it home.* They are making friends. They are living their reward that we here are only dimly aware of. And they have truly become the heavenly angels that they lived as on earth."

Another life. A couple of weeks ago the four of them went to Cape Cod together, as a family. Was it only two weeks? Bill had taken off work and Jen had found a house at the last minute, in Chatham. One night, real late, they all went to see the new Harry Potter movie, *Order of the Phoenix* or something. Hayley and Michaela love those books. Another day they took a bike ride. It was in the afternoon. They rode down Main Street and went off to the right toward the lighthouse, past an inlet, a cool Atlantic breeze cutting the damp New England heat. They were gliding along and suddenly someone yelled, "KK!" One of Michaela's friends from school, her voice carrying in the wind. They all rode to a place nearby and sat outside eating clams, the girls laughing eagerly about summer and friends, the parents chatting like grown-ups. That was a good day.

"This is the second-hardest thing that I've ever done in my life."

Hanna. Black dress, string of pearls, elegant, exhausted.

"The hardest thing came yesterday, when we buried Jen, Hayley, and Michaela. I'm gonna try and draw my strength from Bill and his three girls, so please bear with me."

Shaking. Clutching both sides of the podium as if it's holding her up. Her quick, troubled breaths escape in bursts. But she is breathing. And she can do this. She's telling the story of a family.

". . . When Bill had to leave the state to deliver yet another lecture on diabetes, Jen held the family together. When Hayley had a collapsed lung the week of her graduation, Jen held the family together. When she developed MS, she learned quickly about the disease and never once let it define her or slow her down, once again: Holding. The family. Together."

". . . Hayley was a strong, quiet leader. Emphasis on quiet. Always willing to take the lead, never the credit."

". . . Last but not least, just the youngest, there was KK." Hanna puts her hand on her heart. "My heart aches for KK. She loved to cook, which is also my passion. Given the chance, we could have prepared some grand feasts for the holidays." Hanna's voice rises, quivering. "I promised her this summer that I was gonna teach her how to make the pasta from scratch, and make the gnocchi. Just a little flower and a little egg, mixed with the Italian attitude that only Gram Triano could provide. . . . Losing her at age eleven is possibly the greatest loss of all, because she never got the chance to show us just how great she could have been."

A boyish, blue-blazered young man rises amid the sea of singers and musicians onstage, holding a music folder in front of his chest with one hand. He begins to sing the Ave Maria, accompanied by arpeggios on the piano and harp, a smooth and soaring rendition. High-pitched, like a schoolboy. While he sings, seven girls, all around eighteen years old and wearing black dresses, quietly make their way up the steps to the podium. The orchestra and chorus members seated around the Ave Maria man look over at the girls and purse their lips—they know what's coming. *Friends of the girls.*

The girls whisper a little bit at the microphone, taking their places.

The Ave Maria ends. One by one, the girls begin to speak.

A dark-haired girl, the shortest of the group, her face hidden by the double microphone, her voice clear and wise: "You see, Hayley, your presence in and of itself is brilliant. You have this light about you. And when that light hits someone, its effect is contagious—it spreads from one person to the other. And before you know it, we begin to feel like better people."

It becomes clear that this is a choreographed tribute, the girls having decided that they would take turns addressing Hayley as if she were right there in the room. Each reads her brief, perfect words, then steps back to allow the next friend to step forward.

"Haze, I'll never forget the weekend the eight of us went up to Vermont. You told us you'd have to drive up later and meet us because you were busy that afternoon. We later found out you were busy because you were being publicly recognized for your remarkable contribution to the MS cause. You didn't even tell us."

This is another kind of community, the community of a school, coming together to help, shoring up the crumbled foundation of one of their own. A girl with a daisy tucked into her blond hair, her voice shaky, her eyes bright: "Hayley, we will always feel the magic of your wild side, a side we wish everyone could have encountered. This past year, our senior year, we lived life. I mean, we *really* lived life. No moment taken for granted, and we spent little time apart. Whenever we gathered, fun was inevitable, whether we were outside in the grass, taking road trips on the weekends, or even in the library. The music never stopped, and our crazy times will never be forgotten. This was the *best* year of our lives, and we have . . . no . . . regrets."

A girl in a satin dress and a lock of hair over her right eye, who sniffles after each sentence and looks up at Bill every few words, as if she had written this so he especially could hear it: "Now, as we go ahead in life, we carry your light with us, and with hope, spread the spirit that reigned so vibrantly within that beautiful heart of yours."

The sixth speaker, a tall girl with brown hair pulled back and a glittering black necklace: "Reflecting upon our years as best friends, you have been more to me than I could have ever imagined. I can only hope that I gave you half as much as you gave me. I am truly blessed to have had you and your wonderful family in my life. I love you, Hayley."

The last girl steps up and speaks with calm and clarity, a kind of fullness: "You are our best friend. Our miracle. You are our rock. We love you more with each breath we take and each step that leads us forward."

This group of friends was known around Miss Porter's as the Eight. The seven remaining girls make their way back to their seats.

We rarely talk about the people in our lives this way when they're alive. It is the ritual of death, to stand before the gathered and talk about the memories we hope to carry with us but that we know will never again be as crisp and real as they are at this moment. To eulogize. This service is an onslaught of memories. They beat you down and lift you up at the same time. Beat you down because they're all in the past. Lift you up because they exist at all.

Bill looks over and gives his friend Steve Hanks a little nod.

Here goes.

Hanks helps Bill up to the podium, a hand on his elbow to steady him. Four thousand people suck in quick whispers of air as they watch in disbelief the doctor lumber to the front of the stage. Bill buttons the top two buttons of his unfamiliar suit jacket, pats his breast pocket to find the folded copy of his remarks. Hanks twists open a plastic water bottle for him and adjusts the mike. Bill has lost so much blood and so much family, and everyone is staring at him, and he feels as if he were in another man's body. His new shoes feel strange and the stage is foreign under his feet. You can see the wound on his forehead from the farthest row of seats. Hanna, Ron, Glenn, his parents—everybody is praying that Bill won't drop to the floor right there in Welte Hall. Everyone would understand.

He doesn't drop to the floor. He stands up as straight as he can, takes a deep breath, and speaks for twenty-two minutes. Right away he makes the four thousand people laugh. He brings up his first date with Jennifer that night in Pittsburgh, when he invited his parents to come along and his dad paid. "I was a cheap date, but I've been paying for it ever since," he says. He tells the crowd that he ended up at St. Mary's this week rather than the hospital he was affiliated with, the Hospital of Central Connecticut, because St. Mary's was closer to his home, "but everybody there was beautiful and angels to me and I knew I had to get out for the services, but it did feel safe." He pauses for a few seconds, staring ahead, off script, as if reckoning with a thought. He bobs his head back and forth a little. "Part of me wanted to hide there, and not face things—" His voice begins to crack.

He constantly touches his head. He brushes a hank of hair off his wound, or taps his forehead, or slides a light hand over the cuts in the back of his scalp. The overwhelming energy in his body, finding its way out through his fingers.

"KK Rosebud." He turns around and looks at Michaela's four-foot smiling visage over his shoulder. He talks about her cooking— the balsamic vinaigrette she made just last Sunday. How he used to have to watch basketball games on the tiny upstairs TV if she had dibs on the "clicker" and wanted to watch the Food Network. He does an imitation of her walking around staring at the floor in shyness, his shoulders hunched over, his eyes looking straight down. "But once you got to her, you'd get that smile, and once you had the smile, you knew you were in," he says. He recalls how one day she came home from school crying. "I said, 'What's the matter?' and it was because, when they were getting changed for gym"—he turns and gestures again to her photo. "She's tall and lanky now, but back then she was a little pudgy, and one of the little skinny dwarf girls"—and here he smiles, and the crowd laughs big. Not a nervous, funeral laugh but a hearty, genuine laugh. "That's what we called them together. They poked her tummy, KK's tummy, and said, 'What's that?' And KK was sad. But she had just grown out of it. And maybe it was that that made her stick up for other kids who were getting picked on."

He doesn't talk about evil. He doesn't talk about sorrow. For twenty-two minutes he talks only about his girls, about their lives, their accomplishments, the little things they did that made him feel lucky. He tells stories.

If Jennifer's father, the Reverend Hawke, was reserved in his delivery and if he showed an unbelievable composure at this moment and on this occasion, Bill Petit's comportment in front of an auditorium full of mourners can only be described as a small miracle. The Yankee reserve of Petit's people is the stuff of cultural caricature, but in this instance, Yankee reserve becomes a man's salvation. From his boyhood, he'd been taught that one doesn't complain, and one doesn't indulge the emotions of self-pity or engage in operatic displays of feeling. And so disciplined had he been in the quality of his reserve that Bill Petit, upon experiencing a horror most unimaginable, does not even possess the vocabulary to vilify, or destroy. His instinct is not to turn the attention to his own suffering—to ask *Why me?*—because that has not been a part of his emotional education. The contemporary vogue for public soul-searching and pop psychologizing is as alien to Bill Petit as setting foot on Mars.

He only has words of love. For nearly a week he has been more dead than alive. But he's come here, has struggled to his feet, to tell the assembled that he will spend the rest of his life remembering. And to tell them something else: that he will live in their memories. He will never be released from this, and yet he will live.

At the end, he draws a deep breath, and with his voice faltering and his eyes focused down at the podium, says, "I guess if there's anything to be gained from the senseless deaths of my beautiful family, it's for us to all go forward with the inclination to live with a faith that embodies action—help a neighbor, fight for a cause, love your family." He looks up at the four thousand people. "I'm really expecting all of you to go out and do some of these things with your family in your own little way, to spread the work of these three wonderful women. Thank you."

And the four thousand people rise to their feet and clap for more than a minute.

I understand I'm on the road
Where all that was is gone.
So where to now, St. Peter?
Show me which road I'm on.

—Elton John, "Where to Now St. Peter?,"
from *Tumbleweed Connection,* one
of Bill Petit's favorite albums

EXISTENCE

Summer 2007–Summer 2010

A FEW GUYS at the country club had called or e-mailed Ron to ask what they could do to help. Some other friends, too, guys who knew Bill and knew that Ron would be the point man with the family. That's how it started.

Ron first needed to get through the memorial service, but now he starts to call and e-mail guys back and tell them to come to the club next Thursday after work, around six o'clock. That evening, Ron gets there a little early. He walks upstairs to a colonial-style dining room, summer sun blasting through the towering windows. Outside, the temperature still hovers around 90 even as the sun falls. He doesn't know how many guys will show up, how many of them will be able to take time on a weeknight. Maybe a dozen. But when he gets up to speak on this Thursday night in August after work, there must be fifty men in the room.

A man who's been through what Bill has been through should never have to see a funeral bill, Ron tells them. So I thought we might try to get a little money together to pay for the funeral, he says.

Also, Ron points out, Bill has no clothes. He has no shoes. He doesn't have a belt, a pair of socks, a T-shirt. Ron proposes they all chip in a little extra money to help buy him new clothes, maybe at the club's pro shop—just enough to get him started. And there will be other little expenses that Bill shouldn't have to worry about, so maybe if there's anything left over, they could put it toward other stuff.

"We should just help him out," Ron says.

It's not that Bill doesn't have any money, Ron tells the men. He just shouldn't have to worry. Shouldn't have to deal with any of it, you know? It's not going to be tax-deductible or anything, he says. But we have a man down.

The men nod.

Within five days, Ron collects $77,000.

Moments like that should not be mistaken for examples of "the good that can come out of this," Ron will say later. It's not some silver lining. But when generosity shows itself the way it did at the country club that night, it reminds you that people are basically good, he says. That simple notion—that people are basically good— was difficult to believe in as the rain fell on the afternoon ten days earlier when word started to spread around the state of Connecticut, around America, even around the world that two of us, two human beings, had broken into a house where four other human beings lived, tortured them, and savagely killed three of them. Left the fourth for dead. It was grisly, and when you heard the news, it made you feel grim and afraid.

But you talk about *community*, Ron says. You talk about the good that people can do? Five different guys came up to Ron after the meeting and said, Ron, if you're short, just let me know what the number is. Not all these guys are even best pals with Bill and Ron—not by a long shot. But they are like him. They have families, and they work like dogs to afford a nice life for their wives and kids in a nice part of a nice state, and they play golf on Saturdays to relieve some of the stress. They are a club. They can't imagine what it's like for Bill, and don't want to. So they are doing the only thing they can think of.

These men with their checkbooks pay for the entire funeral. They buy Bill enough new clothes to get him going again. They give some money to the man who had chartered a plane to fly up

Jen's parents. Which reminds Ron that Dick and Marybelle need to get home. He doesn't call the same guy; he calls another guy who Ron thinks might also have a plane. This guy doesn't know Bill very well—they met maybe once, played a friendly round of golf against each other in a tournament. But Ron tracks him down, gets him on the phone. Explains the situation. And the guy sends the plane himself to pick up the Hawkes and take them home to Pennsylvania. Ron is amazed. He says, What do we owe you? I've got some money here in a fund, the guys really came together. What's the cost?

The man says, Don't be ridiculous.

Bad things happen to everyone. And in their aftermath, it is the human instinct to adapt and survive. By and large, people want to live. Biology and human history and our own lives tell us that we are indeed a resilient little bug.

But there is bad, and then there is depraved.

When your family is murdered and the home you made together is destroyed, and you yourself are beaten and left for dead, it may as well be the end of the world. It is hard to see how a man survives the end of the world. The basics of life—waking up, walking, talking—become alien tasks, an almost impossibly heavy weight to lift from moment to moment. You are more dead than alive.

People around Bill, and around the state, even, are starting to ask one another, Just how does a man go about surviving such a thing? How does a man go on?

Bill has stayed at his parents' house on Red Stone Hill since the Friday night of the funeral. Since he got out of the hospital. He lives there now. His own home on Sorghum Mill Drive stands only as a wooden shell surrounded by grass on a quarter acre of earth, fifteen miles away. Plywood covers the windows. Smoke stains mar the siding above them. Inside, many of the rooms are gutted. Others look eerily intact except for a film of soot covering everything. The sunporch, off the back, is a hollow black box.

It is not his home anymore.

He stays in a second-floor bedroom in his parents' house, near the top of the stairs, and spends a lot of time lying on a queen-size four-poster bed, not sleeping. Hanna and Abby have gone to the mall and bought him underwear and shoes and socks, and there were the clothes from the guys at the club—it's amazing what people do for you. The kindnesses.

In addition to Bill Sr. and Barbara, Bill's grandmother, Gram Triano, his mother's mother, lives in the house on Red Stone Hill, too, so there are four of them there. Bill knows every inch of the house but has never lived in it. Each night before he goes to bed, he sets the alarm system. But that doesn't feel like enough to him, so he props a chair-back under the knob of each door to the outside. This isn't so much for his own safety—at this point, he's not convinced he wants to be alive anyway. But his instinct has always been to protect, and it's all he can think of to do to keep his parents' home sacred and unmolested, as his was for so many years, as most people's are for their entire lives. And so he locks down the house against the forces of evil that have been visited upon him.

At first he sleeps maybe an hour, hour and a half a night. He lies awake mostly, thinking about the same questions. Working slowly and without rest, he is building ramparts around his mind to keep out the what-ifs, because the what-ifs are driving him insane. *What if that lock on the bulkhead door had been working properly? That's how they got in, from the backyard. Why hadn't he fixed it?* The haunting questions break through constantly, and he has to try to beat them away. *What if the latch on the kitchen door that led down to the basement had been locked?* A hundred thousand what-ifs. *What if he had heard the men approaching him as he slept on the sunporch and woken up? What if the police had stormed the house five minutes sooner?* You just have to swallow hard and breathe, and sometimes the questions go away for a few minutes. But they always come back.

Bill is trying to rebuild his body, but he can't sleep and thus has little strength. He is bleary all the time, burned out every minute. Beyond exhaustion. During the first few months, the days are bad enough, but at night the nasty darkness covers everything outside, and that's when bad things happen. He doesn't know how much longer he can endure the nights. Three o'clock in the morning. That's around the time the men broke in and his world began to collapse around him. Now it doesn't matter if he falls asleep at 2:45 or if he hasn't fallen asleep at all. At 3:00 a.m. he bolts up and his mind is suddenly back in the hallucinatory panic of that night, the macabre march of horrors unfurling in his uncontrolled imagination even as he sits in the safe peace of his parents' house. His heart starts pounding, the adrenaline sends him to shaking. He sweats. The minutes that made up the seven-hour ordeal roil around in his head, all mixed up—the minutes as he lived them compounded by what he has since learned about what was happening to Jennifer and the girls while he was tied up in the basement.

But even worse, if it is possible to get worse than that, is the moment when he wakes up from what little sleep he manages to get. His punishment for sleeping is a cruel flash of peace, when his eyes pop open and he wonders, for a fraction of a second, if it might all have been a bad dream.

For months afterward, there are people at the house constantly. Fifty to a hundred a day, from eight in the morning until ten o'clock at night. The driveway can probably hold twenty cars, and it seems like it's always at least half full. Relatives, friends, people bringing food, because that's what people tend to bring when they don't know what else to bring: money or food. The amount of food that's coming through the front door is overwhelming. The grocer in town is an old family friend—most of the town, people joke, are old family friends of the Petits—and he has so many orders coming in for the house that he finally calls Barbara and asks if she wants him to space out the deliveries so things don't spoil. Yes, *please*, she says.

Bill keeps thinking how lucky he is to have this family and all these friends. A lot of people, something like this happens, they have no one to help them. He looks at the newspaper sometimes, or the television news—not often, but a glance here and there. And he sees the steady stream of reports of soldiers dying in Iraq and Afghanistan. The months and years after his own tragedy are some of the bloodiest in those two wars, and Bill just thinks how lucky he is not to live in a place where there are car bombs and IEDs and innocent children getting blown up in the streets. This is how his mind is working right now, searching for the logic in his own survival, seeking justification for his own existence.

He doesn't come downstairs a whole lot. He looks out the window at the cars, sees the familiar ones, some he doesn't recognize. There are media trucks out on the street sometimes, and he knows there are reporters trying to get to the house. He just stays upstairs. Gram Triano, his mom, his dad—everyone knows to just let him sleep. *It's dark in there, maybe he's sleeping. Let it be dark.* Hanna is the one who goes to his room the most. Since the day it happened, she hasn't been back to her job at the Italian restaurant in Farmington where she worked as a chef, across Main Street from the country club. She's on indefinite leave—they'll take her back anytime, of course. But right now, she is taking care of Bill. She talks if he wants to talk. She lies next to him on the bed if he's lying down, holds him when he needs to be held—when he needs human contact. She doesn't want to leave him. How can you leave your brother when he's curled up on the bed in the fetal position, crying?

But when it gets late, he tells her to go home. Dennis and Abby and Andrew need her more than ever, he says. Even now, even as this shattered version of himself, this is big brother Billy dispensing advice, seeing through to the truth of things, keeping her straight, like when he told her as a kid to give up gymnastics because she wasn't going to be a dancer, for Pete's sake, and she oughtta play more ball instead.

The mailman, too, is a regular. Every day, some days twice, a truck arrives carrying bins overflowing with letters and cards. Thousands of pieces of mail. It comes from Cheshire, too, redirected. The post office in Plainville is great about it. Some people just write "Dr. William Petit, Plainville, CT" on the envelope, and the post office knows where to send it. Mail pours into the schools: Cheshire Academy, where Jennifer was a nurse; Chase Collegiate, where Michaela had just finished fifth grade; Miss Porter's, from which Hayley had just graduated. All of it makes its way to the house on Red Stone Hill. It fills *rooms*.

And the money. Inside half the envelopes, it seems, are checks. Cash, even. Five dollars. A thousand dollars. Five thousand. Fifty bucks. A few heartbreaking singles. Tucked into drugstore sympathy cards. Or folded into notes composed with careful hands, printed on plain paper, signed at the bottom. Some brief and polite, some long and personal. Some *really* long and *really* personal. Some from children.

"I am sure you have heard this from many people but I hope you know how much your courage and strength has changed my life. When I am having a moment where I am fretting about the small stuff, I think of you and count my blessings," reads one.

From a family that Jen used to babysit for when she was a teenager: "It was easy to see why our son took to his new babysitter very quickly and developed the biggest crush on her. . . . For those that are faithful while on this earth I know when God calls us home it is to a place where we cannot understand the peace, love and wonder of this place called heaven. Jenny and your daughters are there now with the Lord watching over them."

In a child's hand: "I hope you feel better Dr. William Petit Jr."

A lot of religious stuff. CDs of religious music. Josh Groban, songs people find inspirational. Books about Holocaust survivors. Letters from prisoners. Letters from women wondering if Bill needs a friend. Cards from Ireland and China and Italy and from friends down the street. A cake from a baker in Alaska. Cards from entire first-grade classes.

Bill's parents, his sister and brothers, the constant gathering of aunts and uncles and cousins and old friends from the neighborhood who populate the Petits' house in the days and weeks and months afterward—everyone wonders what they're going to do with all the mail.

"We're going to answer it," Bill says.

And so they answer it. The family sits in an assembly line around the table on the porch and writes responses by hand. If there isn't a return address, they go online to try to find it, or call information. A family friend shows Hanna how to catalog each piece of mail in a computer spreadsheet: name, address, type of letter ("simple" for sympathy cards with a short note; "large" for cards that included a donation; "letter" for longer letters), date received, date responded to.

And then everything goes into boxes. That's Barbara.

No one organizes like Barbara. With five kids, you had to. This is the woman who keeps her tablecloths pressed and on hangers in a special closet. For Billy's mail, she instructs everyone to divide the letters into small bundles and place an elastic around each one, then she stacks them neatly in boxes labeled with a black Sharpie in her hand.

They sit for hours each day, in shifts. There is always food and coffee. There are some letters that Billy wants to answer himself, and he does that at the same table, although usually when everyone's not around. Each day, between everybody working together, they answer hundreds of letters. And each day, it seems, hundreds more come in. Not a single piece of mail gets thrown away. Into Barbara's boxes they go.

The 25,000 pieces of mail Bill received after the murders are neatly preserved in his parents' attic.

"I don't know why I did all this," Barbara says several years later, standing in her attic one morning, looking at the rows of cardboard boxes stacked two and three high, reaching almost to the rafters and the insulation under the roof of the house. She stands there for a few long minutes, one hand on her hip, the other resting on the lid of a box. There are at least twenty-five thousand pieces of mail up here. Mail that came for her boy, to make him feel better.

"I don't know why," she says. "I just did."

The Petits didn't plan on starting a charitable foundation. It was not a vision that Bill laid out. But there is so much money. After Ron collected the $77,000 from the men at the country club and paid for the funeral and the clothes and the plane, there was almost $25,000 left over, and nobody wants his money back. And the money in the sympathy cards and letters is adding up, too. Ron talks about it regularly with a couple of guys from the club, and somebody has the idea to start a foundation, to do some good in the girls' memory. Ron tells Bill about this idea, and Bill says: Yes. Good. He isn't sleeping or talking much and can't make sense of anything at all— it's still too soon. Some days, he isn't even sure he will live another year, isn't sure he wants to. But this fund, this foundation, he can see, is a good idea.

One of the men is a lawyer, one's an accountant, and they just start doing it. The first thing they do is set in motion the paperwork process, to establish the Petit Family Foundation with the Internal Revenue Service as a nonprofit 501(c)(3) charitable organization. And almost immediately, somebody, probably Ron, says we should have a golf tournament. Right at the Country Club of Farmington. It feels like half the state of Connecticut is asking what they can do to help, so Ron and the club guys organize it quickly. Everybody pitches in. They run into a bit of good luck right away: The club is throwing a retirement party in early October for the longtime pro, so they'll have tents and all kinds of equipment already set up. The Petit golf tournament can piggyback on that. Perfect.

It's a cold day, even for October. The tents have side flaps and heaters, though, and the club is mobbed from first thing in the morning. Ron and Hanna ask Bill if he's okay, if he's up for this. *Yeah*, he says. They've had programs printed up, but they didn't print Bill's name in there as a speaker because they weren't sure he had it in him. But of course he's going to speak. The way he sees it, standing up and saying a few words is the least he can do for the girls.

So everybody plays golf. There's dinner after, in the tents. Bill stands to speak, and you can hear your own breathing. He thanks everybody, and he has never meant it more in his life. Scores of people make their way over to give him a hug. He does the best he can. The day is a blur.

In the end, the nascent Petit Family Foundation raises $130,000 in a single day, not even three months after the murders. The date is October 15, 2007, the day Hayley Petit would have turned eighteen years old.

Ron Bucchi and Rick Healey, a Petit family friend who's a lawyer, work with the insurance people to figure out the settlements on the house, but there isn't much work to be done—no negotiating, anyway. Thank goodness. "These people were unbelievable," Ron will say later. The insurance companies max out every policy, pay it out in full, never a fight or a question.

At one meeting, toward the end of the process, one of the insurance people begins to weep and embraces Ron and Rick in a hug.

Inside the house is a claustrophobic darkness. After the fire, some of the family were allowed in to look for remnants from the Petits' old life that could be saved, anything meaningful that hadn't been smoke-stained or melted. Some of the furniture was okay. Cindy wanted to find two coffee mugs she'd given Jen for her last birthday. They weren't expensive, but Cindy thought they were sort of cool—the handles didn't attach at the bottom, which made them unique—and Jen loved getting artsy gifts from her artist sister. Cindy couldn't get them out of her head, and she went in to find them. She stepped through the layer of soft ash that covered the floors, shining a flashlight in front of her—the windows were boarded up, and everything was black with soot. She felt around in what was left of a kitchen cupboard for the mugs like a blind woman searching for her Bible, ash clinging to her clothes and skin. Eventually her hands felt the mugs' distinctive handles, and Cindy brought them home with her to North Carolina. She scrubbed them and scrubbed them, washing off the black, until her hands were pruned. Scrubbed and scrubbed and scrubbed the ashes off Jenny's mugs.

At one point, the insurance adjuster needs to get back inside for some reason, and Ron volunteers to take her through the house.

Have you been inside since the crimes? she asks Ron.

No, Ron says. I've been to the property, but not inside.

Don't go in, the adjuster tells him. The owner is your friend? Don't go in. I've been doing this for twenty years, and this is the worst thing I've ever seen. Don't go in.

Ron doesn't go in.

What he decides to do, eventually, as fall becomes winter becomes spring, is take the house down.

Ron has been a trustee to Bill and Jennifer's estate, which was actually in only her name, for as long as he can remember. After the murders and the fire, the house automatically went into the Jennifer Hawke-Petit Trust, of which Bill and Ron are the cotrustees. Ron feels they have to demolish it. Before he says anything to Bill, he sets it all up with his buddy Jimmy Manafort, who owns Manafort Brothers, a big construction company out of Plainville.

Ron says, Jimmy, I gotta take down Billy's house. And I want to do it quietly.

Jimmy gets it. Hooks Ron up with one of his guys, who will head up the job.

Ron tells the guy: Please, we don't want the press there, so when you get the permits to do the demolition, don't specify a date and time. The press will show up. People will be gawking. Some people are creepy that way. Fascinated by this kind of morbid stuff. So keep it a surprise as best you can. And when you take it down, crush it into dust. Crush it as finely as you can. Make it disappear. Because people will follow you to the dump. I don't want to sound paranoid, but they will.

The guy says: Got it.

He calls Ron the morning of. Says, We'll have the house down inside an hour and a half.

The Manafort trucks barrel up Sorghum Mill Drive and surround the property. Three gray dump trucks, each with the capacity to carry a hundred yards of debris. An excavator with a huge claw at its hydraulic end knocks the house in on itself, so that the whole of the Petit family's physical existence is compacted into the foundation beneath it, a grave holding the wreckage of lives that ended in calamity. But it's only the things—clothes, dinner plates, drywall, sinks, carpets, the linoleum of the kitchen floor.

Shovelful by shovelful, the claw grabs messy scoops of the rubble and loads them into the three massive dump trucks. Clouds of dust rise up with each load, some of it settling on the leaves of trees, most of it disappearing into the air. After an hour and a half, the house is now in the trucks, and the trucks drive back down Sorghum Mill Drive, as quickly as they arrived, onto I-84, and all the way to Ohio. Any creep who wants to scavenge this stuff is going to have to travel a long way.

Ron calls Jimmy Manafort. Thanks a lot, Jimmy, he says. You can send the bill to me.

Come on, Ron, Jimmy says. Don't be ridiculous.

There are other trucks there on another day, at the old house. From a landscaping company.

All winter long, Bill had given himself the task of designing a memorial garden behind his parents' home. Its paths and trees and flowers would form the shape of a heart, with an arch at the center.

At the old house in Cheshire one afternoon, men from the landscape company carefully dig up the trees and bushes that surround the house, wrapping the root balls in burlap. Some of the plantings weigh almost as much as a small car, so long have their roots been growing in the soil, so diligently had Bill taken care of them. Later the same day, the landscapers' trucks arrive at Bill's parents' house in Plainville—flatbeds and pickups loaded with trees and bushes. Trays and trays of perennials, the dark soil still clinging to their stringy white roots. There is the chamaecyparis—not any chamaecyparis but the very one from the corner of his driveway in Cheshire, by the basketball hoop. There is the Japanese maple, purple and majestic and delicate, carefully strapped to the truck so it won't topple. One whole truck carries the rhododendrons from the north side of the house, some of them showing raggy tops now that they have been separated. There is the viburnum. Some of Michaela's four-o'clocks.

Bill is not at the house when the trucks arrive. He pulls into the driveway and sees them laid out neatly in the yard, all these beautiful, vibrant plants he raised from when they were tiny—raised with help from Hayley and Michaela, of course, and Abby and Andrew, when they were over. The occasional weeders. And now it is a beautiful sight once again, a bit of his old life resurrected.

The scars on Bill's head eventually heal, and his hair grows back to hide the places where the gashes were stapled together. The last wounded stripe of crimson to disappear under a new layer of skin, the way the grass grows back on the side of the highway after a car wreck, is the one on his forehead—the one everyone can see. It's gone now, and his face is restored.

One night maybe six months after the murders, in the room upstairs in his parents' house, Hanna sat with him as the trees outside blackened with dusk. Bill was lying on the queen-size bed, staring at the ceiling, rubbing his forehead where the red cut used to be. His fingers absently traced its invisible trail, rubbing the area around it as if in search of it.

"That scar's disappearing," Hanna said.

"Yeah."

"Everyone probably thinks that's great. But it's not, is it? The scar told everyone you're not okay. Maybe you want it back."

Billy looked at her, rubbed his head some more, and said, "How'd you know?"

A lot of people are saying, Well, if he could just get back to work, that might take his mind off things. Or if they aren't saying it, they are thinking it.

Bill is fifty-one now. His whole life, he has kept busy. Playing ball as a kid. Leading the kids in the neighborhood to Norton Park like some pied piper, setting up the games, picking teams. Working every angle in high school—good grades, clubs, captain of two sports. Plowed his way through Dartmouth. Med school. Residency, the way it forces you to be superhuman, staying up all night. Setting up a practice. Devoting himself to a marriage. Hustling all week seeing patients, making his rounds, answering his beeper, *being* there. Getting some time on the weekend for a round of golf before going home to his kids and trying to relax. Writing a textbook. Lecturing. Moving up in his field—becoming the director of this and the chairman of that. Fatherhood, the most important job of all. Seeing his mom and dad. Hustling, hustling, hustling.

For fifty years.

And now . . . now he has not a thing to do. Nothing. They took his family, they took his house, they took his clothes and his car, and they stole any sense of purpose he ever felt in the world. And now he spends a lot of time sitting upstairs in his folks' place, staring, weeping, lying on top of the bedsheets, wondering what to do. No situation could be less familiar to him or more antithetical to his previous existence. He has always been one of those guys who just works and works toward some big, vague goal of getting better, getting smarter, having a good life. The things we all want and that he knew how to get. Now, though, now he is somewhere primal, bounced back to the beginning. Back to nothingness, stripped of himself.

Bill misses practicing medicine. Of course he does. Downtown, on an anonymous brick office building on Whiting Street, the white block letters over the rear entrance still read "William A. Petit, Jr., M.D. Internal Medicine, Endocrinology & Diabetes." But there is no way in the world. He can't focus for more than five or ten minutes at once, and when you're treating patients with diabetes and other complex illnesses, trying to do it when your mind is elsewhere is not only difficult but dangerous. Concentration is essential, and it is the one medical skill he lost in all this. The jagged images of that night still rip into his mind every hour of every day, sometimes every minute of every hour. Bill can't concentrate on anything except trying to make them go away. And the way to make the jagged thoughts go away is not to see all your old patients all day and to hear them ask how you're doing, kind though their intentions no doubt would be. And financially, he is okay. He and Jen had some savings, and there was insurance money, and heartbreaking college funds for Hayley and Michaela. Just money.

To sleep, he swallows a combination of medicines that puts him out for eight to ten hours, which would seem good except that it makes him groggy for the next eight or ten hours after he wakes up. And while the sleep is good for his body, sleep is the time when the nightmares come. Between the triggers that hit him all day long and the nightmares that haunt him all night, there isn't a lot of mental capacity for much of anything, let alone endocrinology.

Any doctor will tell you that doctors make the worst patients because they think they know best. Not Bill, not now. He is a willing recipient of treatment. None of the usual doctor's protests that he's fine and everything's fine. It is fairly obvious that he is not fine. Brain trauma is the most severe of his lingering physical problems. Sometimes he has trouble walking on uneven ground, and he has to use the handrails when he goes up or down stairs. Twice he passes out and is brought to the emergency room. Black spots splatter his field of vision, and sometimes he has trouble seeing things between nine and eleven o'clock in his left eye and between one and three o'clock in his right. If he moves his head too quickly, it can make him nauseous or bring on vertigo.

Bill is not about to start seeing patients again. Bill still has trouble finding reason to get out of bed.

But he's trying.

The foundation is gaining momentum. They have a board of directors now, an extraordinary group of people: CEOs, lawyers, loyal family members, people who have busy lives and hard jobs but who want to help. Guys like Mike Chambrello, whose dad coached Billy in Little League and who played on the Cubs when Billy was on the Owls, and who is now the CEO of a huge gaming and lottery corporation. Most have served on other boards, and they know how to get things done. In 2008, they start to meet regularly, once a month. They divide into committees. The meetings are all business. They gather around Big Bill and Barbara's dining-room table. Hanna cooks for everybody. There's wine and soda. Bill, in time, grows comfortable running the meetings.

One of the first objectives is to write a mission statement. They all have ideas for how to put into words what the foundation ought to do, what its goals should be. Eventually they settle on three causes the foundation could potentially support, causes that hew closely to the lives of Bill and the girls. All three causes are important to Bill, but a few people point out that most foundations have a single, unifying mission and it might be confusing to have three. In the end, though, they all agree: So what? These are equally important causes, and none of them can be dropped. The Petit Family Foundation board of directors ratifies its mission statement:

To foster the education of young people, especially
women in the sciences; to improve the lives of those
affected by chronic illnesses; and to support efforts
to protect and help those affected by violence.

There is only one last-minute change. An earlier version read,
"women affected by violence." Rick Bucchi's wife, Ann, points out
that Bill was a victim of violence, too. Why not change "women" to
"those," to be more inclusive? They make the change.

Bill spent many hours writing
thank-you notes and doing Petit
Family Foundation business
on his parents' porch, where he
could see the memorial garden in
the backyard.

By the end of the first year, Bill is spending most of every day
on foundation business. A lot of what that means is that he sits at
the table on the porch and writes thank-you notes. He writes hundreds, maybe thousands, thanking people he knows well and people
he has never met for mailing money to his foundation. Some people
he thanks simply for their expressions of support, for their advice,
and for their prayers. For the kindnesses that some people summon,
without thinking, when they hear about somebody who needs help.

He sometimes talks to Hanna and Ron about moving out of his
parents' house, getting his own place. But why? The house on Red
Stone Hill is beautiful and big. He is surrounded by people who love
him, his mother cooks and cleans, and he can help his dad around
the house. Man, it's a different life, though. For one thing, he tries

to convince his parents to eat dinner a little later than five o'clock. By the time the lunch dishes are put away, it seems like his mother is already pulling the meat out of the fridge and rinsing potatoes for dinner. And then there's the television. It's unbearably loud. The other people in the house—his dad, his mom, his grandmother—are all at various stages of hearing loss, so the TV is turned up to full volume whenever it's on, and he has to shout above it.

If the circumstances that brought about the situation weren't so horrible, the whole thing could be a sitcom.

On some mornings, he goes for breakfast at Saint's on Route 10, a family restaurant with an L-shaped counter, vinyl booths, eggs how you like 'em, and bottomless cups of coffee. He checks his e-mail on his phone, a constant stream of messages mostly about the foundation. The purpose of establishing the foundation was never to help Bill ease back into the world again, but that has quickly become its secondary mission. It is a cause for him to leave the house, to meet people, to write e-mails, to sit on boards and run committees. His whole life, Bill has searched for order in the world, and where he found disorder he constructed a system that made sense to him. When he saw that college was too expensive and too busy, he built a system: give up basketball, enroll in a work-study program, methodically visit the financial-aid office in search of help. Even his habit of cataloging the natural world, teaching anyone who would listen the Latin names of every species of bird and tree and flower, was his way of imposing order on the wild, at least in his mind. It was the same with the foundation. It too was a projection of his mind's need for order, and it became part of Bill's system of defense against the chaos his world had become. Small tasks like writing notes and licking envelopes, large projects like running meetings and helping organize the golf tournament— these were the girders of his rebuilt world, the only one in which he might know how to live.

The foundation's role in Bill's recovery is undeniable, but its primary mission is to give money to worthy causes in memory of the girls. Even by the end of 2008, its first full year of existence, it has awarded $5,000 to the Prudence Crandall Center, a Connecticut domestic-violence support organization. And a group of Bill's classmates from Plainville High, class of '74, gets together to establish a community-service award at the school. The foundation pledges $3,500. The following year, it begins supporting a similar award at Cheshire High School. The board also decides to pledge $8,500 to continue the multiple-sclerosis funds that Hayley and Michaela set up. It has supported a place called Manes & Motions, a therapeutic horseback-riding farm whose clients include veterans suffering from PTSD, a young girl with cerebral palsy, and all kinds of other patients. The 5K road race in Plainville has become a massive community event in central Connecticut, with thousands of participants and dozens of volunteers wearing PFF T-shirts. The golf tournament, too. And the pasta dinners and the speeches and the appearances. The foundation is real. The whole family is a part of it.

Except Abby.

Everyone at Miss Porter's used to call Abby and Hayley "kissing cousins" because they were so close. For Abby, in high school, Hayley was a security blanket. Abby loathed walking to those cold, miserable crew practices, but Hayley made Abby feel better just by being present. Not with pep talks or pats on the butt. Abby just had to know that Hayley was there, and if she could see her hero older cousin, she could find a way to keep jogging or rowing in that godawful cold. She wanted to be around Hayley all the time. The Sunday night before the morning Hayley died, Abby easily could have been over at her house, watching a movie or talking about basketball or Otis or college or how many babies each of them wanted to have someday. Easily. Or Hayley could have been at Abby's house. They had been texting all weekend, as usual.

Abby was sixteen when it happened, going into her junior year. A teenager, learning and figuring out how the world works, only to wake up one morning and find it in ruins. She quit the crew team at Miss Porter's almost immediately. She stuck with basketball, but it would never be the same. The year before, her sophomore year, when Hayley was team cocaptain, Abby had averaged around twenty points per game. Her coach had begun inviting college scouts to see her play. But after it happened, in the 2007–08 season, she wasn't scoring, wasn't feeling it.

Her friends are starting to look at colleges, but in Abby's family, that isn't easy to focus on. The Petits and Abby's family, the Chapmans, always felt like they all lived the same lives, all the time, a big group. That was all Abby had ever known. And now three members of the group are gone, and nobody knows how to function, and everybody is trying to prop up Billy because that's what you do as a family, and Hanna is doing the best she can as a mother and a wife and a sister. She loves her kids more than anything. But there's only so much you can do, and Abby has never felt so alone in her life.

She recoils from all of it. School. Sports. And the storm of publicity and ceremony and mourning that the tragedy has become. She shuts it all off.

The foundation is the worst part, to her. She is "grossed out" by it. She tries to avoid the events, doesn't want to help with anything. When her parents manage to drag her to one of the foundation's functions, she sits in the car or in the corner of the room. To Abby it just seems like people are coming out of the woodwork to claim some kind of closeness with the Petits that isn't real. Abby knew everything there was to know about Hayley. She doesn't want to deal with people Hayley barely knew trying to claim the rights to her memory just because they went to Sunday school with her in third grade or something.

She doesn't talk. Her parents send her to therapy, but she refuses to say even one word, and eventually the therapist gives up. She certainly doesn't know what to say to her Uncle Billy. Her whole life, he has been Hayley's dad. So he wasn't like a regular uncle, Abby will say years later. An uncle's primary role is as your uncle. An uncle is *your uncle*, not somebody's father. Uncle Glenn, he's pure uncle. An awesome uncle, the best, the fun uncle who would swing the girls from his arms and do anything for anybody. Billy would, too, of course, but it was different. Hayley was what Abby and her uncle Billy had in common. He was her soul mate's dad, and with her soul mate gone, it feels as if all the connections are gone, too. What do you do when all the connections are gone? There are a million things she wants to say to him, but whenever she's around him, she can't find a single word.

In the hospital, the day it happened, after they sewed her uncle Billy up, Abby went in to see him. He was lying on the bed, his hair still wet and stringy from the washing of his wounds, his eyes red and distant. Not mighty, goofy Uncle Billy. He turned his head, took her hand and squeezed it a little, and said, "I'm sorry I couldn't save your best friend."

Bill still makes it out to basketball games. The UConn games he and Hayley used to love so much. Now he goes with his dad, with Hanna, sometimes with Andrew. They talk about how the teams are doing, but no one pretends that the routine has the same fun to it, or that the anticipation fills the car the way it used to. The Huskies split their home games between Gampel Pavilion, a bright and raucous basketball stadium on the UConn campus, and the XL Center in Hartford, about a half hour to the west. At both arenas, people recognize Bill from the newspaper or the local news and they stare at him, almost as if he were disfigured in some way, a man with some shocking physical malady that you can't help looking at even as you know you should look away. In their eyes is a mix of curiosity and awe. Everyone in the state, it seems, knows what happened to him, every horrid detail, and they are curious about what a man looks like after he has come out on the other side of that. They are curious about how he acts and whether he smiles. Will he stand and cheer when the team scores?

And they are awestruck, still, by the fact that he is alive at all.

The first games he went to after it happened, in the late fall of 2007, were tough. Walking into Gampel—the crush of students, their cheeks painted blue and white, crowding through the turnstiles; the familiar smells of nachos and pizza from the food stands; everything blazing under the lights shining down from the stadium's huge, round golf-ball ceiling—Hanna found herself swallowing hard, trying to hold back tears. It caught her off guard, the feeling of breathlessness, but . . . these games were just such a big part of their *thing*. And then, suddenly, the scene that surrounded them was utterly familiar but strange and empty at the same time.

Even several years into his new life, when Bill walks in front of Hanna, moving with the crowd through the stadium corridors toward their seats, she can hear the people whisper:

Is that Dr. Petit?

I think that's his sister.

Look, there's Dr. Petit.

The thing is, he does cheer. He smiles sometimes—Billy has that quick flash of a smile that comes all at once, his mouth hanging open a little, and it takes you by surprise. There is mischief in the smile. And so sometimes, when he's out in public, at a game or appearing at an event for his foundation, Bill Petit looks pretty good. And people say to Hanna, Wow, he's doing so well. And Hanna thinks, Yeah, at that moment you saw him, maybe he was. But he doesn't always do so well when the game's over and the daylight fades into another punishing moonless night. Or when, in the middle of a conversation, the sadness suddenly obscures him like an eclipse. He doesn't always do so well at three in the morning.

A lot of times, when he's on his way somewhere, he says at the last minute that he doesn't want to go. He becomes paralyzed. He says that when he shows up at these places and there are people around, he doesn't know what he's supposed to say. How he's supposed to look. Whether he can smile. Whether it's okay to stand up and cheer. What will people say if he does? Does a man who has had his whole life ripped away from him *smile*? Would the act of cheering at a basketball game dishonor his wife and daughters? Will people think he doesn't care? Will they mistake him for a man who is healed?

Who am I supposed to be?

One day, sometime in the first year or so after it happened, Ron and Bill took a drive. An old friend from Plainville had become a well-known psychologist out in California. Writes books, goes on TV. He was going to be in Boston for a couple of days on business, and Ron and Bill drove up to meet him for lunch halfway between Boston and Hartford. When they were driving back, not talking a whole lot, a nondescript stretch of I-84 flying by the windows, Ron suddenly understood something about his friend. It just hit him: The best physicians, he realized, have the ability to flip a switch and turn off the human emotions that could cloud their judgment when they're working with a patient. It's an essential skill, because if you get sad every time someone is suffering, you won't have the clear mind required to treat them. The best physicians know how to detach.

Ron was driving, and he tried to put this into words for Billy. One of your problems, Ron said, is that you feel guilty because there are starting to be times when you can flip the switch in your head. You're learning how to detach, just a little. And you feel guilty about that. About being able to turn off that switch. You feel guilty for turning it off long enough that you can smile.

Bill didn't say anything. Just stared ahead at the taillights moving through the dusk. But after a minute, he reached over and tapped Ron on the knee, and after forty years of friendship, Ron knew what Billy meant with a tap on the knee.

. . .

People talk about closure. That's a word Bill has been hearing a lot. People ask him about it, with a hopeful rise in their voice at the end.

You think you'll find some closure, Dr. Petit?

What do you think will give you closure, Bill? When the men who did this go on trial, when they get sentenced?

Give 'em the death penalty. That'll give you a little closure, right?

These things—personal tragedies—they don't go away. That's what people don't know, and what he never really understood before now. You don't get over them, and they don't close. The best you can hope for is that you figure out, little by little, how to get through your days. How to cope. People remarry, they have another child, they buy a new house. And as days add up to years, the sting may wear off when the bad thoughts creep into your head. You learn to live around the bad thoughts. But the marriage, the kids who are gone now, the house that burned down—it's not like you can put those parts of your life away. He doesn't blame people for wanting him to have closure—for wishing or assuming that it even exists. People want him to be happy and move forward, because it's easier for everybody when nobody is grieving, when everything's okay. People want to believe this is possible for him. But becoming okay is not Bill's goal, not what he finds himself marching slowly toward. He heard a phrase once about what the worst kind of pain can do to your heart: It rips a jagged hole. That's what this feels like. A jagged hole in his heart. The sharp edges may wear down over time, but the hole will never go away. The state could kill these two men a hundred times and it won't bring closure.

But that's exactly what Bill wants the state to do.

THE FIRST TRIAL

September 13, 2010–December 2, 2010

"TRAGEDY TO triii-al! Front paaa-age!"

A young woman wearing a plastic rain poncho stands on the corner in front of the Superior Courthouse in New Haven, hawking the local paper, the *Register*. The sky at 8:00 a.m. is low and the color of pavement, spitting down a pebbly drizzle over the city. A line of television trucks hugs the curb along Church Street like boats at the dock, their extendable arms rising like masts, rooftop dishes searching for satellites beyond the clouds. The cameramen and sound technicians sit in their trucks eating bagels, ready to do a live shot at any moment.

Lawyers and reporters and friends and gawkers file into the lobby, lining up to place their briefcases and handbags on the baggage scanner and walk through the metal detector—belts off, keys and cell phones in the bin. Judicial marshals, all business, wave them through one by one. Upstairs, on the sixth floor, a few dozen people wait in the hall outside Courtroom 6A, hoping to get a seat. Around 9:30, a half hour before the proceedings will begin, the chief marshal emerges to announce that the courtroom is filled to capacity. A few people approach the marshal to plead for a seat, but there's nothing he can do. *It's the fire code, ma'am. I suggest arriving earlier tomorrow.* These are the people who won't make it into the courtroom for the morning session of the first day of testimony in *State of Connecticut v. Steven Hayes.*

There's another metal detector at the entrance to the courtroom itself. A marshal sits at a table searching everyone's bag by hand. If anyone makes the metal detector beep, a second marshal waves an electronic wand over his or her body. Bill was already seated inside the courtroom but stepped out to go to the men's room. When he walks up to reenter, he doesn't walk through the metal detector like everyone else. The marshal gestures for him to step around, and he hand-frisks him—Bill Petit, pillar of the community, being felt up for a weapon. The marshal looks almost apologetic. But if Bill minds the indignity, he doesn't show it. He knows they have to do this. He is about to enter a courtroom in which he will be seated ten feet from one of the men who killed his family, and they need to make sure Bill doesn't have any ideas. People try things.

Bill thanks the marshal and walks inside.

The courtroom is paneled almost entirely with wood the color of honey: the jury box, the bench, the witness stand, the clerk's box, the stenographer's station, the shelves that hold volumes of Connecticut statute along one wall, the uncomfortable Catholic-school benches that spectators must endure. A judicial marshal stands at each of the five doors—one that leads to the judge's chambers; one used by lawyers, court personnel, the jury, and the defendant; one to the jury-deliberation room; one to a small office; and one to the hall, for the public. The carpeting is blue-flecked industrial. The room is shaped something like a stop sign. Half of it is devoted to gallery seating, six rows with an aisle down the middle, the rows getting shorter as they reach the back of the room. The white ceiling is dotted with round recessed lights, like a planetarium. Next to the jury box, an oil portrait of a distinguished-looking gray-haired judge hangs on the wall.

Reporters fill the first two rows behind the defense table, the on-air talent dressed up and made up, the newspaper writers taking shorthand notes in skinny notepads or tapping at the keys of laptops. Producers from the national morning shows work their smartphones and scan the room for possible interview subjects.

The first two rows behind the prosecutor's table are reserved for the Petit and Hawke families, but the extended clan is so big it spills into the whole section. Barbara and Bill, Glenn, Hanna and Dennis,

Dick and Marybelle Hawke, Cindy, the aunts and uncles and cousins, good friends, neighbors from Sorghum Mill Drive, colleagues of Jen's from Cheshire Academy, members of the church—everyone is here. Bill sits in the first seat of the first row. He wears a blazer and slacks and chews gum in quick turns of the jaw, as if mincing it. He wears his wedding ring, a band of yellow gold, as he has for more than twenty-five years. He has combed his hair back—it has grown more gray than black in the three years since his family was murdered. It just about covers the white scar running down the back of his scalp.

Bill does not once look at Steven Hayes as two marshals lead Hayes to his seat at the defense table. This is not the first time since the murders Bill has seen in person the man who raped his wife and crushed her larynx with his bare hands, the man who appeared to Bill as only a dim shape in the darkness that night. Hayes was present for the jury-selection process, which Bill attended regularly. But this is the trial, and the room is charged with a kind of humming undercurrent now. Everyone seems hushed, on alert.

Hayes looks small. On July 23, 2007, he was a burly man with a shaved head, thick arms, and a snarl. But he must have lost eighty pounds since then. He's meek. His face sags, and his bird-backed, slope-shouldered frame drops like a sack of corn flakes into his blue upholstered office chair. He wears baggy pants with no belt and a too-big oxford shirt whose collar gives a wide berth for his pencil neck. He swivels almost imperceptibly in the comfortable-looking chair, flanked by his two public defenders, the bald, methodical Patrick Culligan and the more charismatic lead man, Tom Ullmann, who has a neck beard and whose ties, the courtroom will soon learn, are always exactly four inches too long. The lawyers' chairs are about a foot taller than Hayes's.

Off to the side, in the spectator section, sits Jeremiah Donovan, the lawyer who will represent Joshua Komisarjevsky, the other man caught fleeing the Petit house in Jennifer's minivan, at his trial next year. He's a charmer, Donovan, and the reporters who know him keep an eye on him and try to chat him up when he walks by. (It's never difficult to chat up Jeremiah Donovan.) He's tall with bristly white hair. His suit pants are stained.

Every woman in the state of Connecticut has thought about what she would have done had she found herself in Jennifer Petit's impossible situation that morning: standing in the safe confines of a bank, her captor circling in her own minivan outside, waiting for her to emerge with the money he and his friend are stealing from her and her husband, all while her two children remain tied to their beds with pillowcases over their heads and she doesn't even know where her husband is. The two men have told her that if she just gives them the money, they'll leave the house and no one will get hurt. They are polite to her, even when they tell her that if she tries to get the police involved, they will kill her family.

Jennifer had options. She could get the money, tell the bank manager to send the police to her house immediately, and leave. She could stay inside the bank and call the police, which would keep Hayes circling while the cops rush to the house to ambush the other man. Or she could do exactly what the men have told her: Get the money, don't call the police, and let the man drive her home, in the hope that the criminals will do exactly what they say they will do, which is to end the nightmare and leave her family in peace.

From the testimony of a junior teller and the bank manager who were on duty on the morning of Monday, July 23, 2007, the 117 people in the courtroom learn that this is what Jennifer did:

She walked into the Bank of America branch in Cheshire, trying to appear calm. It is a freestanding building in a suburban shopping area, one-story brick with cupolas on top like a little schoolhouse, with a parking lot out front. She waited for the next available teller, a young woman named Kristin. She gave Kristin an account number and requested a withdrawal of $15,000. Kristin checked one account and saw that there wasn't enough money in it. They checked another account, a home-equity line of credit, the one of which Hayes and Komisarjevsky had found a record at the house. Kristin asked Jennifer for identification. Jennifer said she didn't have any on her but that she needed the money. Kristin told her that wasn't possible—not only did she need ID, her husband would need to be present to cosign for the withdrawal. So Jennifer told Kristin there were two men holding her family hostage in her home, and that she had to bring them the money right away or they would kill her daughters and her husband. She said they were being polite and she just needed the money. Please. Right now.

The teller excused herself and quickly walked over to get the manager, Mary Lyons, a friendly woman who had worked for Bank of America for more than thirty years. Kristin whispered the situation to Mary, showed her the piece of paper with Jennifer's account number written on it. The protocol in this situation, Kristin says, was that the bank employees try to determine as quickly as possible if it's a real crisis or some kind of scam. Mary walked over to Kristin's teller station and calmly asked Jennifer for identification. Jennifer held open her wallet to show that she didn't have any, because the people in her house had taken it. What she did show Mary in her wallet were two photographs of her daughters. Mary looked up at this woman, and she could see the whole terrifying story of the last six hours in Jennifer's eyes. Right then, Mary Lyons knew the woman was telling the truth.

Now Mary Lyons sits nervously on the witness stand, re-creating this ungodly scene. She is being questioned by Gary Nicholson, the senior assistant state's attorney.

"Can you describe for the jury, if you would please, what Mrs. Petit's demeanor was like during this period of time when she was attempting to get the $15,000 from the bank?" Nicholson asks.

"Yes, she was—she seemed quite calm. She seemed very, to me, brave."

"Did you look at her eyes?"

"Yes, we did—after I saw the pictures, we looked at each other and I knew right then that she was—what she was telling me was the truth, and I needed to help her and let her get out of the bank. . . ."

"During the time that Mrs. Petit was at the teller counter, was there any discussion concerning whether or not she wanted the police to become aware of the fact that she was withdrawing this money?"

"I think she said something to the effect that, 'Nobody can know about this because I have to get back with the money.'"

At the bank, Mary authorized an immediate $15,000 cash withdrawal. Jennifer took the money and calmly walked out of the bank, hoping that Mary Lyons wouldn't call the police.

Given her options, Jennifer Petit decided that the only thing she needed to do was get back to her children. Maybe it was not even a decision. Maybe it was instinct. Maybe it's what any mother would do if she found herself standing in that bank.

"At this time, Your Honor, the state would like to offer state's exhibit number 6," says Nicholson. State's exhibit number 6 is a 911 call that Mary Lyons made as Jennifer was leaving the bank. A marshal dims the lights in the courtroom. On a large white screen facing the jury, Nicholson projects a series of grainy black-and-white images from the bank's surveillance cameras. One shows Jennifer in a white blouse, jewelry neatly in place, glasses on a chain around her neck as she often wore them, standing at the teller's counter, waiting. Doing everything right. She looks calm and brave, like Mary Lyons said. She looks as if she understands that these are the most important few moments in the entire forty-eight years of her life.

The recording of Lyons's voice fuzzes through the courtroom speakers: "We have a lady who is in our bank right now who says that her husband and children are being held at their house. The people are in a car outside the bank. She is getting $15,000 to bring out to them. If the police are told, they will kill the children and the husband. They have their faces covered. She is petrified. They told her they wouldn't hurt anybody if she got back there with the money. She believes them."

Bill's left arm rests on the edge of the bench, his hand to his cheek as if it's holding up his head. Both his legs bounce up and down. He looks up at the picture now being projected on the screen: the last picture taken of his wife. The white rectangle of the screen reflects on each lens of his glasses. He has seen these photos before, but not like this, in this room, and he stares up at them again now. The last picture was captured by the security camera inside the ATM in the lobby of the bank. It shows his wife, his good, good wife, walking out the front door of the bank at 9:23 a.m., clutching her bag with the bands of cash inside it, very much believing that she was about to go home and save her family's lives.

And then the state calls Dr. William Petit Jr. as its witness.

It's strange. The worst, most haunting parts of Bill Petit's testimony at the trial of the man who killed his family are not those in which he describes his own torture but rather the parts of the ordeal when he didn't know what was going on. His being beaten in the head, his being blindfolded and dragged into the basement and tied up for hours—he reports these chronologically and without emotion. The questions that sound so innocuous are the ones that give you chills. This is the prosecutorial talent of Michael Dearington, the state's attorney who looks like a white-haired Irish priest out of a John Ford movie. He has this way about him that makes you wonder sometimes if he's all there—he fumbles, he withdraws a question, he gets the exhibit number wrong. But as his questioning goes on, you see that what he lacks in finesse he makes up for in the methodical, metronomic way he is building this case, question by question, exhibit by exhibit, fact by fact. His direct examination of Bill is constructed of dry exchanges that contain details both horrible and banal:

> PETIT: Yeah, I called home on the cell and asked if we had any plans for dinner and they said, Yes, we'll throw something together here. Stop by a farm stand and see if you could find any corn or fresh vegetables.
>
> DEARINGTON: And did you, indeed, look around for a stand?
>
> PETIT: I did, but at 6:30 or so, everybody had locked up for the weekend. . . .
>
> DEARINGTON: Did you hear anything that would suggest to you that someone was going into the refrigerator?
>
> PETIT: Twice when I was down there [in the basement], somebody came downstairs, down the stairs and walked directly in front of me over to the refrigerator, took something out—I'm assuming a can because it sounded like a pop top—and went back upstairs. That happened twice. They didn't say anything either time. I could just vaguely make out the outline of somebody going by through whatever was over my head at that time.
>
> DEARINGTON: And what was in the refrigerator, as best you could recall?
>
> PETIT: Mostly soda, a little bit of beer that was left over from the graduation party a month before. . . .
>
> DEARINGTON: At some point, did you hear any thumping-type noise?
>
> PETIT: I did hear, right around that same time, three loud noises that I couldn't understand what they were, as if someone were throwing twenty- or fifty-pound sacks on the living-room floor, it sounded like. . . .

DEARINGTON: You referred to those as zip ties or some such thing?

PETIT: I am not sure exactly.

DEARINGTON: The material, what type of material was it generally?

PETIT: Hard but flexible plastic.

DEARINGTON: And did you keep any of those in your house?

PETIT: No . . .

PETIT: Well, unfortunately, it was nonfunctional because sometime—perhaps a month earlier when I was getting ready to go to work early in the morning, I came down into the kitchen and Jennifer had come down and I didn't see her. I called, she was down in the basement, I went down in the basement, and she said she was having a hard time opening this lock, which is a deadbolt. And she had essentially disassembled, disassembled the lock to open the door so that she would be able to get things from the basement to the patio.

DEARINGTON: And so on that particular day, neither locking mechanism was working, is that correct?

PETIT: That—the deadbolt was not functional, no. . . .

DEARINGTON: With respect to exhibit 125, do you recognize that wallet as looking familiar?

PETIT: That looks like the wallet that Hayley didn't carry on a regular basis. And after graduation, she had received a number of gift cards, we had just obtained that Bank of America ATM card and a credit card for her to use when she went to college. . . .

PETIT: Jen kept her jewelry in the bedroom in a jewelry box. I don't—I think she accepted the black pearls at Christmas

and wasn't as, wasn't especially—didn't think my taste was
that great that year, and I think it stayed in the jewelry box
for the most part. . . .

DEARINGTON: I'm going to show you what is marked as
exhibit 37 for identification, I believe. I'll ask if you
recognize that, Dr. Petit?

PETIT: It's a Louisville Slugger baseball bat that we had for
a long time in the garage and in the basement. I think I
received it from my—via my brothers and father, who some
time back had several package stores. It has the Ronrico
Rum name on there, probably was a giveaway with some
marketing that they were doing. . . .

Bill's testimony ends without ceremony or drama, and there is
no cross-examination.

Juries are made up of people, and people do unexpected things,
and after lunch on the second day of the trial, the first really weird
thing in the case of *State v. Hayes* happens.

The judge in the case is Jon C. Blue, twenty-one years on the
bench, more than a dozen as a trial lawyer before that, midwest-
erner, towering helmet of white hair, enunciates every syllable.
Grandfatherly. Stern if he needs to be. And firmly in control of his
courtroom. He announces after the daily one-hour lunch break
that one of the jurors, a Mr. Lively, would like to address the court.
In Blue's tone you can hear that he's anxious to learn what this is
about. And so he calls Mr. Lively to sit in the witness box and tell
the court what's on his mind. Mr. Lively unfolds a piece of paper
and reads:

"As a juror in this case, I am confused by the presentation of the
state's case, and bewildered by what seems to me a lack of preparation on their part. The physical evidence is poorly organized and
the order of its introduction seems to be arbitrary and casual. But

for me, what's worse, the evidence being presented to us has no explanation with it and no contextualization. It's as though . . ."

Jesus. Who is this guy? Mucking up the works. The problem with people doing weird things in a jury trial is that it creates the possibility of a mistrial. And one could argue that Jon C. Blue's most important job here, for however many days this trial goes on, is to avoid a mistrial. That, and to try to avoid handing the defense any reason to appeal. It's all very tenuous—every objection, every motion, and every weird thing like this is a test for Judge Blue.

Blue glowers at Mr. Lively.

Tom Ullmann, meanwhile, is probably thrilled with Mr. Lively. For one thing, Mr. Lively is not impressed with the state's presentation so far, which could bias him in favor of the defense. But also, a loose cannon on the jury is not such a bad thing for a defense team looking for any reason to move for a mistrial.

Blue responds to Mr. Lively's announcement first by effusively praising all of the attorneys on both sides, saying they are four of the best in the state. Ullmann and Judge Blue, neither of whom have ever seen anything quite like this in their long careers in the courtroom, take turns questioning Mr. Lively. They cajole him for ten minutes, affording him multiple opportunities to say that he can continue to be faithful to his oath as a juror—those are the magic words that would mean he could possibly remain as a member of this jury.

> THE COURT: Let me just ask you this. Based on what you
> know now, I need to know your answer. Knowing
> what your responsibilities are going to be, that you have to
> base your decision—because of your oath, you have to base
> your decision on all the evidence, and you have to follow
> the instructions of the court, can you assure us that you
> will be faithful to your oath? Or can you not so assure us?
> You tell me.

THE JUROR: I could be faithful to my oath.
THE COURT: All right.

Blue thinks he has him.

THE JUROR: Yes, I can do that.
THE COURT: And you could assure us?
THE JUROR: To the best of my ability.

Blue does a double-take.

THE COURT: You say "to the best of your ability"?
THE JUROR: That's what I'm doubtful about.
THE COURT: You are doubtful about your ability?
THE JUROR: Yes, to focus on the right things in this trial.

Blue hears this, looks up at the lawyers, and snaps out one last question:

THE COURT: Are there any follow-up questions?

You can hear it in his voice: We're done here.
Mr. Lively is gone.
Blue arguably had no choice but to dismiss the juror from his service, but the fact is, there is now one less juror available in the case of *State of Connecticut v. Hayes.* Every case starts with twelve jurors and four alternates. There are now only three alternates, and it's only lunchtime on the second day. If Bill Petit is worried about this, or frustrated by this Mr. Lively for interrupting the delicate procession of a case that Bill would like to see resolved swiftly and without undue drama, he doesn't show it. As is his custom, Bill does not show anything at all.

. . .

Each morning, whoever is going to court that day meets at the house on Red Stone Hill, and whoever's going to court usually means the whole crew. Bill, of course. Dick and Marybelle Hawke. Cindy. Barbara and Bill Sr. Glenn. Hanna and usually Dennis, when he can get off work. Aunt Bev and Uncle Larry. They pile into a couple of cars and drive the forty minutes south to New Haven. No one says much on the ride. Bill's stomach turns the whole way, every day. He wants none of this. But he goes for the girls. There is guilt in why he goes. He goes because he believes his presence will help bring the killers to justice, and that is the one, last thing he can do for his girls, the girls he could not save. He knows it's irrational to think that way, but that's the way he thinks.

The state allows the family to park in a special lot directly across Church Street from the courthouse. When they arrive, Bill gets out of the comfort of the car and steps into the bracing downtown air, like walking out of the bathroom after a shower, the warm cloud of humidity dissipating around you. The reporters are always huddled out in front of the courthouse, and they click on their recorders and take the caps off their pens. The cameramen heave cameras onto their shoulders. Bill and his family wade through, saying little more than *Good morning*.

Andrew Chapman comes along once in a while, if he doesn't have school. His sister Abby, though, does not. She is just starting her sophomore year at the University of Vermont, on the cold shore of Lake Champlain, far away from Plainville, far away from Cheshire, from the Petit Family Foundation and its road races and golf tournaments, far from Uncle Billy's sad room upstairs in her grandparents' house, from this suffocating courtroom. At school she has met nice kids from all over the country. She is joining a sorority, making good friends. But she doesn't tell anybody. Doesn't tell a single person of the horrors that have befallen her family. This makes her feel like a fraud, because there's this huge thing that nobody knows about her, but that's the point: She doesn't want anybody to know. She rarely goes home to Plainville on school breaks. With her new friends, she goes anywhere but home. If she doesn't acknowledge the past, Abby tells herself, it won't seem real. So she makes a new life, or imagines one.

One day, Abby is sitting in the student center with some friends. There's a television on, tuned to one of the news channels, and she looks up and sees her Uncle Billy's face. He's walking out of the courthouse, her grandparents and her mom by his side. Abby looks away, pretends not to notice.

Bill arrives one morning wearing his dress-up version of golf clothes, or his golf-club version of dress clothes: tan slacks, gray blazer, black mock turtleneck with a tiny white Nike swoosh on the collar—a pro-shop shirt. Outside in the hall, in the line of people waiting to get in, he spots two of Jen's old friends from Cheshire. They are both named Deb, and Bill stops to hug them both at once.

"D squared," he says quietly, with a weak smile.

Inside, he takes his seat on the harsh wooden bench, shifting every few minutes because these things kill your back. His stare is blank, his unlined face frozen.

Captain Robert Vignola, a twenty-three-year veteran of the Cheshire Police Department with a bullet head and metal shavings for eyes, sits in the chair on the witness stand. He fires a glare at Steven Hayes that could knock down a brick wall.

Nicholson, the prosecutor, has a mustache and broad shoulders and looks like a detective from the Chicago PD, and together he and Vignola are a couple of bulls charging through what exactly happened on Sorghum Mill Drive on the morning of July 23, 2007. Nicholson projects an aerial photo of the Petits' old neighborhood.

Bill's leg is bouncing fast.

Vignola tells the court that he was at his desk at Cheshire police headquarters when he got a call from dispatch at 9:27 reporting a possible hostage situation at 300 Sorghum Mill Drive. Mary Lyons, at the bank, had looked out her office window and had seen the car as it pulled away, and she relayed the plate number to the 911 operator. Vignola ran the plates on the car, the Chrysler Pacifica. The car was in Jennifer's name, matched to the address. He and another detective jumped into an unmarked car and sped to the neighborhood, with another two-man unit following behind them. He radioed a fifth officer, who was off-duty working a second job, doing construction. That officer ran to his car, left the construction site, and sped toward Sorghum Mill. He was on pace to get there first, and he radioed Vignola and requested permission to do a drive-by of the house for a visual, which Vignola granted. Vignola also ordered marked cruisers to close Sorghum Mill Drive to traffic at either end.

About ten minutes after receiving the initial call, Vignola himself arrived and did a drive-by of the house. He saw the Pacifica already back in the driveway, along with Hayley's old Mercedes. He drove slowly, saw no lights or activity in the windows. He circled the block and parked so that he had a line of sight to the house.

Over the radio, a police dispatcher told him they had located the home phone number for the house, plus cell-phone numbers, but Vignola ordered that no one call the house just yet. He knew that in the 911 call, the bank manager had made it clear that according to the wife, the intruders said they would kill the hostages if the police showed up. You don't risk that, not yet. Right now, what he needed to do was establish a perimeter around the house. He had no idea how many intruders were inside—the wife had said two, but that wasn't certain enough to act on. He was ordering men to the woods behind the house, and there were now two vehicles within sight of the house, and backup on the way.

Protocol.

On the aerial photograph projected in the courtroom, Vignola uses a laser pointer to show the jury where he was positioning his men. For each new post, Nicholson adds a small red arrow. Bill follows this closely, looking up at the screen each time Vignola points to a new location, as if hearing it for the first time.

Next, Nicholson asks for state's exhibit 15a, and a marshal dims the lights. Bill shifts in his seat as he looks at a picture of his former house. It's a beautiful house, just as he remembers it: the cream-colored clapboard, hunter-green shutters, the lush lawn he labored over, orange flowers by the road, tall trees all around. The American dream, pretty much. But if you look closely at this particular photograph, you can see black smudges above the front door and the upstairs windows, from the smoke.

Sitting in his unmarked car, Vignola did not take his eyes off the house. Suddenly he heard on the radio that there was a man in a neighbor's driveway saying, "Dave, Dave, Dave." Vignola stiffened, asked for more information, but before it came, he saw a suspect running from the Petits' house.

"Tell us what you saw, Captain," Nicholson says.

"Mr. Komisarjevsky"—Vignola later learned that this was Joshua Komisarjevsky, the younger of the two intruders—"ran to the car with a bag in his hand, placed the bag in the car, quickly reversed, very, very quickly—that's when another officer [who had a view of the back door] stated that there was movement from the suspects. Moments later, Mr. Komisarjevsky was in front, Mr. Hayes was behind him running to the vehicle. Mr. Komisarjevsky came around, went into the driver's side, Mr. Hayes went into the passenger's side."

Vignola flipped the sirens on, yanked his car into gear, and flew up to the mouth of Bill's driveway. Jennifer's Pacifica, now driven by Komisarjevsky, screamed down the driveway about a million miles an hour. "Hang on," Vignola told his partner. The Pacifica slammed into Vignola's car. He jumped out and pointed his 40mm semiautomatic pistol at the Pacifica, shouting, "Police!" Another detective closed in, pointing a tactical rifle at the vehicle, and a third approached the passenger side, shouting orders. But the Pacifica peeled around in a 180—almost hitting the officer with the rifle—ran over a stone wall and a swath of Michaela's four-o'clocks at the bottom of the driveway, and started speeding down Sorghum Mill Drive. It disappeared around a corner and there was a loud crash.

Joshua Komisarjevsky and Steven Hayes had driven head-on into the two parked police cruisers that had set up a roadblock, then rolled to a stop.

Bill's eyes are closed, and he rubs the spot on his forehead where the Louisville Slugger first met with his skull about seven hours before the crash Captain Vignola has just described.

With the suspects out of view, Vignola says he turned his attention now to clearing the house. Nicholson asks, "Did something catch your attention concerning the Petit residence?"

Bill opens his eyes.

"We saw a large plume of smoke coming from the back side of the residence."

The first thing Ullmann, the public defender, said in his opening statement on the first day of the trial was that his client did it all. Pretty much everything the state says he did, he did. Broke in. Watched his friend beat Dr. Petit with a bat. Tied up the girls. Bought gasoline. Drove Mrs. Petit to the bank. Brought her back and raped her. Strangled her. Ran from a burning house in which he knew at least two living people were restrained, unable to escape.

His plan, he told the jury, was to ask them to consider the troubled life his client lived before that night, and to spare his life.

Now, two days later, Ullmann stands up to cross-examine Captain Vignola. The jurors fix their eyes on the lawyer. Each juror has been given a W.B. Mason spiral pad to take notes in, and a few open their notebooks to a fresh page, their pens ready. A middle-aged woman in the second row of the jury box slides her glasses up the bridge of her nose.

"Good morning, Captain Vignola."

"Good morning," Vignola says to Ullmann. Clipped, official.

Ullmann asks Vignola when, exactly, on the morning of July 23, 2007, he knew various bits of information: the license-plate number of Jennifer Petit's Chrysler Pacifica, the telephone number to the Petit residence, the family's cell-phone numbers. He is smooth, Ullmann—a veteran. The tilt of his voice is almost conversational, his pitch low and casual. Vignola says he found out all of this as he and the other officers set up a perimeter around the house.

"No one made an attempt to call?" Ullmann asks. A tad sharper now. Challenging.

"No, they asked me if I wanted to make that call [to the Petit house], and I advised them that I was going to wait a couple of minutes for a better inner perimeter, more people, for the safety rescue," Vignola says.

Bill's eyes bounce back and forth between the lawyer and the witness with each question.

Ullmann raises his eyebrows. "Almost twenty minutes altogether where no phone call was ever made . . . from any police officer into the home?"

Now Vignola narrows his eyes at Ullmann, a look of either confusion about what the lawyer is implying or anger because he knows precisely what this lawyer is implying.

In the press section of the public seating, a seasoned on-air reporter for one of the New Haven stations whispers to herself, "They're putting the cops on trial."

"That is correct," Vignola hisses to Ullmann.

Ullmann plows ahead, asking Vignola why no one approached the residence. He projects onto the overhead screen his own aerial photograph of the neighborhood. He asks Vignola where every officer was, and with each answer, Ullmann marks an X on the map. Not only does each car get an X, but each officer in each car—he is trying to crowd the map with as many X's as he can, to show the jury just how many Cheshire police officers were set up around 300 Sorghum Mill Drive in the thirty-some minutes between the 911 call and the time the suspects fled.

Next he projects a log of the radio calls made between Vignola, headquarters, and the various officers who were on the scene—the time, in hours, minutes, and seconds, that each call came in, along with a summary of the call. Ullmann cranes his neck up at the screen, peering at it through his glasses, referring to a hard copy in his hands.

The lawyer's implication is clear to everyone in the room, not least to Captain Vignola: that if his team had stormed the house, they could have stopped Ullmann's client, Steven Hayes, from raping Jennifer Hawke-Petit and could have stopped the men from burning Hayley and Michaela Petit alive, but instead they just set up their perimeter, allowing all of that to happen. What this has to do with his defense of Hayes is unclear.

When Judge Blue asks the state whether it wants to follow up after Ullmann's cross-examination, Nicholson jumps up and asks Vignola to once again explain that everything he did was protocol, by the book.

"And did you, sir, have any idea what Joshua Komisarjevsky or Steven Hayes were doing in that house?"

"I had absolutely no idea that there was any act of violence," Vignola says. "If we had any information whatsoever that there was violence, I would have been the first one through the door."

The volley goes back to Ullmann, who stands up to re-cross-examine Vignola. He tries a few paths to try to get Vignola to admit fault. Vignola shuts those down. Then Ullmann asks a question that's really a statement, the kind of thing lawyers say to get on the record, knowing it will draw an objection: "The fact of the matter is that with all this setting up—and not excusing what happened in any way—it's too late, correct?"

Nicholson: "I'm going to object to this."

Judge Blue sustains the objection.

Ullmann is already walking back toward his seat. "I have nothing further."

Bill's head is bowed, his eyes closed.

They march on, these lawyers, clinically dissecting the night the world ended. Bill clenches his eyes and worries the scar on his forehead, now a faint plum-colored line. "As you were going up the stairway from the first floor, did you have any concerns for your safety, sir?" the prosecutor, Nicholson, asks. Rick Trocchi, a volunteer firefighter who owns pizzerias, is on the stand. Nicholson is asking him about when he first entered the Petit home, minutes after the two perpetrators fled. Bill sits hunched over, his arms hanging like thick anchor line on his lap. He knows what's coming.

"The stairs had been burned and they were structurally compromised, we could tell, especially as you went up, indicating that they were losing—they had lost some structural stability," Trocchi says.

"All right. And in addition to the stairs being compromised structurally, did you have—was there also some problems with the visibility going up the stairs?"

"Yeah, there was very little visibility and it was very hot up there as well. We could feel the heat through our gear. Our gear is very, very thick. If you could feel the heat, it's very hot."

"Now, you indicated that you found a person at the top of the stairway leading up to the second floor, is that correct, sir?"

"Yes, sir."

Nicholson handles a manila folder that he says contains two photographs and asks that the marshal pass them to the judge. Only the judge and jury will see these pictures—they won't be displayed on the screen. They are photographs of the person Trocchi saw at the top of the stairs. The judge asks Nicholson to establish who it was.

Nicholson nods. "Let me just ask you, sir," he says to Trocchi. "At the time, did you know the identity of that person?"

"No."

"Have you subsequently learned who that was?"

"Yes."

"Who was it?"

"Hayley Petit."

"All right."

The marshal takes the folder from the judge and hands it to the first juror in the box, who opens it to see a color photograph of a seventeen-year-old girl lying facedown on what looks like the surface of Mars—black and gray soot, craters of burned carpet, ash all around her. Her head had landed just inside the door to the bathroom, across the hall from the only bedroom she ever knew. She wears a T-shirt and sweat shorts. Hayley Petit had escaped. After hours of struggle, she had actually escaped from the rope and nylon restraints around her wrists and ankles. She had fought and fought, covered in the gasoline that Steven Hayes had bought and poured on her, to free herself from captivity in her own room. But the trail of gas led right to her bed, and even all her stamina and all her strength and all her love were no match for a fire so hot that firefighter Trocchi could feel it through his gear a half hour later. She had used up everything.

Bill watches the jurors open and close the manila folder containing the two photographs of his older girl. Some look away. Some just stare. They try not to look at Bill. One woman's eyes crinkle up with the unmistakable tears of shock. The only sound in the packed room is the *ffftt-fffftt* of a courtroom artist's pastels on paper.

Bill just watches them, unmoving. Then his body starts to flinch and fidget, the energy searching for a way out. He scratches his chin. He rubs his lips with his fingers. He flicks each finger off his thumb, and the gold wedding ring that he has worn for twenty-five years catches the light. He is willing himself to be in control, but then his shoulders start jerking up and down. A little at first, and then more, and then he is biting his lower lip. Throughout the trial—throughout his life—Bill Petit has been Mr. In Control. Now and at all times he has maintained an impossible stoic comportment. The emotional range of statuary. The Petit way is to give up nothing. To charge always and only ahead. If you appear in control, then goddammit you will be in control. Oh, *goddammit*. In front of all these people, Bill's composure has abandoned him. He desperately taps his fingers, trying to make it go away, trying to stop. *Ffffftt-ffffftt*. Hanna puts a hand on his back. The manila folder passes from hand to hand. Bill squeezes his eyes shut and lowers his head. No one in the courtroom knows where to look.

The white corner of a crumpled tissue pokes out of Bill's fist. He absently tugs his shirtsleeves so they extend beyond the sleeves of his blazer just so, a small, futile grasp at something like control in a situation that feels, with the passing of each excruciating, airless minute, as if every dehumanizing nightmare he's ever had is playing endlessly in a loop in his head. And he can't crawl out of it. Anyone who has heard or read about what happened to Dr. William Petit— and especially any husband or father—can't help but try to imagine what it was like for this man the night it happened, or the morning after, or in the months that followed. But he is a name in the newspaper, and we read names in newspapers all the time. When we read those stories, the human instinct is to imagine what it was like for this person named Petit, because there but for the grace of God go we. We can force ourselves to picture it for maybe a few seconds: our wife's body, strangled and burned on the floor of our own living room; ourselves trying to get plastic ties off our wrists in our own basement; our own children, gasping for breath in their beds, wondering where we are; our parents and our brothers and sisters, staring at us in our hospital bed the next day, their eyes red and puffy. And then we can pull ourselves out of it. We can look over at our wife and smile, we can tousle our kids' hair. We can take a deep breath and go mow the lawn or something. But Bill is enduring the unique and cruel human experience of having lived it and now being forced to live it again—or maybe he is forcing himself to live it again. It is a mounting psychic torture, the only thing worse than the physical torture to which he was subjected, and the expression on his face tells the world that for Bill Petit, this recurring nightmare beggars belief.

Jay Markella, a lieutenant thirteen years now with the Cheshire PD, is not on the witness stand for very long—maybe thirty minutes. He arrived on the scene, he says. He tried to enter the house, he says. It was too hot, he says. "The air was hot when you breathed it—you could feel the burning in your throat." The fire department sprayed more water inside, he says. Eventually he and four other officers were permitted to enter, their weapons drawn, to make sure no additional suspects were hiding in the house, he says.

The state shows a photograph of the upstairs hallway, a narrow black corridor with flame-scarred walls receding toward the ghost of a dresser sitting at the end of the hall. Markella says he walked down the hall and entered a room on the left.

Mike Dearington, the white-haired state's attorney, asks him, "And did you go into the bedroom?"

"Yes, I did, sir."

Bill watches, giving away nothing.

"What did you observe in the bedroom?"

"There was a bed that ran next to the wall there, adjacent to the wall, and that's where I found Michaela Petit."

"On the bed?"

"Yes."

Following procedure when entering a piece of evidence or a photograph into the record, Dearington hands Ullmann a manila folder and says to the judge, "I'm showing counsel exhibits 76 and 77 that are currently marked for identification." Exhibits 76 and 77 are photographs of Michaela's body on her bed, her hands still tied. Ullmann, his cocounsel Patrick Culligan, and the defendant, Hayes, study the photos for a moment, their faces pinched as if they're scanning a note for typos.

Judge Blue asks if there is any objection to these being entered into evidence.

"No, sir."

Bill watches them looking at the photos, which again are not visible to the courtroom. Bill's body is tensed up now, as if the coils inside him are tightening. He is not so much watching as trying to brace himself.

Dearington asks, "Did you go in for the purpose of ascertaining whether there was any life left in Michaela?"

"Yes, I did."

"What did you do?"

Markella looks like a cop: shaved head, squared-off jaw, balls of muscle for shoulders. He answers as flatly, as businesslike, as he can. "Michaela was lying on the bed," he says. As the police lieutenant soldiers through a bleak description of the scene in the little girl's bedroom, Bill is crying once more, his shoulders shaking. He runs a hand back through his hair. Bill Sr., sitting next to him, puts an arm around his son, rubs Bill's back, squeezes his shoulders tight, the old man's long fingers trying to knead out his boy's pain.

After the jurors again perform the crushing ritual of passing the manila folder from one to the next, trying not to glance over at the silently weeping man seated a few feet away, Judge Blue announces that he's going to dismiss them early today. "We understand that this has been a pretty harrowing experience," he says to them. He saw the photos, too. "It's one thing to appreciate that, it's another thing to go through it. Obviously, if we could spare you, we would, but we can't." He tells them they can feel free to give each other hugs if they need comfort, but, as usual, "do not discuss the case among yourselves or with anyone else."

One afternoon, Jeremiah Donovan, Joshua Komisarjevsky's lawyer, sits in the front row of the spectators' gallery as state's attorney Dearington questions Paul Makuc, a detective for the state fire marshal. Dearington is asking Makuc about the restraints that were used to tie Hayley and Michaela Petit to their beds. He asks for state's exhibit 90 to be projected on the screen. It's a chilling, awful photograph of Hayley's charred room. If the courtroom was quiet a moment ago, it's suddenly so quiet that, sitting there, you feel hot and a little sick.

The mattress, what's left of it, is black. The fabric covering the box spring has been incinerated, exposing the metal coils inside like a tangle of barbed wire. Periwinkle-colored paint blisters off the walls in grotesque blotches, and the pictures that Hayley had taped to the walls above her bed—at perfect angles and evenly spaced, like paintings in a museum—have peeled off like dead skin. Her pillows are two blackened shapes, the pillowcases still pink at the edges. The nylon stockings and rope that Hayes and Komisarjevsky used to tie her hands and feet are melted onto the bedposts like wax around a candlestick.

The spectators, frozen, stare at the photo with a kind of dazed horror.

"You've indicated that accelerant"—gasoline—"was poured up on the bed and came down," Dearington is saying. His voice, dry as wool, sounds somehow muted in the stifling silence of the windowless room. "Can you tell where the pour ended, or perhaps began—that is, the end of the trail where it comes down off the bed?"

Makuc, who is tall and pale and baby-faced, answers, "The pour extended from the edge of the bed along the east wall of the room."

Suddenly, a blaring cell-phone ringtone cuts through the silent tension, so loud a couple of people jump. Everyone looks around in shock. The ringtone is the Three Dog Night song "Joy to the World":

"Jeremiah was a bullfrog! Was a good friend of mine!"

Judge Blue looks as if his head is about to launch off his neck from the anger. "Excuse me!"

Jeremiah Donovan leaps up and jams his hands into his pockets, searching frantically for his phone.

"That's me, Your Honor. I'm sorry," he says, and walks quickly out of the room.

Outside the claustrophobia of Courtroom 6A, Bill Petit's world continues to reconstitute itself. He still lives with his parents on Red Stone Hill, still goes for breakfast at Saint's. Still sits at the head of the long table on the glassed-in porch, doing the work of the Petit Family Foundation. The organization, his organization—it couldn't exist without him—is three years old now. Requests for grants roll in constantly, and Bill reads them all. The idea is to grow the foundation to a point where it's self-sustainable—where it can live off its own interest. Five million in the bank is a good goal. That leaves a few million to go. People still send single dollar bills sometimes. And Bill still writes them a note, thanking them.

Basketball season is coming up. This will be the start of the fourth season without Hayley, his UConn buddy. He still goes to the games, of course, still follows the news—reads up on every new recruit, looks at the schedule to see how tough it is. The Huskies aren't looking too good this year. The men's team, anyway. They've got a freshman coming in, Kemba Walker, out of the Bronx, looks like he might be a star. But all the preseason polls are picking them to finish near the bottom of their conference. They enter the season unranked in the nation, something the team isn't used to. They are expected to be terrible. The Petits still have season tickets, and they'll still pile into the car a dozen times this winter to make the haul up to Hartford or Storrs for the home games. But it won't be the same. It's a little harder to care about Kemba Walker and the preseason polls right now. (In six months the team will beat the odds and defy all the predictions. UConn will barely survive to play in the postseason tournaments, but when they do Walker will lead them to an improbable eleven consecutive victories and the national title. Bill will be there to watch.)

Still, the perpetual motion of Bill's brain needs an outlet. He's not a practicing physician anymore, but the instinct to help people was not killed that morning at his home three years ago. That survived. And so he has found a new outlet, one he believes gives him purpose. A few times now, he has driven the twenty-five minutes from Plainville to Hartford to testify before the Connecticut General Assembly, the state legislature. A bloc of Democrats is trying to abolish the death penalty in Connecticut, and Petit wants to stop that from happening. Last spring, six months before the start of the trial of Steven Hayes, he testified against the repeal. When he goes to Hartford to speak, he is afforded three minutes, like every other member of the public. The first time he went, he and Hanna had to wait nine hours for their turn. But he makes the drives and he sits and he waits, and then he says what he feels he must say. He also speaks out in favor of laws that would mandate harsher punishments for people who commit violent crimes. He has testified in Hartford several times in favor of a three-strikes law for violent offenders.

But for the most part, Bill's world during these few months at the end of 2010 is small. Each morning, he wakes up—or, more likely, simply rises from his bed after being awake for at least an hour or two, sometimes all night—showers, dresses, combs his hair back over his faded scars, and rides with his family to New Haven. Even before they get into the car, the nausea starts to churn his stomach. Every day, he knows no part of the next eight hours will hold anything good for him. He knows that from the minute he steps out of the car in the special reserved parking lot on Church Street, each following minute will be worse than the last.

The cameras are always waiting for him. That's a new, weird thing in his life. Reporters, cameramen. The TV people: men wearing suit jackets and ties with jeans or khakis because the camera sees only their torsos. Women with heavy makeup and perfect nails. They look different from the newspaper people, who mostly wear a more workaday version of business attire—rumpled sport coats, lived-in pantsuits. They clutch laptops and reporters' notebooks (narrow enough to slide into a breast pocket) and palm-sized digital recorders and a handful of extra pens, and they work their butts off all day, not missing a word.

It started when he was in the hospital right after it happened, but he was oblivious to it then. He was protected. In the intervening months and years, reporters and producers have tried coming to the house, calling, showing up at Petit Family Foundation events, sending letters. He doesn't begrudge them doing their jobs, most of them, as long as they're not rude and don't hound him and his family at home. A few of them even covered jury selection back in the spring. But now that the trial is real, now that it's happening and is hitting the front page of the Connecticut papers most days, not only does the crush of reporters fill up the allotted two rows of seats in the courtroom, but the spillover takes up most of the next four rows, too. Most are local press—the *Hartford Courant* (a news reporter plus a blogger), the *New Haven Register* (also a team of two), the local CBS affiliate, the Fox affiliate, and the New Haven channel, WTNH. The *New York Times* has a man there every day, a seasoned legal reporter with New York swagger, and the Associated Press guy is always present. The national morning shows—*Today*, *Good Morning America*—seem to be sending people every day. *Inside Edition*. CNN. Fox News. Bill says hi to a few he's come to recognize because they're respectful and nice and they show up diligently—Robert Goulston from Channel 3, Erin Cox from WTNH, Alaine Griffin from the *Courant*.

Each morning, twenty tickets are given out—actual pink cardboard tickets on which numbers are written with a Sharpie by the external-affairs person from the Connecticut judicial branch. A ticket guarantees a member of the press a seat for the entire day's proceedings. If you don't have a ticket, you become a regular member of the public, hoping for a seat, and at least a couple dozen members of the public are showing up every day, too, sometimes more, so it's highly competitive. The problem is that there's an hour break for lunch, during which the courtroom is emptied and locked, and if you don't have a ticket, you might not get a seat after the break. On the first day, the reporters showed up as early as 7:00 a.m. But back then, nobody knew how competitive things would be. Nobody figured on the documentary filmmakers and the national magazine reporter and the *two* courtroom sketch artists and the national news producers coming up from New York City and taking hotel rooms across New Haven Green just so they could be there every day with their dreams of landing the big interview with Bill Petit. And so the reporters started arriving earlier and earlier: 6:45, 6:30. Then 5:45, 5:15. Sometimes by 6:00 the line was already at least twenty people long—the day's tickets were already taken. At 8:00, the exterior courtroom door was unlocked, allowing the reporters to get out of the elements and into a large vestibule outside the lobby, arranging their belongings in order, everyone keeping their place in line. As the trial stretched deep into the fall and the mornings grew colder, the reporters took to dropping their handbags and briefcases in a line as placeholders and returning to the warmth of their cars or seeking refuge in the bagel shop down the street once it opened at 5:30. When the courthouse itself opened at 9:00, the reporters filed in (again in the precise order in which they had arrived), passed through metal detectors, and proceeded to the sixth floor, where once again they arranged themselves in line and awaited the external-affairs person to come around with the tickets. The courtroom was unlocked around 9:30, and the day's proceedings started at 10:00, five hours after the first reporters had dropped their bags down on Church Street.

The live trucks run their cables along the curb, their telescoping satellite poles extended high above. When the Petits pull their small caravan into the private lot across the street, men wearing jackets with TV-station logos hoist cameras onto their shoulders and point them at Bill, a ritual by now in which the cameras try desperately to capture him while he practices obliviousness. It's the same when he enters Courtroom 6A: The reporters, trying to look casual, sneak looks at him and tweet his arrival. Even the judicial marshals, stationed around the room like turrets, follow him with their eyes, curiously. Bill just tries to look like a man walking into a room.

Jeremiah Donovan has pulled some stunts in his thirty-one years as a trial lawyer. There was the time in the courtroom he jumped up onto a bale of marijuana that was being used as evidence in a drug case. Or the time he was defending the founder of the Latin Kings gang and recited the nicknames of 124 gang members from memory, an attempt to show that there were so many guys with the same names that the state didn't even know for sure which one had been killed. Then there was the mob trial in which he drew giant cartoon thought bubbles on photographs of his client, showing his alleged inner motives. But today, he makes a statement—in public, to the press—that tops them all.

The Hayes trial is still going on. Next year, Donovan will stand in the same courtroom and defend Joshua Komisarjevsky, the man who committed the atrocities in the Petit house with his friend Steven Hayes. Donovan shows up at the Hayes trial frequently. He studies the state's case, the defense, the jury's demeanor, Judge Blue, the reporters, everything. He takes notes. He is looking for ways to sharpen and adapt his strategy for the next defendant, his client. He makes sure to be there on this particular day, because the medical examiner for the state of Connecticut is testifying. The medical examiner testifies that Komisarjevsky committed an unspeakable violation of Michaela Petit.

Donovan loves a good piece of legal strategy and he is a student of political maneuvering. He and his wife, who is also his law partner, have spent the past few years reading biographies of every United States president, in chronological order, because he felt that American history represented too wide a gap in his general knowledge. Now that he's done with that, he's reading the *Aeneid* in Latin. When Donovan gives a dinner party, he approaches it as a complex series of problems to be solved, an attitude that eventually led to his devising a system for cooking perfect risotto—a delicate dish in which rice cooks slowly on the stove with constant stirring, absorbing liquid a little at a time until it reaches the perfect creamy texture and consistency—in the microwave. He never, ever ends a sentence with a preposition, sometimes smiling as he threshes his way through the syntax, trying to get the words in the right order. ("The rule of cross-examination is, never ask a question [pause, smile] the answer to which you do not know.") He is a solver of intellectual problems.

Today, Todd Bussert, Donovan's young, hard-charging cocounsel, has the idea that Donovan should talk to the reporters. While their client, Komisarjevsky, sits in a six-by-nine-foot cell at Northern Correctional, a maximum-security prison, Hayes's lawyers are making Komisarjevsky out to be the worse of the two. Donovan expected this. What he was less certain of was that Hayes's lawyers would introduce evidence suggesting that Komisarjevsky had raped Michaela in her bed. That Komisarjevsky had, in fact, sodomized her.

Since he first met Komisarjevsky a few days after the crimes were committed in 2007—more than three years ago now—Donovan has taken him at his word. Not as a matter of habit—Donovan has had plenty of clients whose word wasn't worth a bag of spit. But Komisarjevsky confessed to so much: beating the father, tying the girls to their beds, stealing money. He even said that he performed oral sex on Michaela and ejaculated on her. Heinous and cruel acts, Donovan concedes, but different from rape. And the fact that Komisarjevsky was so clear in his confession that he didn't rape the girl—well, Donovan believes him.

In the courtroom, the state medical examiner is testifying about Michaela's autopsy. Bussert is following the courtroom Twitter stream—mostly tweets being posted by reporters sitting only a few feet from Donovan. He tells Donovan that everyone is writing about the medical examiner's testimony that Komisarjevsky raped the girl.

Maybe you should say something, Bussert suggests. To clear things up.

Donovan agrees, but it's going to be tricky. All the lawyers involved with both cases are under a gag order by the punctilious Judge Blue. But Donovan just can't let this pass, because if he does it will get repeated to the point where it's accepted as fact. Picking a jury for Komisarjevsky's trial is going to be difficult enough without his client getting branded as a child rapist on top of everything else. So, shortly before the 1:00 p.m. lunch recess, he and Bussert ride the elevator down to the street to make a statement.

Outside, it's balmy for late September in Connecticut, well into the 70s and humid. The TV reporters in the sixth-floor courtroom have apparently called down to their camera trucks outside to let them know Donovan is coming down and plans to speak, and a cluster of microphones has been assembled. The automatic door slides open and Donovan's lanky frame descends the concrete steps to the sidewalk. He walks up to the mikes, winces out a quick, awkward smile, and says softly in his weatherbeaten Boston accent, "Are we ready?" And then he says, "I've been concerned because in watching televised interviews with the Petit family, I realized that they're under the misimpression that on the night she died, the younger Petit daughter was anally raped. When Joshua Komisar-jevsky was arrested, he gave a very detailed description of what had happened that night, and in that statement, he explained what happened. It's been supported by the three expert witnesses—the DNA expert, the chemist, and the chief medical examiner—and I've explained how that was done. And it'll be a long time between now and the Komisarjevsky trial, and I just don't want the Petit family to believe that on the morning that she died, their second daughter was the subject of an anal rape, because that just is not what happened. I know this is probably small solace, but it's just something that I felt I had to say."

There is a kind of awful banality to the way a murder trial has to be run. There are procedures, of course. And legal phrasings are exchanged constantly—motions filed, exhibits entered into evidence. There is a lot of waiting. It can feel strangely clinical sometimes, but for Bill, every procedure that's followed, every witness who is called to the stand, questioned, cross-examined, and finally dismissed brings the trial that much closer to the blessed moment when it will be over, when they will stop having to pound these facts into his head hour after hour. He sits every day in the first seat of the first row, saying nothing, showing nothing, doing nothing. Just waiting, watching the court reporter tap out the millions of words being spoken by these lawyers and the witnesses and the judge, praying for the day when the spool of white paper ceases rolling out of her machine.

Because of this, any disruption to the regimented course of events is like a punch in the chest. That incident with Mr. Lively, the juror who complained about the prosecutors—something like that can derail the whole operation, wasting months of preparation, jury selection, and all the rest of it. Or the stunt Donovan pulled on the courthouse steps, that sickening stunt. When these unexpected things happen, you fear the worst: mistrial. A mistrial would be a disaster.

And so when Tom Ullmann, Steven Hayes's lawyer, walks into court one morning and announces to Judge Blue that his client experienced some kind of a fit in his prison cell the previous evening and urinated all over himself, you can feel the courtroom tighten. *Oh, God, what's this now.* "It seems to me like there were seizure-like symptoms," Ullmann says. "I don't believe he had any sleep last night. We're ready to proceed with the next witness, but I will alert the court if I don't think we can proceed any further." Bill listens to this intently. Judge Blue hides any feelings he may have about the defendant's having urinated all over himself the night before, assuring Ullmann that the court will make every allowance for Mr. Hayes's health.

A week later, Judge Blue himself gets sick and the trial is postponed for two days. Another scare, something the defense could pounce on.

It is autumn now. Through the huge plate-glass window in the sixth-floor hallway outside Courtroom 6A, the shadows across the Yale University campus, all brick buildings and oak trees and church spires, stretch farther than they do in midsummer, and the leaves are turning from green to crimson and gold. The trial is in its third week, and the hard wood benches in the courtroom aren't getting any more comfortable. One Tuesday, Bill Sr. brings a folding nylon camping chair to sit on, which makes it a little easier for his aging frame to stand the discomfort for six hours. Big Bill has closed his eyes a few times during the trial, the fatigue getting the best of him during slow moments. Bill worries about the jury seeing this.

When Hayes walks into the courtroom that morning, as he does each day just before things get going at 10:00, he shuffles his feet.

His eyes are red. His clothes look new and baggy, as usual, and he is not permitted to wear a belt. He hasn't shaved today, which is unusual for the trial so far. He looks like hell. He shakes hands with Culligan and slumps into his chair.

You can smell the gasoline in the courtroom. A forensics detective is on the stand today, and the state is introducing evidence that has been stored in metal canisters since it was analyzed after the murders. A piece of the T-shirt Hayley had worn to bed Sunday night, July 22. A scrap of denim from the jeans Jennifer put on to go to the bank. Michaela's torn shorts. You can still smell the gas, thirty-eight months later.

On the projection screen, the state shows a photograph of the scorched kitchen. It barely looks like a room. But if you look closely, there, in the sink, appears to be the pasta pot Michaela used when she was cooking Sunday dinner. The teakettle sits on the stove, where it always was. A cupboard door hangs off its melted hinges, and a shelf has fallen cockeyed.

The state shows more photographs—ghostly stills floating in the dimmed chamber, each one broadcast for minutes on end, a slow torture for Bill. While the photos remain on the screen, the lawyers and the witnesses speak of them in the context of his family, repeating their names a hundred times a day—*Jennifer. Hayley. Michaela. Jennifer. Hayley. Michaela. Jennifer. Hayley. Michaela. Jennifer. Hayley. Michaela.* Over and over, each mention of their names like a knifepoint into Bill's skin.

Next: a photograph of the charred living room, the furniture arranged just as Jen liked it, with the oriental rug she had finally bought unrecognizable beneath the wreckage. Now, in the photograph, it's a black scab on the floor. Bill looks up at the photograph, turns his head away. You can see a dark cloak in the middle of the room: the place where Jennifer's body lay. She'd had to be identified by her dental records. There is a macabre routineness to all of this, as if Bill were being forced to watch some twisted fire-safety video featuring pictures of his own home.

Another man from forensics takes the stand, this one short and nervous, with a bureaucratic mustache. He testifies that he recovered text messages from Hayes's and Komisarjevsky's cell phones, a thumbed-out conversation between the two men early on the evening of Sunday, July 22, 2007, the night they would break into Bill's house. The images of the texts are displayed in court:

"I'm chomping at the bit to get started. Need a margarita soon," Hayes wrote.

An hour passed after Hayes sent his text, and he didn't hear back from Komisarjevsky. At 8:45, he typed: "We still on?"

The response, two minutes later: "Yes."

"Soon?" Hayes wrote back.

"I'm putting kid to bed hold your horses," came the response. Komisarjevsky was father to a five-year-old daughter, a little girl he was apparently tucking in for the night.

A half hour later, Hayes got antsy again and texted, "Dude the horses want 2 get loose! lol."

There were photographs, too, on one of the phones, the man testifies. The photos aren't shown in court, but he is asked to describe them. The pictures depict a young girl tied to a bed, he says, without clothes on, and a man's genitals.

On his way out of the courtroom, the man from forensics has to walk right past Bill.

"I'm sorry," he whispers.

At almost eleven o'clock that night, Bill sits in his room upstairs in his parents' house and composes an e-mail, which he sends to legislators in the Connecticut assembly. In it he urges them to consider a law like Chelsea's Law in California, which gives automatic life sentences for sexually assaulting a minor on the first offense. "It would be the moral and ethical thing to do," he writes. "Special exemptions can be carved out for extenuating circumstances (hard to think of many)."

In Connecticut, murder trials have two parts: the guilt phase and the penalty phase. In the guilt phase, the prosecutors go first. They must try to prove that the defendant is guilty beyond reasonable doubt. They must establish that the defendant committed the crime with which he is charged. When it's their turn, the defense tries to establish reasonable doubt—even a remote possibility that the defendant could be innocent. The jury's decision—guilty or not guilty—must be unanimous. If even one member of the jury has doubts about the defendant's guilt and refuses to vote guilty, the trial is over. There is no penalty phase.

If the jury is unanimous in finding the defendant guilty of at least one capital crime, the penalty phase comes next. This is the defense's show. The defendant's lawyers try to demonstrate that while the defendant may indeed be guilty, there were mitigating factors that explain why he might have committed the crime, and because of those mitigating factors, the defendant should not be put to death but should instead be given some lesser punishment, usually life in prison without the possibility of parole. Mitigating factors could include things like mental illness or a troubled childhood.

At the end of the guilt phase of *State of Connecticut v. Steven Hayes,* the jury is sent into its deliberation room, adjacent to the courtroom itself, at 11:30 on a Monday morning. The clerk, a calm and efficient young woman, is charged with bringing into the jury room all the exhibits that were entered into evidence during the trial—photographs, posters of aerial photographs showing Bill's old neighborhood, the blood-blackened baseball bat Joshua Komisarjevsky used to beat Bill's head, which was found leaning against

Michaela's bed. Long minutes pass as she checks the neat assembly against the official list, like a warehouse manager readying a truck on the loading dock—everything is numbered and cataloged and accounted for. At one point the clerk drops one of the many metal canisters that hold bits of physical evidence collected from Bill's old house. The can clangs loudly to the floor of the room like a cymbal crash, and the top pops off. Everyone looks. Inside could be any number of terrible things—a shred of Jennifer's burned jeans, or Hayley's gas-stained shorts, or a swatch of the melted hallway carpet, now reduced to a grotesque curio in a canister in a courtroom in New Haven.

Almost the moment the door closes behind the jury, Judge Blue disappears into his chambers, and Courtroom 6A quite suddenly feels rudderless. After weeks of stilted, official behavior, an unfamiliar mood settles over the room. A few people look around as if wondering, Is it okay to talk now? Can I go to the bathroom? It is, and yes. Because now it's just waiting.

Bill stands as if rising during intermission, jiggles some change in his pocket, and whispers something to Hanna. A few people stretch. The reporters all pull out their smartphones in unison, clicking and scrolling. There is a quiet rush on the three electrical outlets around the perimeter of the seating area as people charge their phones and laptops. The marshals remind people to keep the noise down.

When Bill and his family walk out of court at the end of the day, the jury hasn't yet reached a verdict. There are seventeen charges against Hayes, six of them capital felonies, so the twelve civilians have a stack of legal paperwork before them and a procedure to follow. It was never going to be a five-minute decision, Bill knows that. Is it just the red tape that's keeping them in there?

Out on Church Street, the news-truck guys have arranged a bouquet of microphones at the bottom of the courtroom steps, as they often do on the days the press hopes Bill will make a statement.

He walks by without stopping. "No thanks, not today," he says. "Appreciate it." The cameras follow him across the street anyway, all the way to his car.

The next morning, back in Courtroom 6A, Bill flips through a magazine, barely looking at what's on the pages. As lunchtime approaches, there is a loud knock from inside the jury-room door. Bill looks up. No one speaks, but the hundred people in the room hurry to their seats, their spines stiff. Reporters flip to a fresh page of their notebooks. A judicial marshal cracks open the door, nods quickly, and motions to the clerk. The clerk goes to get Judge Blue, who emerges from his chambers and assumes his seat behind the bench. The jury files into the jury box. Between yesterday afternoon and this morning, they have spent a total of just over four hours in the deliberation room. The marshals are sent to retrieve Hayes from his courthouse holding cell, where defendants wait during deliberations.

When everyone is in place, Judge Blue turns to the jury and says, in a voice louder and clearer than even his usual loud, clear voice, "Have you reached a verdict?"

The jury, sober and in unison, replies, "Yes."

Hayes and his lawyers stand. Dearington sits, his hands folded on the table in front of him, waiting to hear whether he has proved Hayes's guilt beyond a reasonable doubt on at least one of the capital felony charges. The foreman hands some papers to the marshal, who passes them to Judge Blue. The judge reads them in silence. Hanna is shaking. Big Bill holds her tight, his huge hand on her tiny shoulder.

Blue peers over his glasses at the jury and says, "This is your verdict and so say you all?"

"Yes." Strong. Loud.

Bill isn't in his usual seat. He's at the other end of the first row, next to Jennifer's parents. He reaches over and puts a hand on his father-in-law's shoulder. Everyone stares straight ahead.

After the verdict is read, Bill shakes hands with Dearington and Nicholson, and he even smiles for about two seconds. He hugs his family. On every capital count, the jury has found Hayes guilty. On all but one of the lesser charges, too. But Bill feels no joy. Relief, maybe. A little. But certainly no joy. In one sense, sure, he wanted this day to come. In this new universe in which he lives, the news is good. But it's a warped victory, and the relief it brings is hollow. Bill doesn't want to live in this universe at all.

There is hardly a break. Thirteen days.

When the penalty phase begins, Judge Blue addresses the jury and describes the duty now before them—deciding whether to give Steven Hayes the death penalty—as "grave and awesome."

The guilt phase left the image of Hayes as a mouth-breathing thug, a brutish and depraved miscreant who thundered into a beautiful home and raped and strangled and burned people alive. Court proceedings can be clinical—those numbered metal canisters containing evidence, the stilted legalese even when talking about the most personal parts of a life. But as the evidence against Hayes mounted, he was reduced to a smaller and smaller person, a darker shadow. The flanks of family and friends around Bill, in turn, became larger-than-life in their humanity, the secondary victims who showed up every day as if it were their sacred duty, dressed with a respect for the courtroom and steeled, as best they could be, against the violence that would be replayed before them. The gaunt man seated at the defense table was marginalized. He became dumb evil, pure and simple.

Hayes's lawyers, Ullmann and Culligan, veteran public defenders, must bring him to life somehow, and as they begin the penalty phase they strike a tone that is not fiery, not self-righteous, not too aggressive, but assertive. They are here, doing this thankless job, because they believe everyone should have legal representation and because they don't believe in the death penalty, and they aim to spare Steven Hayes from it. And so they introduce a parade of witnesses who testify about his tormented childhood, and about his previous life as a rather inept petty criminal. A former deputy sheriff from Hayes's hometown talks about him as if he were her grandson. "Yes, he was very proud of becoming a father," she says when asked if she knew him when his son was born. She describes him as a "klutz," and it almost sounds loving. "He just wasn't all that good as a criminal," she says. She calls him a follower. "Definitely a follower, definitely—without question."

One day, not long into the penalty phase, Christiane Gehami, the owner of a small restaurant in the suburb of West Hartford, tells the court she employed Hayes the previous fall, washing dishes. "He was good-natured, he was jovial, he made people laugh," she says. "He blended." Gehami has small eyes that dart around the room, and her voice is confident. Toward the end of her testimony, her real purpose as a witness is revealed. Ullmann asks her about the time when Hayes, her jovial dishwasher, introduced her to a friend of his, Joshua Komisarjevsky.

"I took one look at him and I thought I was looking at the devil," she says. "My skin crawled. My hair stood on end."

At this, Hanna, who for weeks has endured hour after hour, day after day of excruciating, horrifying testimony with a face as stone-solid as her brother Bill's, smiles in disbelief at this seeming attempt to exculpate Hayes and buries her face in her hand. This is too much.

Hayes's thirty-year history of burglaries is presented in great detail. He used to drive to a local reservoir, in the same stolen car every day, and knock out car windows when their owners went for walks, snatching purses and wallets. He was friends with prostitutes, his lawyers establish, and did a lot of drugs. But one of the most painful parts of the penalty phase for Bill is the testimony from the mental-health experts. One guy from Texas, a clinical and forensic psychologist, testifies at length about a slide presentation titled "Violence Risk Assessment," an academic consideration of whether Hayes would be likely to show violence toward other inmates and prison guards while serving a life sentence. "In prison lore," the man says, "it has long been recognized that convicted murderers make some of the best inmates."

At one point, even Hayes yawns as he sits through the data being presented to try to save his life.

A psychiatrist with an office on Madison Avenue in New York talks about how Steven used to blame his younger brother for everything so Steven wouldn't be the one to get beaten by their father. "It was a sad, horrible situation," the doctor says. Hayes's father, apparently, would make the boys go into a room and beat each other up to see who would get whipped. "This is sadistic," he says. This doctor has interviewed Hayes extensively, and his testimony sometimes seems like a stand-in for that of Hayes himself, who isn't taking the stand. For example, the witness reports that Hayes told him that the night before they broke into the Petit house, Komisarjevsky took him around to several other houses in Cheshire and broke in to them. He wanted to show Hayes how easy it was.

At 8:15 on the morning of November 1, the reporters are assembled in their customary line in the hall outside the courtroom, briefcases and backpacks snaking along the linoleum floor, in order. Judge Blue appears, grinning under his high cap of white hair, holding up a plastic Ziploc bag like it's a fish he just caught. He announces to the reporters that he made chocolate-chip cookies yesterday, and they are welcome to have one if they like. The reporters smile nervously. It's a bizarre but lovely gesture, and the cookies are better than average.

A couple of hours later, when everyone is settled in and wait-ing for the day to start, Blue makes an announcement. It seems that on the previous Friday afternoon one of the alternate jurors—there are only two left by this point—passed a note to one of the judicial marshals. The juror is a woman with spirals of dark curls; the mar-shal a man, well over six feet, brown hair, friendly face. Blue says that in the note the juror suggested "what I'm going to call an as-signation, or a meeting." The note, which Blue has in his possession, reads, "Sunday, 5 p.m., Side Street Grille, Hamden."

She was asking the marshal out on a date.

The jurors, as everyone in the room has heard Blue instruct them at least twice a day for weeks, are not to discuss the case outside the courtroom, nor are they to associate with anyone connected to the case in any way. Holding this note, Blue tells the courtroom, "I'm a romantic at heart, but not in here." Looking like a beleaguered high-school principal, he motions for the clerk to call the juror in. Alone, without the rest of the jury.

She walks in and is shown to the witness box. She sees the note. Her face is strawberry-red and she keeps covering it with her hands.

"If I could spare you the embarrassment, I would," Blue says.

The juror finds her voice and offers weakly, "But you said as long as we don't talk about the case—"

"Sure," says Blue. "I also didn't prohibit you from walk-ing naked across the New Haven Green. But this was, excuse my French, a goddamned stupid thing to do."

Nervous, incredulous laughter sneaks out all over the room—except from the two rows where the Petit family sits. They are not laughing, because this isn't funny. Blue tells the juror that he is al-lowing her to remain on the jury in her role as an alternate. "What you did was certainly a matter of spectacular poor judgment," he says. But, he concludes, he can't see how it affects her impartiality, so she can remain.

Bill's leg rockets up and down like a metronome as the woman slinks out of the room.

On November 4, the day the two sets of lawyers are scheduled to make their closing arguments, a cold, dismal rain beats down on New Haven. Today, the members of the jury will listen to the arguments, and they will go back into their deliberation room and decide, collectively, whether the first man to be brought to trial for the murders of Jennifer, Hayley, and Michaela Petit will be sentenced to life without the possibility of parole, or death. Today, Bill will move a day closer to the rest of his life.

Tom Ullmann places a slide on the overhead projector and squints up to make sure it's straight. The jury watches Ullmann shuffle around and looks up at the screen to see what he wants to show them. When the image appears, a few of them scrunch their faces with incomprehension. Most stare blankly. Judge Blue leans on his elbows in front of him and peers up at the screen. Bill tilts his head toward the screen, as he has done so many times to see what new horror or indignity it will visit upon his eyes.

The image is a photograph of a man pushing a rock up a hill. It looks like Sisyphus. "When I first received this case when it came in the office, about a week later, having interviewed Mr. Hayes, I put this photo on my bulletin board," Ullmann says, speaking like a professor in freshman English. "That's Sisyphus"—as it turns out— "and Sisyphus is a Greek story—mythology about a person who was burdened and has to always push this rock to the top of the mountain, but he can never get to the top because by the time you get there, the angle of the mountain and the weight of the rock, it always rolls back down, and so you are always burdened with pushing that rock up. It's an unrelenting and unforgiving burden. It's only effective if you have a conscience. It preys on your mind and weighs heavily on your soul. Only Steven Hayes's death can free him from that burden. That's when he gets to the top of that mountain. Why would you want to relieve Steven Hayes of this burden?"

Ullmann's argument hammers this one note. He contends in a smooth and even voice that for Hayes, life in a tiny prison cell, racked by remorse and suicidal thoughts, would be "a fate worse than death." He compares Hayes to a sick horse that would need to be shot in the head to escape its misery. Don't put Steven Hayes out of his misery, Ullmann pleads. Let him suffer. Alive.

And then, toward the end of his speech, he says this:

"Your Honor, may I have Mr. Hayes come up here for a moment?"

Hayes rises from his swivel chair and shuffles to the area in front of the jury box, standing slump-shouldered before his adjudicators. A new kind of tension sucks in the walls of the room. Hayes has been in this room every day, walking in each morning and walking out each afternoon. But now he is being presented almost as an exhibit. "This is a human being," Ullmann says. "You may not like him, you may hate him, you may despise what he did in this case, but he's not a rabid dog that needs to be put down. . . . His greatest freedom is what you just saw occur, walking from that desk to here—that's it." The jurors stare at Hayes, or at Bill. Ullmann ends his argument, his last substantial words on the record in the case of *State v. Hayes,* by quoting Martin Luther King Jr.: " 'The ultimate measure of a person is not where they stand at moments of comfort and convenience, but where one stands at times of challenge and controversy.' Where do you stand?"

Judge Blue is not one to let poignant moments linger, so as soon as Ullmann stops speaking, he asks Dearington to begin his closing argument. Compared with Ullmann's smooth, big-picture, morally focused oration, Dearington's thirty-minute presentation is mostly a jumbled mess. He spends most of it wandering through the minutiae of the evidence. The approach, in theory, continues what has been the state's strategy all along: Stick to the facts without passion or prejudice, calmly elucidate the jury's legal responsibilities, and by the end, the pile of facts will leave them with no choice but to find Hayes guilty and sentence him to death. It has seemed effective so far. Dearington comes across as a dry, wizened veteran, and Nicholson a straight shooter. But now Dearington is just confusing people. In this last-chance summation, he is missing an opportunity to nail this thing shut, sometimes nearly losing the jury to sleep as he meanders through the lawyerly details.

"The basis for the statutory mitigants apparently, and it's up for you to decide—well, I withdraw that. The legal basis for the statutory mitigants are that the defendant's mental capacity was significantly impaired but not to the point of rising to a defense, number one. Number two, the defendant's ability to conform his conduct to the requirements of the law was significantly impaired, but not so impaired in either case as to constitute a defense to the case. And then there's this third one. . . ."

The jurors look lost. Dearington continues:

"Again, a nonstatutory mitigant, if you find one has been proven beyond a reasonable doubt, is not an automatic bar to the death penalty, to imposing the death—"

Here Judge Blue actually interjects, a rare move for a judge while a lawyer is in the middle of a closing argument in a titanic death-penalty trial.

"Nonstatutory mitigant need only be proven by a preponderance of the evidence, sir," Blue says.

Dearington looks up. "Did I not say that?"

"You did not."

"I stand—clearly, they need only be proven by a preponderance of the evidence. Now, here's the statutory mitigants that are being suggested to you—and you will have a list of them. His bad childhood—"

"You are now talking about the *non*statutory mitigants?"

"Nonstatutory mitigants."

"Which will be explained. Proceed," Blue says.

"Now, getting back on track . . ."

The jury may not completely understand this exchange except to note that the judge had to step in and correct the lawyer, and that probably isn't a good thing for the lawyer.

It's not that what Dearington is saying isn't true or logical or important. But the presentation is somewhat incoherent and technical, and if there's one moment in the trial where he should want to be impassioned and clear, this is that moment. Not mired in nonstatutory mitigants for a half hour. He does get in some shots at the defense's attempt to turn Hayes into a sympathetic character, and the avuncular Dearington's efforts to dish out zingers are endearing.

"Sisyphus. Very interesting. I'm not sure of the connection in this case, because [in the image of Sisyphus on the projector] I don't see a mask, I don't see a gun, I don't see a bucket of gasoline, I don't see him breaking into a house. . . ."

"I hasten to point out, there's not necessarily a correlation between abusing drugs and committing violent crimes. . . ."

"I assume most of us have not experienced such a childhood [as Hayes's]. On the other hand, it doesn't mean that everyone who is brought up in an unfavorable family situation turns into Steven Hayes. . . ."

Toward the end of Dearington's drifting monologue, Blue pipes in again, this time saying flatly, "You have five minutes remaining." It almost seems as if he's trying to help Dearington out, reminding him that he has a mere five minutes in which to inject some life into his summation.

In his last five minutes, Dearington rushes through the more emotional part of his argument. He sounds vaguely panicked. But then, at the very end, he pauses, inhales and exhales, and picks up three unmarked manila folders from the table, the same manila folders that hold the same horrible photographs the jurors were asked to pass among each other in some of the worst moments of the trial. He does not open them. He just holds them. "I know you know what's in these three folders," he says. He turns to look for a moment at the projection screen, which shows a radiant photograph of Bill, Jennifer, Hayley, and Michaela. He motions to the screen and says, "That's how they looked the evening before, when they were sitting down for supper with Dr. Petit." He turns to the jury again, still clutching the manila folders. "And I know you've seen what's in these folders. And you know how they were left by this defendant."

It is masterful.

Bill is trying every day to claw his way back into a world he's not even sure he wants to live in. The end of the world visited a loving family in a small Connecticut town one night, and he alone survived it. Damaged almost beyond repair, but alive. Still, he decided soon afterward that the only thing his wife and daughters would want him to do is to go on, and so he is going on. Life abides. Life wants to live, and he is doing his best to live it, against some of the impulses in his brain. He has thought of suicide—of course he has. He has had all the thoughts. Guilt. The wish that he had died in that fire.

But he has decided to live, because life abides.

And yet at every turn, it seems that the end of the world was not enough for Bill Petit to have to endure. It's not going to be that easy. For three years, he endured the aftermath, propped up by Hanna and Ron and his parents and entire towns of people. He was, slowly, regaining his strength, resuscitating parts of himself that had almost slipped away. But this trial. This trial has beat him down again—a slow, plodding assault on what's left of him. It has introduced new horrors to his fragile mind, incited new outrage in his bruised heart. It has deepened the wounds. We all hope for a clean break when there is something in our past we want to leave behind—some accident, some betrayal we're trying to live down, some illness we have overcome, some mistake we can't unmake but spend our days trying to erase. But this trial, and the second one looming next year, is like a scab being ripped off. Did he have to attend the trial? Not legally, no. There was no formal obligation. But yes, he did, because it's a small thing he can do to make it up to his wife and daughters that he couldn't be there for them. A small thing he can do to help bring the men who killed them to justice.

And so right now, he is sitting flipping through a magazine in a small, windowless room, an unused office appropriated for him and his family, where they wait for twelve strangers united only by the fact that they all live in New Haven County to decide whether to kill or not to kill the first man. He wanders back into the claustrophobic courtroom, whose center is oddly dim while fluorescent bulbs light up its hexagonal circumference, as if the room were the base of a spaceship. Reporters sit on the floor, swiping their smartphone screens. A man pulls a novel out of his backpack and reads. A woman answers her cell phone but is ushered out by one of the marshals, who stand sentry at every exit. People pass gum and mints and do crosswords. Bill's handheld device is the kind you don't see much anymore, the kind that requires a stylus. He pokes and scribbles on it, sitting in his regular seat in the front of the public gallery. He can't think about why he's here. Why he's trapped here on this stupid uncomfortable bench instead of taking a patient's blood pressure in his office on Whiting Street, then calling Jen to check in about dinner, then picking up Michaela over at the Poissons', then reminding Hayley that the first UConn game of the season is next weekend up in Storrs. When one of his neighbors or an uncle or friend walks by, almost out of habit they give his shoulder a squeeze. He turns his head just a little each time, never letting these quick expressions of love go unacknowledged. There's a snack bar downstairs, run by a friendly blind man named Dave. Dave sells candy and chips and drinks and even cooks bacon and toasts toast and makes hot sandwiches. Heck of nice guy, Dave. You have to tell him how much money you're handing him. Bill tries not to snack too much, but sometimes the family gets lunch from Dave, partly to avoid facing the reporters and onlookers and the occasional anti-death-penalty protester outside. This waiting is awful. One morning, the jury had to start its deliberations twenty-five minutes late because one of the jurors couldn't find a place to park. Another time, Bill was sitting in the family waiting room with the door open and overheard a reporter in the hall answer his phone and say loudly, "Hi. Good. I'm bored, but I'm good." The jury deliberates all weekend, Saturday and Sunday both. On Saturday, word comes from their sanctum that they don't want to break for lunch at the appointed hour. Maybe they're close! Bill stands against the wall, hands folded behind his back, chatting quietly with Jen's dad. But nothing comes of it. Fifteen minutes later, the jury breaks for lunch. On Sunday, you can hear feverish bursts of clapping from inside their room, but nothing comes of that, either. What everyone on the outside is listening for is a knock. That signals . . . something. Could be anything. A knock on the door means the jury might have a procedural question or might need some testimony read back to them or might be hungry. Or they might have reached their decision.

Monday morning. That's when the knock comes. The fourth day of deliberations. Tom Ullmann whispers to one of the reporters, a woman from the *Hartford Courant*, that this isn't a question about procedure and they don't want pizza. It's time. Everyone gets into position. Bill sits at the far end of the bench, as he did for the verdict in the guilt phase. Long minutes fall off the clock on the wall as the parties are assembled—the judge, the clerk, the court reporter, the attorneys, Hayes. Bill sits without expression. The jury finally enters, looking serious to a person.

For each of the six capital counts—the counts for which Hayes could be sentenced to death—there may be aggravating or mitigating factors. Aggravating factors mean Hayes will get death—unless the jury finds that there were mitigating factors that outweigh the aggravating factors. There are three possible aggravating factors here: that Hayes committed these crimes "in an especially cruel, heinous, or depraved manner," that in committing any one of the crimes he knowingly caused grave danger to another person, and that he committed these crimes while in the act of committing a crime for which he had previously been convicted, in his case third-degree burglary. The state made an easy case for all three of these during the penalty phase. Mitigating factors include the defense's offerings about Hayes's character and his troubled background of abuse and addiction.

In the first of the capital counts, the murder of two or more persons, the clerk asks the jury whether they found the aggravating factors.

Yes.

She asks them whether they found any mitigating factors.

Yes.

She asks them whether the aggravating factors outweigh the mitigating factors.

Yes.

That's it. Death.

Hayes turns around, looks at the courtroom for a few seconds, then swivels back around. The reporter from the Associated Press, here since day one, thumbs a news update into his BlackBerry, his hands shaking. One of the jurors wipes tears from her eyes with a quick brush of the back of her hand. A sketch artist in the front row of the media section, at the opposite end of the courtroom from Bill, starts hurriedly scratching out a beautiful pastel portrait of Bill with a single tear running down his cheek, even though he is all the way across the courtroom and doesn't appear to be crying. Jennifer's mother, Marybelle, gently chews gum. Dennis, Hanna's husband, holds his head in his hands. Big Bill turns his head just enough to look down the row at his son, who isn't moving a muscle. The older man looks flushed and drawn, and his mouth hangs open a little. Hanna dabs her nose with a tissue.

The procedure is repeated for every count. Every juror is asked, again and again, whether he or she believes beyond a reasonable doubt that death is the appropriate punishment.

"... on the fifth count, murder of a person under sixteen, Michaela Petit ... that death is the appropriate punishment ..."

Yes, yes, yes ...

"... on the tenth count, murder of a kidnapped person, Jennifer Hawke-Petit ..."

Yes, yes, I do, yes ...

It goes on for an hour. Six capital felonies, each carrying the penalty of death.

At the end, when it's all over, Bill leans back, slings his arm over the back of the bench, and tucks in his lips like an affirmation. The judge asks the marshals to escort the jurors, whose job is now done, from the building for their safety. Bill stands, hugs Dearington, hugs his mom, and hugs Hanna for a long time. An old friend squeezes Bill's shoulders and whispers something that makes him chuckle. Big Bill shakes his son's hand, but they don't smile. Bill has been unburdened for the moment, but somehow he doesn't feel any lighter. This isn't happiness. Maybe it isn't even relief. The best you can say is that it's better than the alternative. In the little windowless waiting room, Bill takes in a deep breath of air and lets it out slowly. And he puts on his coat.

Outside, the TV cameramen wearing parkas check their microphones with fast hands, breathing hard. Newspaper reporters stand in front of the cameras, inadvertently blocking the shot, and the TV guys ask them to move—"No, no, no, you gotta get *lower!*" This is the moment. This is when Dr. Petit might finally speak, after months of sitting there, stolid and mannequinned, wondering and remembering and probably stewing and raging inside—this is when he might interpret it all, and answer questions even. And everyone is going live with it, so you have to *siddown* in front! Reporters genuflect before the cluster of microphones, flip to clean notebook pages, check pens for ink, pull digital recorders from their bags and hold them close to where the doctor will be standing. The guy from NECN, tall with blow-dried hair, shouts into his cell phone to someone back at the station, "Are you *fucking* kidding me?" The two middle-aged guys who are making a documentary about the case for HBO huddle with their cameraman. The veteran *New York Times* reporter looks serene and ready.

A gale screams out of the blue sky down Church Street in front of the courthouse, whipping the U.S. and Connecticut flags on the pole. One of the TV stations has set up a small white tent in case of rain, but the wind blows it down like the flame on a birthday candle. Then, through the glass doors, the TV guys see the Petit family members and friends emerge from the elevators, and they scramble behind their cameras. The newspaper guys click on their recorders. The radio guys switch on their wireless mikes.

Everyone is in place.

Bill is wearing a white turtleneck, a maroon V-neck sweater, and a blue overcoat. The moment he steps through the sliding doors, his salt-and-pepper hair is shellacked over to one side of his head by the wind. It's long, but not as long as he has let it grow at other times since the murders. Sometimes it has been way down over his collar.

He speaks without written notes. He talks about justice being done, about the jury's admirable commitment, about the fact that he was fortunate to have had insurance and been relatively affluent, because the funds for victims' aid in Connecticut are paltry. He says it wasn't his decision to reject Hayes's plea bargain at the outset of the case—guilty in exchange for life in prison—but rather Dearington's, although he agreed with it from day one. His voice is sure and clear.

As soon as he stops speaking, the questions begin. The first is, What was he thinking when the jury announced its verdict? "What was going through your heart, what was going through your mind?" is how the reporter phrases it.

Rev. Hawke, standing behind his son-in-law, bites his cheek. Bill Sr., at Billy's left, puts a hand on his boy's back. Bill's hair blows forward on his head, and he looks down.

"I was really, ah—"

He raises his eyebrows, licks his lips a little. Fighting.

"I was really, ah, crying, crying for loss."

He shakes his head a little, as if to shake away a bad thought. He shrugs, trying to shrug away the emotion that is overwhelming him.

"You know—"

His voice comes off its hinges.

"Probably many of you have kids, ah . . ."

More than ten seconds pass. He is trying to get the words out. He hates this, every second of it. Dick Hawke looks up at Bill. Bill Sr. looks down at the sidewalk. Hanna squints through the bitter wind.

"Michaela was an eleven-year-old little girl," Bill says, shaking his head, raising his eyebrows, attempting to explain the inexplicable one more time. "You know, ah, tortured and killed . . . in her own bedroom . . . you know? Surrounded by stuffed animals. And . . . Hayley had a great future. And was a strong and courageous person. And Jennifer helped so many kids. At Children's Hospital in Pittsburgh and at Strong Memorial in Rochester and at the Yale Children's Hospital and Cheshire Academy, and she cannot do that. So I was really thinking of the tremendous loss. . . . I was glad for the girls that there was justice, because I think it's a just verdict, but mostly I was sad for the loss that we had all suffered."

Robert Goulston, CBS Channel 3, upbeat guy, always respectful, asks if there was ever a moment when Bill didn't think he could do it—didn't think he could come here every day and sit through it. Bill bobs his head and almost chuckles.

"There was, ah—every day when I basically didn't want to get out of bed, and—nothing against you guys, but I didn't want to park the car and walk across the street. I didn't want to get my picture taken for the hundred-and-fifty-thousandth time. I didn't want to sit here and listen to the things that were being said in the courtroom. There were a thousand times I wanted to jump up and scream out."

Somebody asks about closure—"the healing process"—now that the verdict is in. It sounds like a morning-show question, the kind designed to get someone to either cry or become angry.

"I don't think there's ever closure," Bill says. He has thought about this. "I think whoever came up with that concept's an imbecile."

This is what happens when you take everything from a man—from *this* man. He's left standing on a sidewalk, talking through the wind, feeding the five-o'clock broadcast. There's a jagged hole in his heart, a heart that was once filled with happiness and God and ambition and joy and the everyday love and pain of being a father and a husband. Raising those girls—he tried so hard to get it right, or at least more right than wrong. Every day, he tried to live up to their admiration of him. He tried to make Jen know that she was an even better person than she made him feel *he* was. Now, every night and every day of his changed life, he stands as if in a burning house, holding a bat stained with scab-black blood, swinging it with those oxen shoulders and the force of his strong, fifty-year-old frame, screaming—screaming for his girls, for his life. And then, when the fire is out, when his blackened house hisses under wet smoke, he whispers that he is not okay. Now he is trying to fill the hole again. He hasn't had a good day yet—he might never have a good day again. But he is trying to fill the hole.

That African prayer from church the day before they died:

Will we stop building a better future because of evil?
No! Our God will deliver us from evil.
Will we concede our dreams for our world, your Creation,
*   because of evil?*
No, God will judge all evildoers.

When a man loses everything the way Bill has, there is a danger of falling to a place where his heart will be rendered dark and useless. Where he won't care much about the future. Where he won't trust love, won't bother to hope. Bill has felt sometimes as if he is dangling over that place, has felt like he might fall in—has felt, even, like he might *want* to fall in.

But maybe Bill could trust again. Maybe he could love again. Maybe if he keeps telling people about the good these three women brought to the world, and if he has the faith that people will listen to him and will go out and do one kind thing, maybe the hole will start to fill in. Maybe faith is enough.

His next chance to tell the world about the girls comes a month after the day the jury condemns Steven Hayes to death. Judge Blue must formally sentence Hayes, and a date had been set: December 2, 2010. On sentencing day, the state allows the victims of a capital crime—the surviving family members are considered victims—to make a statement just before the sentence is officially handed down by the judge.

Court begins at ten, as usual. But last night, Bill decided the family would get up early and make a stop. December 2 also happens to be the day that the Hospital of Central Connecticut, where Bill used to spend most of his waking hours, is bestowing the inaugural William A. Petit, M.D., Physician Service Award, a prize the hospital created in Bill's honor. Steve Hanks, Bill's friend who stood by his side as he spoke at the memorial service five days after the murders, would be giving it out on behalf of the hospital. Bill was supposed to be there. But yesterday Bill asked his dad to call Hanks's assistant, Doreen, and let her know that unfortunately Bill wouldn't be able to make it to the small ceremony because of the sentencing.

Of course Hanks understood.

But it didn't feel right, not going, because it would allow Hayes to rob the world of yet another piece of joy, this time a proud moment for a doctor who had done good work. The award was established to recognize a doctor's "spirit of altruism, commitment, and excellence." The first recipient, a doctor from Southington named Anthony Ciardella, had organized a medical mission to Haiti last year in which he and other doctors from the hospital helped victims of the massive earthquake. This was supposed to be a special morning for Ciardella, and Bill decided at the last minute that he wouldn't let the sentencing ruin it.

Just after 8:00 a.m., Bill walks into a beige, fluorescent-lit hospital meeting room with floor-to-ceiling window blinds and a patterned carpet. Hanks is there, and Ciardella, and some other doctors. Bill speaks for a few minutes, praising Ciardella, and poses for a few unsmiling photographs. At 8:30, he shakes hands all around and walks back out to the car.

The nausea chews at his stomach more than usual as the Petits' caravan rolls south on the cold pavement toward New Haven. Courtroom 6A is filled to capacity again. Familiar faces surround Bill. Even Ron Bucchi, who attended the trial only sporadically because of work, is here today. Several members of the jury are here, too, having waited in line with the reporters to get in, seated among the general public. A reporter asks one of the female jurors what made her come today. "I just wanted to see it through," the woman says as she takes her seat. Tom Ullmann, the lead public defender, strokes his beard. Today he has managed to tuck his tie right into his pants. Next to him, Hayes sits in his swivel chair, his neck sticking out of a blousy orange prison jumpsuit. He whips around to look at the big elementary-school clock in the back of the room. His shoulders sag, his eyes are small and black, his cheeks wilted like deflating balloons.

As the state officially disposes of Hayes, *impact* is what Bill chooses for his first word, because that's what the law calls these things: "impact statements." And the impact just pours out of him: how Jen tried to hide her MS from the girls when she was first diagnosed; how Michaela loved to spy on Hayley so she could learn to be like the big girls; how he and Hayley used to stay up working in their little home office until after midnight sometimes. How she would be a senior in college by now. The details are his, but the story is the story of every family, ordinary and beautiful.

"I grieve because she never got to love someone—"

Here he just stops. He rubs the place on his forehead where you can barely see the scar anymore, rubs it over and over. His hulking shoulders shake in silence as the tears escape from under his glasses. Judge Blue looks around the room—there is nothing to do but wait. No protocol. And as Bill cries, Hayes stares over from the defense table without blinking—long minutes of unbearable silence pass, and the man who poured gasoline on the girl while she was still alive just keeps staring at the man who raised her.

The pause seems as if it might never end.

But then, finally, Bill picks up again.

"—because she never got to love someone for a long time. She had a friend who was a boy and who still thinks about her. He is now a senior and a basketball player. If he called on a Sunday night at seven o'clock, and she had been studying for six hours and looked washed out, she jumped up and got her basketball clothes on, because that is what they did—they played basketball together and chatted. She loved it and probably loved him."

Otis.

Bill goes on for pages about each girl. Of Michaela he says, "I learned many things from her teachers after she died that I wish they had told me before. One teacher said she always made an effort to go over to someone who was ignored by others in the class. Other children told me she stood up to the older kids on the bus when they tried to make the smaller and younger kids give up their seats." He never knew any of this when she was alive.

Toward the end of his statement, Bill says, "I am not sure what my own hopes and dreams are, if any."

Bill stands and walks back to his seat. There are no affirming nods from his family, no squeezes of his hand to say, "Good job." That is not their way. The row of faces points straight ahead, and Bill sits. It's done. He is done.

Ullmann makes a last statement, declaring that anyone who supports the death penalty is as bad as his client. "We are all Steven Hayes today," he ventures to say. Then Hayes himself stands and mumbles through an apology. And that's it.

Judge Blue announces loudly that he "will make no apology for being the instrument of the law" and sentences Hayes to death on each of the six capital felonies of which the jury found him guilty. When he says to Hayes, "May God have mercy on your soul," a weird silence seizes the room. Hayes actually has to sign a form, an odd piece of bureaucracy. The marshals step into their positions behind Hayes and at every door. And eventually, everyone stands, the judge exits without ceremony, and it is over. The state of Connecticut will kill Hayes, it is now official, but the ritual makes for a strange anticlimax to a grueling trial. If in the age of therapy and confession we expect or demand closure from these proceedings, there is no closure to be found here even now, certainly not for Bill Petit.

People begin to drift out of the room, taking one last glance to see whether something else might happen. Five or six of Bill's family and friends huddle around him as he sits in the front row with his head in his hands. Mike Dearington sits nearby, and the marshals stand guard, waiting, looking as if they will wait forever if they have to—the courtroom is closing down, but they've been in the room and heard every detail, and they aren't about to ask Dr. Petit to leave. Bill is off somewhere else. He is in his bedroom, alone, or on a beach somewhere, or standing on the rubble of his house. He closes his eyes, and he is nowhere.

HELP A NEIGHBOR, FIGHT FOR A CAUSE, LOVE YOUR FAMILY

Spring–Fall 2011

THE OPRAH WINFREY SHOW had been sending a producer to the Petit Family Foundation 5K Road Race for a couple of years running, and to the Hayes trial, too. Winfrey wanted Bill's story for her show. All the big TV shows did—*Today, Good Morning America, 60 Minutes*. Bill had asked his friend Rick Healey, the lawyer, to help handle the media requests that began immediately after the murders, when Bill was still lying in a daze at St. Mary's Hospital. Rick has been a solid buffer, respectful to every reporter, from the local newspapers to the national TV shows, even as he offers them very little—no special access to Bill, no one-on-one interview, the prize they all want. The core of decision makers on interview requests is Bill, Rick, Hanna, and Ron. Rick usually presents the options, without offering much in the way of opinion. Bill, Hanna, and Ron each have a vote. ABC has been making a strong case to do a prime-time special, but the Oprah request has made sense from the beginning.

After the verdict but before the sentencing, Rick had started talking to the producer in earnest, telling the producer that he would need to review the show before it airs, because Bill was to be a witness at the next trial, and there are certain things he can't talk about on TV. He also asked for some time to mention the foundation on the air. When he said that Bill wasn't going to talk before the sentencing, because doing so would detract from his impact statement, things got a bit complicated. Oprah had a trip planned on November 29, and Hayes's sentencing was scheduled for December 2. The producer suggested filming the interview before the sentencing, and promised not to air it until afterward. Rick said no, because then both things would suffer—Bill would be thinking about the impact statement during the interview, and then having already done the interview would weaken his statement at the sentencing. Both have to come from the heart. Between Thanksgiving, Oprah's trip, and the sentencing, there just wasn't time for Bill to get to Chicago, where the show was taped, and back by the time they wanted to air the show.

Okay, the producer said to Rick. What if Oprah comes to him?

When? Rick asked.

December 3, the day after the sentencing.

Big Bill and Barbara had watched the Oprah show for years, usually in the kitchen while they got supper ready. One day, at the house on Red Stone Hill, Billy and Hanna tell Barbara they've decided to give the interview to Oprah.

"I want to go," says Barbara. "I want to be in the audience!"

"We're not going to Chicago," Hanna says.

"What do you mean you're not going to Chicago?" Barbara asks.

"She's coming here."

"What do you mean she's coming here?"

"She's coming to your house," Hanna says.

Well, Barbara just about falls through the floor.

No one can know. To the local press, the very fact of Oprah Winfrey jetting into Connecticut to interview Dr. William Petit would be a news story in itself, so Rick makes sure no one says a word.

Barbara cleans for days. Two days before the interview, a crew from Winfrey's production team arrives at the house. They traipse through each room, scouting for the location for Bill and Oprah to sit and talk. They take digital photos of every square inch of the first floor. The next day even more people come, fifteen or twenty. They set about moving furniture and removing pictures from the walls—that's why they took all those pictures, so they would remember exactly where to put everything back—and carefully running cables across the shiny hardwood floors. They set up a makeshift control room out of view of the couch and chair where Winfrey will conduct the interview.

Part of the deal is that Hanna will appear with Bill for part of the interview. A few days before the taping, the producers ask Hanna what she's going to wear. I don't know, Hanna says. She can hardly focus on the interview because she's working so hard on her impact statement. Finally, after the sentencing, she and Bill and the rest of the family are having lunch, and Hanna tells Bill she has been so focused on the sentencing that she hasn't even thought about tomorrow's interview with Oprah Winfrey.

Me, too, Bill says. He asks her if she wants to come up to the house tonight so they can talk about what they're going to say. He tells Hanna that Oprah has these little blue cards she uses to make sure she hits all her points.

Hanna smiles and says maybe they should make their own little blue cards. Make sure they hit all their points. "All right, see you later," she says.

But Hanna is spent. The buildup to the sentencing, and the inevitable exhale, has left her feeling exhausted. She falls asleep watching the UConn women's basketball game on TV and never makes it up to Red Stone Hill, and wakes up at four the next morning feeling bad for not going up to help Billy prepare for Oprah—who by this point will be in Plainville in a matter of hours. She waits until six to text Billy, in case he's sleeping. (He isn't.)

"You up?" she writes.

"Yeah."

She says she's sorry she didn't make it up to the house last night.

Billy says, Don't worry about it, I crashed, too. Just come over a little early and we'll figure it out. She goes up to her parents' house, and she and Bill just stare at each other. They're numb. Finally, he says, "It'll be fine."

Big Bill and Barbara look out the window as Oprah Winfrey pulls up their driveway—her window is down, and they can see her in the backseat. She is lovely and gracious and thanks them so much for allowing her into their home. The furniture is completely re-arranged. All the ringers on the telephones are turned off, and the clocks that chime have been disabled. The producers tape a note to the front door asking people not to knock or ring the doorbell—heaven forbid a neighbor should stop by with a loaf of banana bread today, of all days. Bill Sr. and Barbara are stationed in the kitchen. Ron Bucchi and Rick Healey stand in the makeshift control room down the hall, watching and listening to a live feed of Bill and Oprah from the living room.

Bill's pressed pink shirt matches the flowers on the coffee table. It also nicely complements Oprah's eggplant-colored cardigan. They sit almost knee to knee. She looks Bill in the eyes, which are tired and puffy, and says, softly, "So we're here in your parents' home. You've come back home."

They talk for nearly three hours.

Three months after the sentencing and the Oprah interview, Bill arrives at Cheshire High School one morning alone and walks up the knoll from the parking lot, squinting against the low, late-winter sun. It's chilly, and he walks with his hands shoved into the pockets of his jeans. He wears his hair, damp from the shower, combed straight back into a fringe of curls that sweep the collar of his baggy white golf shirt. The belly of a man who hit fifty a few years ago pulls slightly at his fleece vest. Across the lot behind him, suburban Saturday-morning traffic drifts up Main Street. Above, under a dry, blue March sky, two swallows chase each other around the sun. Bill walks slowly—he always gets a little queasy at these benefits, as the people are coming just for him, and he is required to be social. Being social has never come easy for him, but now it can be excruciating. Outside the doors, one of those inflatable castles for kids to jump around in is set up on the sidewalk. He stops.

A boy, four years old, blue-eyed and sandy-haired, sits on the sidewalk. Not many people are around yet—it's nine-thirty, and the basketball tournament doesn't start until ten. The boy is unstrapping the Velcro on his shoes and jimmying them off his little feet. Bill bends at the waist with his hands on his knees.

"Hey there," he says to the boy. He arches his eyebrows hopefully and holds up a hand for a high five. Seeing Bill around a child, you notice that his cheekbones are high and wide, like rock faces. The boy looks up at the giant hand but quickly scrambles into the inflatable castle. Bill stands up straight again. "Ah, he doesn't want to talk to me," he says. His voice is deep and rusty and the words rattle out unevenly, as if they are the first he's spoken since waking up. "He wants to play." He drops his jaw a little and laughs to himself, then turns and wanders into the school.

He still doesn't much like doing these things, but he does them all the same. It's part of his work, the work of the foundation. It is his life, or his best attempt to remain among the living. That Bill is himself alive is a sort of miracle and a reality to which he has still not fully acclimated. Even in settings like these—safe and comfortable, surrounded by smiling faces—Bill seems to be floating, half here and half gone.

Inside, the halls are rumbling to life. Vast, fuzzy trapezoids of sunlight glow white on the linoleum, bending up the walls. A pimply kid with a brown, bushy mop sits smiling at the welcome table, his hands folded next to a box marked DONATIONS. Gray-haired women lay out foil trays of homemade chocolate cupcakes and baggies of frosted cookies—EVERYTHING $1, reads a sign on the table. The ping of basketballs hitting the gym floor echoes in the halls. People nod and smile at Bill as he makes his way in, and he nods back and offers up a "G'mornin'." A woman wearing a tracksuit stops to hug him, standing on her tiptoes. "Heyyy," he says quietly.

In the gymnasium, kids from college on down to grade school shoot around and basketballs whiz everywhere. Soon the adolescent voice of a local kid home from college scratches out through a speaker, announcing that Dr. Petit is going to take the ceremonial first shot of the tournament. Bill hams a funny uh-oh face, fakes a nervous smile, and shrugs at the crowd. Someone bounces a ball to him. He turns it over in his hands a couple of times, rotating it, squeezing it, the ball hard and cold, same as always. He dribbles hard, pounding the ball into the shellacked hardwood like he has done—could it have been a million times in his life? He walks slowly to the free-throw line, a goofy wink at the drama of the moment. There's no drama, really, because it doesn't matter if he misses, but—well, come on, you don't want to miss, do you?

Feet planted on the line, he dribbles three more times, then shoots, his elbow snapping like a piston, firing the ball off the end of his fingertips as if not a day has gone by. A few hundred eyes follow its arc toward the rim. The ball bangs the front, takes a bounce back onto the heel of the rim, and falls through the net.

Bill's eyes go wide and he pretends to wipe sweat from his forehead. Everyone claps, and, the moment over, kids peel themselves off the walls and fill the gym back up with noise. Bill feels pats on his back, feels his hands grabbed and shaken. *Nice shot!* Then he walks over near the door, out of the way, kind of bobbing along. *Close one!* The boy from the inflatable castle is there, on his father's shoulders. "Hey!" Bill says. He holds out his fist for a fist bump. The boy grins this time, but he turns away again shyly. "Awww," Bill says.

Bill Sr. comes over, chucks his son on the shoulder. "Nothing but net," says the old man.

They cleaned out Michaela's locker at school after she died, and in it there was a quote taped to the inside of the door: "You must be the change you wish to see in the world." Gandhi. She had posted the same quote on her Facebook page, the one Bill didn't know she had.

When he saw the quote, it hit him hard. It became the driver of the foundation, the reason they do everything they do. It's printed on the cover of the brochure: "Be the change." It's stamped onto pink-and-green rubber Petit Family Foundation bracelets. It's what the girls did all the time, as if by instinct. They were the change they wanted to see in the world. Jen took the job at Cheshire Academy—and, in fact, went into pediatric nursing in the first place—because she wanted a world in which children could be healthy and thrive. Hayley started Hayley's Hope because she wanted a world in which MS didn't exist, so that her mother might be healthy and live. Michaela, on the weekend before she died, e-mailed a group of her fifth-grade friends asking if they could help her raise money for animal rescue shelters because she loved animals and knew she could help them. For all three of them, being the change came naturally.

And Bill is starting to see now that other people in the world were like this, too. For a long time, it was so hard to appreciate goodness. He saw it every day, in the form of the thousands of cards and letters and checks that were mailed to his parents' home. But as his foundation digs deeper into the needs of people around Connecticut, as more and more people give money and show up at the events, the hole in his heart is slowly filling in, or at least its edges are becoming ever so slightly smoother. And as more and more people give money, the foundation is able to turn around and give it to more causes. In 2010 the board increased its annual pledge to the Prudence Crandall domestic-violence shelter from

$5,000 to $10,000. The amounts given for the community-service awards at Plainville and Cheshire high schools are higher. They give a $7,650 grant to the Cheshire Public Schools to support educating girls in the sciences. In keeping with its mission to help people with chronic illnesses, it donates $500 to a research foundation for chronic regional pain syndrome, a debilitating neurological ailment. Two thousand dollars goes to the Bristol Hospital Parent and Child Center, which prevents and fights child abuse.

There's a new event that started in the fall of 2010, during the trial, three years after the murders: the Ride for Justice. A motorcycle rally, of all things. It was amazing. Three thousand bikers showed up.

Bill stood in the parking lot as they rolled in and met as many of them as he could. They waited to shake his hand or give him a hug, biker after biker. One man, wearing a leather jacket with the sleeves ripped off and tattoos running up his arms, looked Bill in the eye and said very quickly, "I'm sorry for your loss. It's an honor to ride for you today." Bill stood on a riser under a blue-and-white circus tent and spoke to the crowd sitting in folding chairs. He thanked them, and when his voice caught, and he couldn't speak for a moment because he felt the tears welling up, they just stood and clapped for him for a minute. Afterward, there were just so many of them, and he kept hugging them—men and women his own age who rode Harleys and wore bandanas around their heads and called him Doc and clapped his back until it hurt.

It is now spring of 2011, and more evidence of the good that people can do makes its way to Bill through the conduit of the Petit Family Foundation: Hanna got a call a few weeks ago from a fourteen-year-old boy in Philadelphia. Never met him before. His family holds an annual fundraiser at their home, he said. A big auction, makes tons of money. This year, they want to do the whole thing for the Petit Family Foundation. So Bill will drive down to Philly for that. Have to show up.

A guy called from Utah. Does an annual charity golf tournament, and this year he's chosen the Petit Family Foundation as the beneficiary. So Bill will fly out to Utah for that, probably with Ron. Have to show up.

Ron is worried about this next trial coming up in the fall. The lawyers for Hayes, Ullmann and Culligan, may have been the opposition, but they were respectful. They didn't cross-examine Billy at all, even. But this guy Donovan, some of the statements he's made—he's not going to make this easy for Bill.

Ron sees Bill at the next board of directors meeting at the house on Red Stone Hill. Hanna has made a big batch of Italian wedding soup for everyone. Big Bill and Barbara have set the table, and there's red wine and soda out. Then they start arriving, these CEOs and doctors and lawyers on Bill's board—Bill knows a lot of smart people. They serve themselves from the buffet and review the committee reports—development, finance and investment, grants, the golf tournament. Bill mentions a little girl who, not long ago, told her friends she didn't want birthday presents and asked guests to make a donation instead—she raised $400. The foundation's holdings are up to $1.8 million. Its board will give out a total of $113,600 in 2011, topping $100,000 for the first time. It still supports Manes & Motions, the therapeutic horseback-riding center, this year with a $7,300 gift. Justice for My Sister, an organization supporting gender equality especially for women immigrants, is awarded $5,000. Safe Haven of Greater Waterbury: $5,000. The goal for the foundation's endowment is still the $5 million that would make it self-sustaining. Then they could hire some people to send the notes and organize the spreadsheets and keep the records so Bill knows whom to thank, so he wouldn't have to do so much of that stuff himself.

The thing is, Bill would end up doing most of that stuff anyway.

After the meeting, Ron and Hanna and a few others hang out and talk. Eventually, Bill goes up to his room. Books and papers and

Bill Sr., Bill, Ron Bucchi, and
Rick Bucchi at the golf club,
where Bill found peace both
before and after the tragedy.

albums of family photographs cover most of the queen-size bed—
Bill sleeps at the edge of the mattress. When blackness disappears the
world outside, and when Bill is trying to fall asleep, that's when the
what-ifs and the bad thoughts try to stab their way into the fragile
equilibrium that he has worked so hard to achieve in his mind.

*What if Jen had just stayed inside the bank instead of coming
outside with the money? What if he had gone upstairs to bed after he
turned off the lamp by the couch?*

Every night after he gets into bed, even when his light is out,
he hears a soft knock on the door. His grandmother, Gram Triano.
The door opens and light leaks onto the walls of his room.

"Bill?"

Her voice is soft, as if she's trying to wake a toddler from a nap.

"Bill?"

He rolls over.

"Yeah, Gram?"

She shuffles into the room and gently pats his shoulder.

"Are you okay?"

He has met someone. He didn't set out to, but he did. Her name is
Christine, and he thinks about her a lot. The way her laugh can just
knock you over from across the room—it's a beautiful laugh, honest

and funny in itself, as if she laughs from her soul. And they come so easily to her, her little bursts of joy. They catch him off guard, and he likes that. He thinks about how she absently tucks a wave of blond hair behind her ear when she's taking a photograph, and squints just a little.

Christine worked as the marketing director at the country club—she took photos, did internal advertising for events, wrote the monthly newsletter, redesigned the Web site. She also tended bar in the Founders Room. She didn't know who Bill was when he would come in, which is to say that she didn't know he was "Bill Petit" from the news. When it happened, she was traveling the world as a member of Up With People, the community-service entertainment group founded in the 1960s, and the news of the murders had passed her by.

How about her? Ron said to Bill one afternoon after a round of golf. *The girl behind the bar.*

Bill shrugged. He didn't even know how to think about something like a girlfriend.

Eventually Christine went back to Boston, where she was studying photography at Boston University's Center for Digital Imaging Arts. For her final project, she was required to volunteer her services to a nonprofit organization. She called Bill Petit, the good-looking guy from the club, who, she now knew, had lost his family and had set up a foundation in their memory. She asked him, by any chance would the services of a photographer be beneficial to the foundation?

Bill remembered who Christine was when she called. Knew she could crack a joke, knew she was pretty. It took him about five seconds to say yes, Christine was welcome to take pictures for the foundation.

Christine was nervous when she came to Bill's parents' house to take pictures of the memorial garden Bill had created in the back-yard, her first assignment. She liked Bill, but she didn't know he liked her, too. She thought *maybe*, but . . . then, as they were walking through the garden—him pointing out the different species, her taking pictures—he stopped, looked at her, and reached up and touched her earring, told her he liked it. She walked away, started taking pictures again.

Bill is drawn to her. When he is around her, his own laughter surprises him. She shoots more and more for the foundation, so he sees her, and he likes seeing her. But there's something inside him that flinches at his own attraction to her. He wonders if his feelings are . . . correct. It's been about five years. He wonders whether Jennifer would approve. He wonders whether Hayley and Michaela would approve. He wonders if he should be feeling the way he feels about a woman who is not his wife, who is not Jennifer, the woman who died trying to save Bill and their girls. And so, for a while, he pushes the feelings down. For a long time, really. He wonders whether the feelings will dissipate like the smell of lilac in the wind, a momentary richness that you forget as soon as it's gone. He wonders whether this is a passing thing, a normal, human reaction. Just a part of the process.

But he is fairly certain it's not a passing thing. Christine's presence strengthens the world he has built for himself since the tragedy, and that strengthens Bill. And so, after letting the thoughts and feelings roil around in his head for too long, he decides it's probably okay to feel good about something. It's probably okay to feel good about Christine.

She photographs the golf tournament in 2011, a warm June day under cotton-ball clouds and a pale blue sky. The volunteers wear Petit Family Foundation golf shirts. Early in the morning Christine takes pictures of the dozens of golf carts parked in neat rows outside the clubhouse like cars at a dealership, a scorecard and rule sheet clipped to each steering wheel. Bill's foundation shirt is bright crimson. He has let his hair grow as long as it's been in years, over the ears, and it curls up in gray wisps from under his baseball cap.

He gets nervous before these things, but the brilliant sunny day helps, golf helps, and having all his friends and family around helps. And seeing Christine helps. Her sunglasses are pushed back into her wavy blond hair, and she wears a Petit shirt the color of the sky. A silver heart dangles from a bracelet around her wrist.

A lot of people knew Bill Petit even before the tragedy, and he wonders about being seen in public with a woman. But that summer, he and Christine take hesitant first steps into a relationship. They hang out at Christine's place and order in, or go for walks in the woods, or just drive, Christine sometimes taking pictures out the window.

But you can't eat in every night. One evening, not long after the golf tournament, Bill takes Christine out for dinner. He takes her to Apricots, a charming place right on the Farmington River, been there for decades. This is the first real date when Christine feels Bill is okay with being seen with her in front of other people. Not that he was scared before this, but—people stare at him. They probably judge. *He's dating? Who is she?* He shouldn't care, and he doesn't, but it's just easier to be private about things.

Enough, though. He has spent so much time being unhappy, and thinking he can't be happy. To him, Christine is happiness. She radiates it. It's not that she's insensitive to the daily trials of being Bill Petit—not at all. She somehow understands as if by intuition when to laugh and be normal. She does not feel the need to affect solemnity in his presence. She also knows when to let him disappear into the sad silences that sometimes envelop him. Tonight is a time to be happy. She is happy, and he is happy. After dinner, they sit outside and watch the river slide by. He reaches over and touches her cheek. She smiles. They sit. Up the river somewhere, off in the direction of Unionville, they can see fireworks over the trees. It isn't even the Fourth of July.

The wind blows where it pleases.
You hear the sound, but you cannot tell where it comes from
Or where it is going.

—John 3:8, tweeted by Bill Petit, March 2015

THE SECOND TRIAL

September 19, 2011–January 27, 2012

O NE YEAR after Jeremiah Donovan ran from Courtroom 6A, "Jeremiah was a bullfrog" blaring from his cell phone, he is there once again. It's September 19, 2011, the first day of *State of Connecticut v. Joshua Komisarjevsky*. About a hundred people are stuffed into the spectator seating area. Donovan strides down the center aisle just before 10:00 a.m. The first two rows on one side of the gallery are filled with reporters squeezed in hip to hip. He smiles at them as he walks by, saying, "Hi, hi, good morning. Hey—hi! Hi." He's like an upperclassman on the first day of school after summer break. There are deep crow's-feet splayed out from the corners of his eyes, because he flashes quick smiles all day, almost like a tic. He plops his briefcase on the defense table and ambles over to say hello to the court reporter. The normally reserved clerk stands, flips her hair, and giggles as she talks to him.

The briefcase is a black doublewide with two combination locks on top, from which Donovan has never removed the plastic ties that keep the numbers set to 0-0-0. He begins piling folders and papers on the table, yellow Post-its jutting out at odd angles, notes written in the margins. He pops open a laptop, scratches out a few last-minute thoughts on a legal pad. If a society can be defined by the tenacity of the legal defense it provides those who are accused of the most depraved crimes, then Jeremiah Donovan could be regarded as a great compliment that our society pays itself. For, as one of Connecticut's leading criminal defense attorneys, he throws himself into his cases, relentlessly defending some of Connecticut's very worst, often as if his own life is at stake, in the firm belief that the survival of our justice system depends on it.

In the service of his clients, Donovan's tactics are notorious.

The state's attorneys, Mike Dearington and Gary Nicholson, are the same stalwarts from the Hayes trial. Bill sits behind them with Hanna, his parents, the Hawkes, all come again to this room to relive everything. Soon it will begin. The photographs, the 911 call, the psychiatrists attesting to the troubled childhood of the accused. A bad acid trip on a loop. Bill is miserable and his stomach is tight, and he is wary of this guy Donovan.

This is the part Donovan relishes. When he got to Yale Law School in 1974, across town from here, he liked it okay, but law school is all about the case method. The professors tried to animate cold, dry principles by explaining how they're applied in actual cases. It was interesting, but Donovan wanted to see some *lawyering*. Any chance he had he ran over to the federal court on Elm Street to watch trials. He loved the drama the lawyers acted out, each in his appointed role—"the interplay of intellect and experience," he calls it. A person can understand the rules of evidence on a technical level, but when you see a sharp lawyer deftly flinging those rules at an adversary, winning even some small, evidentiary ruling that keeps out an exhibit—well, that was a thrilling thing.

Then he started hanging around the United States attorney's office in New Haven. He says he asked if he could be an intern— back then you just asked, apparently—and they said okay. Interned all three years and served as an editor at the *Yale Law Journal*. By the time he graduated, the assistant U.S. attorneys were practically treating him like one of their own. Once, they sent him up to the correctional facility in Danbury to argue a case in which the inmates were suing the prison over mail they said was being wrongfully opened. Representing the inmates was one of their own, G. Gordon Liddy, who was serving his Watergate sentence. As his first witness, Liddy called the warden, who seemed to Donovan plenty angered about being questioned by one of his charges. This was Donovan's first court appearance. He thought all of it was wonderful.

By 10:02, Komisarjevsky is seated at the defense table with Donovan, his attorney. In his mug shot, Komisarjevsky was skinny and tanned, a flop of brown hair over his forehead, a pointy chin that was almost handsome. He sits in court now clean-shaven and heavier, round, even—not fat, just bigger. His hair is cropped short. He wears a black suit, a crisp white shirt, and a tie. He smiles and chats with his attorneys, makes notes, looks around. He is, at least in court, the opposite of the lumpy Hayes.

Donovan wheels his chair around and stares at the section of the courtroom where Bill sits with his family and friends. Each of them wears the heart-shaped lapel pin painted with the logo of the foundation, a mother bird folding two chicks in her wing. It's odd the way Donovan is just staring at the Petits, even creepy. But then you see why he's doing it: He wheels back around, stands, and says to Judge Blue, "Your Honor, I count twenty-one Petit Family Foundation pins in the courtroom today." He refers to Bill and his family and friends as the "Petit posse," a term he came up with. And he says with sarcasm that having them all sit so close to the jury box—which is where the court has directed them to sit—wearing their pins amounts to "effective prosecution."

Surely, even with his back to the gallery, Donovan can hear people gasp and scoff at this bit of theater. But he makes his point calmly before sitting to wait for the jury to arrive. When they do file in, Donovan's entire team—himself, cocounsel Walt Bansley, and Todd Bussert—stands in unison. Komisarjevsky stands, too. Donovan has coached them all to do this. It's an old-fashioned move, just like when Donovan sometimes refers to opposing counsel as "my brother." A bit of showmanship.

The prosecution doesn't stand once.

· · ·

After college, in the early 1970s, Donovan roamed around Europe and Asia and eventually found himself sleeping on the roof of a Bangkok hotel while he awaited his orders from the Army. He had no money. There was a little restaurant at the Army base where for twenty-five cents you could get an egg and toast with coffee. They let you refill your coffee as much as you liked, which Donovan would do, so that he could fill his cup mostly with whole milk, for the calories—he had started his trip at 165 pounds and was down to about 145. He was always good with languages, and he picked up Thai quickly. The waitresses in Bangkok smiled as he tried to talk to them in their language, and whenever another customer didn't finish his toast, they always brought it over to the American, Jerry. He had the gift of being able to talk to anyone.

"Proceed, Attorney Donovan."

This is the deep, midwestern voice of Judge Blue once again. Donovan needs his gift of oratory today, the second day of *State v. Komisarjevsky*. He stands and clasps his hands behind his back, revealing the green suspenders that match his repp tie. He is tall and lanky, with a thatch of hair that runs from black to white.

"May it please the court, as I will every morning, I notice that there are twenty-three Petit Foundation pins in the audience. What's most disturbing to us, I suppose, is that Dr. Petit is wearing one," Donovan says to the judge. The working-class Boston is still thick in his voice, so that *doctor* is *dawk-tah*. "We anticipate that he will be the first witness."

"Thank you. Proceed," Blue says.

"I do have a request with respect to witnesses, that is, the witnesses being ordered not to wear the pins," Donovan says.

Donovan has already tried this at a previous hearing, so he is simply renewing his request here for the record, knowing full well what Blue's ruling will be.

"You know," says Blue, "if we're talking about the pins that were the subject of the hearing, I think I've made my ruling on that. I don't view the pins as disruptive or inflammatory, sir, so your objection is noted. Obviously, you could cross-examine him on the pin to your heart's content. Sir, is there anything else I should address?"

Blue is asking this as a formality. The assumption is that there is nothing else. But Blue knows Donovan.

"Yes, Your Honor. I want to put on the record our objection as to the background of the victims, what they did that day—their accomplishments."

By "accomplishments," he is referring sarcastically to what Bill, Jennifer, Hayley, and Michaela did on that Sunday, July 22, 2007, their last full day alive as a family. The fact that they went to church together, that Bill played golf with his father, that Michaela cooked dinner for the family—Donovan wants all of this kept out. This objection, too, has already been the subject of a hearing, and Blue shut it down then as he shuts it down now.

Donovan is not done yet. Next, as a preemptive move, he wants to limit the number of photographs of Bill's bludgeoned head that can be admitted into evidence. One is acceptable, Donovan argues, but there are three that the state intends to submit into evidence, and that is too many. He even offers up an argument that because one of the photos is of the back of Bill's head, Bill would have no way of truthfully testifying that it is definitely his head.

"The other two photographs seem to me to have minimal probative value that is far outweighed by the prejudicial effect. As Your Honor knows, and the record will reflect, those show photographs of Dr. Petit lying on a pillow, I assume at the hospital, and the pillow is soaked with blood. I have heard of waving the bloody shirt in front of the jury, but this is the first time I've heard of waving the bloody pillow," Donovan says.

A few members of the Petit family allow the faintest hint of shock to show on their faces.

"With respect, the objection must be overruled," Blue replies. "I can understand why it's made, but the photographs are not cumulative, and they are not—obviously, while they are disturbing, I do not believe that they are so horrendous as to be prejudicial. And the adage that I typically follow is that the defendant may not object to the jury seeing photographic evidence of his handiwork, and I think that fits here."

There are several ways to impeach a witness on cross-examination, according to Jeremiah Donovan.

You can bring up his obvious interest in the outcome of the case as a factor that might color his testimony. But Bill Petit—how can you do that with Petit? He lost his wife, his two daughters, his home, his interest in work, his whole life, and he himself was left for dead. Spending time establishing that this witness has an interest in the outcome of the case would make a lawyer look stupid, because of course this witness has an interest in the outcome of the case.

You can go after his prior inconsistent statements. But Petit's head was beaten like a grapefruit by the man sitting at the defendant's table, using the bat that's now sitting on the evidence table in front of the court clerk, a bat still blackened with Petit's dried blood. Prior inconsistent statements? If anything, that would make him more sympathetic.

You can impeach a witness by questioning whether he was really in a position to see what he says he saw. But Petit doesn't claim to have seen much. After the cranial bashing, Hayes and Komisarjevsky covered his head and hauled him down to the basement. That's about all he remembers.

The thing of it is, he's not a witness at all, really. He is a living exhibit. And you can't impeach an exhibit.

So when the state finishes questioning Bill, and the judge says, "Your witness," Donovan has a challenge before him. He likes an intellectual challenge, and he likes talking to people, but he's not particularly looking forward to this.

"Thank you, Your Honor."

Donovan establishes that Bill gave three statements to the police: two the day the crime occurred and one a couple of weeks later. He does this quickly and with the calmness of a professor. He establishes that Bill attended the first trial in this case, of Steven Hayes, last year. He establishes that, due to the fact that Bill was not sequestered during that trial and was in fact allowed to sit through every minute of it, Bill has seen all the evidence and heard all the testimony already.

"Yes, sir," says Bill over and over, showing nothing on his face, revealing nothing in his voice. "Yes, sir."

"Fair enough," says Donovan finally. "Now, can you, as you sit here today, tell the jurors how much you really remember and how much you are trying to put together from the things that you heard other witnesses testify to during the Hayes trial?"

Dearington, the prosecutor, objects immediately. Without even asking the grounds, Blue says, "Overruled."

But Bill doesn't take Donovan's bait. "I believe what I've testified to is to the best of my own recollection," he says, his voice flat, eyes on Donovan, as calmly as if he were recounting some arcane fact from an endocrinology textbook. "I was making a concerted effort . . ." Donovan is already looking down at his notes, preparing his next question.

Donovan is smart. But Bill Petit is not only an extraordinarily sympathetic witness, he is extremely intelligent, too, and not just book smart. He is quick, he thinks three steps ahead, and he is calm.

Even for Donovan, this is hard.

Next the lawyer tries to get in the point that one of the men who invaded his home actually put some pillows under Dr. Petit after they brought him to the basement, presumably to make him more comfortable. Bill says he doesn't remember telling the police that they put a pillow under his feet. Donovan knows he said this, because he has Bill's sworn statement. In this situation a lawyer usually asks the witness whether it would refresh his memory to take a look at the statement.

"Did you say that, 'It was strange, they put a pillow under my butt and my feet and that they covered me with a blanket?' Did you say that?"

"That's what they wrote down. I don't recall saying 'under my feet' at this time," Bill says.

"Would it refresh your recollection to take a look at the written statement?"

"I trust that's what's written there, but I don't—"

And here Donovan strays just for a moment from the taut script of a delicate cross-examination and conjures a little of the Jeremiah Donovan who once jumped on a bale of marijuana in court, who acted in the Hasty Pudding show at Harvard, and who made his way from England to Bangkok alone, bullshitting with strangers the whole way. He places his hand on his heart and says, with self-effacing charm, "Don't trust *me*, sir."

Before they can catch themselves—and in *spite* of themselves—just about everyone in the courtroom chuckles. This is a quick moment, but to Donovan's strategy of winning over the jury and poking holes any way he can, no matter how bad they might make Bill Petit feel, it is essential. With no way to impeach this witness, Donovan does the next most effective thing. In this most horrible and joyless of trials, he actually gets them to *laugh*.

Bill finds it more difficult to maintain his composure in this trial with Donovan leading the defense, but somehow he does. Donovan routinely objects to the most innocuous of things, moves for a mistrial regularly, lets nothing slide. He will do anything to create confusion or take the jury's attention off the core facts of the case.

He sees his duty in this case as keeping Joshua Komisarjevsky off death row. That's it. And he will do anything to fulfill that duty.

Bill doesn't crack.

Christine is here most days. That helps. She doesn't sit next to him, though. The victim's advocate, a person appointed by the court to help families through the trial process, advises them that it wouldn't look good if Bill and Christine sat together. Especially with Donovan trying the case. They don't want to give him any bait, any information he could twist in an attempt to puncture the jury's perception of Bill, because Donovan is the type of lawyer who just might try. So Christine sits behind Bill.

While the Petits sit impassively, day after day, Christine is not so accustomed to keeping emotion off her face. She marvels at their stolidity because, jeez, you can't believe some of the stuff Donovan pulls. But when she occasionally reacts the way most people would—a muffled gasp, a *can you believe this?* face, a little nudge and a whisper to the person next to her—there's no response from the family around her. This is somewhat amusing to Bill, and in fact it's part of what draws him to her: She is true to her emotions. She lets them show. Not too much or in a way that would offend anybody—nothing like that. But the contrast between Christine and his family is stark. At social gatherings, or even when it's just the two of them, she makes him laugh. With a perfectly timed roll of the eyes or a conspiratorial smile across the room at a moment when he was thinking the same thing, she makes him feel like smiling without thinking too hard about it, and that's something he hasn't been able to do for a very long time.

This trial, however, is not amusing. She is aghast, mostly, but she quickly adopts the Petit stone face, even if she wants to scream sometimes. Now Donovan is looking at the notes he will use to question William Shute, special agent, Federal Bureau of Investigation. The prosecution contacted Shute three days ago to request that he travel from his office in the J. Edgar Hoover Building in

Washington to New Haven so he could testify as an expert witness about the locations of the cellular communications towers in and around Cheshire, Connecticut. Before the call from Dearington's office, he had never heard of the Cheshire murders.

The state is interested in the period during the morning of the crimes when Hayes left the house on Sorghum Mill Drive to fill the cans with gas and made several cell-phone calls to Komisarjevsky, who was back at the house. The FBI agent doesn't know the particulars of this case but has experience using cell towers to track mobile callers, and the state is using him to help establish Hayes's rough whereabouts on the morning of the attacks.

In preparing for the trial, Donovan has read that, according to some experts, cell-tracking science is not science at all. And he believes that this agent, Shute, has been asked by the state to say that the radii of the cell towers are whatever is most convenient for their case. And so Jeremiah Donovan goes on the attack. He's researched the hell out of cell-phone-tower range, and he's done the calculations to show the range to be a certain number of miles.

But Shute is too loose with his numbers for Donovan's taste. Two miles, 1.7 miles—he's all over the place.

> DONOVAN: Isn't it true, sir—didn't you testify that the radius
>   of the cell-phone tower is approximately two miles—you
>   have chosen to use 1.7 miles and 1.5 miles, isn't that right?
> SHUTE: One point seven miles, to me, is approximately close to
>   two miles, sure.
> DONOVAN: Well, let's see how close 1.7 miles is to two miles.

Shute shifts in the witness chair, looking a little annoyed but also a little nervous about where this lawyer is going. He is perhaps guesstimating with the wrong lawyer. Jeremiah Donovan, after all, will not even end a sentence with a preposition.

DONOVAN: You know the formula for computing the area of a
    circle?
SHUTE: Sure, sir.
DONOVAN: What is it?
SHUTE: It's pi r—is it pi r squared?
DONOVAN: Pi r squared?

And here Nicholson, the assistant state's attorney, objects. His
tone suggests that Donovan is wasting the court's time. Blue allows
it, but he's keeping Donovan on a short leash.

DONOVAN: So it's a 2.5, the radius squared would be—
BLUE: Where did you get 2.5? The witness said two miles,
    didn't he?
DONOVAN: Didn't you testify that the average is two to three
    miles?
SHUTE: In this geographical area, the towers are separated by
    about two to three miles.

So Donovan is dealing with two different numbers now, range
and distance. He's drawing pictures on the overhead projector, towers and circles, and he's doing math longhand. His giant magnified
hand moves around the screen, scribbling out long division. The
jury, after days of nightmarish evidence and wrenching testimony,
is rapt, and some are even showing a hint of a smile. They appear to
be allowing themselves to be entertained.

DONOVAN: Would you agree that 2.5 squared equals 6.25,
    right?
SHUTE: Sure.
DONOVAN: Now, I'm going to embarrass you: Do you
    remember the value of pi?

SHUTE [so taken aback that he just goes ahead and answers]:
3.14, something something something?

BLUE: I believe this is why God invented calculators. [*Smirks.*]

DONOVAN: If there is a mistake from the defense team, please
let me know.

BLUE: For those of us who went to high school in the pre-
electronic-calculator era, this is what high school was.

DONOVAN [scribbling away, really sweating the math]: So, 2.5
miles is about 188 square miles?

BLUE: You know, Mr. Donovan, I do have an adding machine
here, could you use this, it's—if you multiply 186 by three,
which is an approximation, you get 18, so that indicates
your decimal point may be off.

DONOVAN: And may it please the court, I would ask the court
to take judicial notice that this calculation comes out to
19.625?

BLUE: Yeah. Call it 20. Go ahead, sir.

DONOVAN: I wonder if we could do the same thing, I'll ask my
brother counsel to do the same thing with—

BLUE: With what number?

DONOVAN: The figure that is used on—the smaller figure that
is used on this, which is 1.5 miles, 1.55. [Pause.] 7.54. So,
I mean, there is a pretty considerable difference, is there,
between the radius—between the square footage that is
covered when the radius changes?

And everybody looks at Special Agent William Shute, including
Judge Jon Blue, eyebrows raised, lips curled up at the edges, and the
jury, too, who never expected this kind of theater. Shute stammers,
and the examination trails off a few minutes later. Joshua Komisarjevsky watches with apparent interest, but it's unclear whether he
realizes that his attorney is doing every blessed thing he can think
of—including taking half an hour to try to discredit some poor FBI

agent who never heard of this case until three days ago and whose testimony about the radius of a cell-phone tower doesn't mean a damn thing—to save his life.

The jury found Komisarjevsky guilty of all seventeen counts against him, including the six capital felonies that carry the death penalty. That's why Donovan is standing before the court on day one of the penalty phase. If the Petit posse didn't like him during the guilt phase, they are going to like him even less now. The Jeremiah Donovan Show is just beginning. And the first thing he does is—once again—say something unimaginable.

Part of what the state had to prove in the guilt phase was that the victims of these murders—Jennifer, Hayley, and Michaela Petit— died in a manner that was heinous, cruel, or depraved as defined by the law, which seems like a given in this case. Not to Donovan, though. Not that he's going to admit in court.

"At least with respect to the death of Hayley Petit and Michaela Petit," he says, "as Your Honor will recall, the testimony of the medical examiner was that when one dies from smoke inhalation, what happens is that in a matter of seconds one is overcome by smoke. During those seconds one suffers some confusion and pain in the throat and the lungs, and then one is fortunately unconscious while the—while the breathing of the smoke causes the death of the person. So with respect to the deaths of Hayley Petit and Michaela Petit, their actual deaths were not, in the defense's view, committed in an especially heinous, cruel, or depraved manner."

And again you can hear the muffled gasps. Donovan knows full well that everyone in the room is thinking about the heinous, cruel, and depraved six hours the girls were tied to their beds, and then the endless, terrifying minutes when the intruders poured gasoline all over their rooms, and the fact that those two girls knew at the very end that they were going to die that morning in their home.

Donovan gets nowhere with Judge Blue on this motion. But he knew he wouldn't. He had to state it for the record. There will be appeals someday, probably, and so Donovan makes as many of these motions as he can think of, hurls the next one at the judge as quickly as he can rule on the last one.

Now, he's going to tell a story.

Donovan stands in the middle of the room. He got a haircut, and his hair looks darker than usual, more black than white. He puts his glasses on as he peers down, then looks up at the jury and whips them off.

Donovan knows how to tell a story. At the elite Jesuit boys' school he attended on an academic scholarship, he read the *Odyssey* in Greek. Twice. By the time he got to Harvard, college seemed easy by comparison. But Bill isn't in the courtroom to hear Donovan tell this story, one of the few times in either trial that he excuses himself. Bill doesn't want to hear this. Doesn't care that Komisarjevsky was adopted when he was two weeks old, and that his biological family suffered from various mental disorders. Doesn't want to know that Josh's adoptive parents took in a fifteen-year-old foster child when Josh was four years old, and that that boy began sexually abusing Josh, including raping him, almost immediately, and burned his skin with cigarettes. Doesn't want to hear that Komisarjevsky's parents were evangelical Christians who made him recite Bible verses while he did his chores, or that by the fifth grade he was sneaking out of the house, wandering alone in the woods at night, and occasionally walking into people's homes and stealing women's underwear—or that his parents knew about this and didn't do enough to stop it. Bill doesn't want to hear about how Josh sexually molested his younger sister, and that his parents knew about this, too, and didn't seek sufficient professional help for him, because they felt these things were best dealt with in the family and in the church. The chanting, the group humiliation that was practiced in the Komisarjevskys' church, the rejection of medicine and psychiatry, the speaking in tongues, the yelling and the coldness that pervaded the Komisarjevsky home—none of this does Bill Petit want to hear. Because how can any of this be relevant now that his girls—Hayley, so good to everyone, and sweet Michaela, who helped him plant flowers, and Jennifer, his beautiful Jennifer, twenty-six years his Jennifer, such a good and gentle soul—now that his girls are dead, how can any of that matter?

Donovan tries to make it matter. One afternoon, deep into the penalty phase, when most of that biography has been established through a parade of defense witnesses, he calls Frances Hodges. The marshal in the back of the courtroom opens the door. A woman walks in, about thirty years old, with heavy black eyeliner and her dark hair teased above her head. She wears a teal blouse, black nail polish, and tiny rings in her nose and lips. She has sad eyes.

Hodges, who was Komisarjevsky's girlfriend when they were teenagers, is a delicate witness. She's nervous. She sits in the witness box and folds her arms, and her eyes pinball around the room—the jury, the judge, the hulking marshal standing against the wall over her left shoulder. The Petits. When her eyes land on Komisarjevsky, whom she hasn't seen in at least a dozen years—since long before the crimes of July 23, 2007—she stops. He looks so different now. He was a skinny kid, but good-looking, and she used to gaze into his deep brown eyes. Now, after prison—four years since the murders, plus some long stretches before that, for burglaries—he looks pale and thick, doughy even, his brown hair shaved close. Like a prisoner.

He doesn't look at her.

"Miss Hodges," Donovan says. She sits up and snaps her eyes to him, licks her lips quickly in preparation to speak. Donovan stands between Komisarjevsky and the jury box, his arms folded like a professor's, with a folder of pages in front of him. He uses a voice that is calm but proper, soothing but polite. "I would like to start off by letting the jury know something about your life history."

Among the first things the jury comes to know is that Fran Hodges did not have a very happy childhood.

"We used to have church meetings," she tells Donovan, her voice at once confident and heartbreakingly fragile, "where the leaders of the church would present what they said were science-based presentations of evidence that the prophecies of the end times, in the Book of Revelation, were coming true or had already come true, and that we were in the final stages of the end of the world."

Fran and Joshua lived in the same religious community as teens, so in this witness Donovan has effectively found a surrogate for Joshua—someone who can speak firsthand about what his life was like, because she lived it with him.

As a girl, Fran was taught to wonder whether she would one day witness her mother burning at the stake as her father looked on. She was made to feel that her faith was "inadequate." She assumed that she herself would have to die for her beliefs at some point—it was inevitable, her parents said. Fran became depressed and anxious even before adolescence. She cut herself deliberately, pulled out her hair. She feared anyone who was not a member of her church, mostly because she hadn't ever really met anyone who wasn't. As a teenager, she participated in community outreach programs for the Evangelical Bible Church. One of her missions was to try to spread God's love so that she might help cure people of homosexuality. In the church in which she grew up, she tells Donovan, homosexuality is "an abomination," and she was taught to go out and spread that definition of love the way Girl Scouts are sent out to sell cookies. She knew nothing of the outside world. She was, she says, "born into being a misfit." But trying to cure the gays seemed to trigger something in her mind. She began to feel conflicted about her faith.

She didn't know what to do, and she felt alone in her state of conflict, until she met Josh Komisarjevsky.

DONOVAN: Did he also have the same kind of inner conflict?
HODGES: Yes.
DONOVAN: What was his mood as you became friends?

She looks at Komisarjevsky as if to ask for help finding the word. He stares down at the table.

HODGES: He was sad.
DONOVAN: Okay. How would you describe your mood?
HODGES [still looking at Komisarjevsky]: I was sad.

Donovan is gliding through the examination. He sees that Fran Hodges is pretty and sweet and vulnerable and captivating, somehow, in the way she speaks. He is talking to her with empathy, because maybe that will help him pull off the impossible, which would be to make the jury feel empathy for Komisarjevsky. Or at least to understand him, a little.

"You have no idea what morality looks like in an applicable, culturally acceptable way," Hodges is saying. "So I left the church and I just—there was this wake of wreckage behind me. I had absolutely no moral conscience after leaving. I felt like I was damned to hell."

Donovan puts his glasses on, then takes them off again. He takes a step forward, then back, looking down as he speaks and then up at Hodges. The jury watches him now, their heads ping-ponging between the witness and the lawyer. Donovan asks Hodges about another boy who was the model child in that church community, the kid everybody thought was great.

"John," she says, nodding. "He was moral, and genteel, and generous, and humble."

Donovan looks up at her, his eyebrows arched, like a Saint Bernard hearing the doorbell. "Did he have any aspects of his life that the community might have looked upon as an abomination?"

He uses her word, *abomination*.

"John was gay," Hodges says, looking straight at Donovan.

Without passion, Donovan says, "How did he react to that?"

She says that her friend John lived a life of crushing self-hatred and repentance, and that he apologized to the entire church for "his moral failings."

"Was that kind of similar to the cycle of repentance and sin that you felt you were going through?"

Donovan is coming to the end of his notes, and you can feel him going through the questions—this has gone from a heart-to-heart to a dry examination. But if you watch Fran Hodges, you can see she is starting to crack, talking about this John.

"Yeah, I think we all just felt trapped."

Donovan looks down at his notes and asks, almost as an afterthought, "What finally happened to John?"

"He jumped out a window."

He is still looking at his notes, shuffling papers, so he doesn't see Fran's body suddenly begin to convulse as soon as she can get the answer out, doesn't see her soft face crinkle into sadness as the sobs tumble from her in silence.

He is still looking down when he asks, "Things are better for you now, Fran?" And then he looks up at her. And he sees that she is overcome. He recoils, and looks down at the carpet, as if out of respect, or shame.

"Ah, we need to take—ma'am, why don't we do this. Let's take a five-minute recess," says Judge Blue.

Fran leaves, leaning on the marshal who escorts her as she walks.

Donovan stands motionless, his jaw hanging open a little, his arms slack. He is blindsided by her breakdown, and yet it probably helped him.

• • •

It doesn't work. None of it matters. In the end, the jury finds that Joshua Komisarjevsky should be put to death. After the sentencing, Donovan gives an interview at his home, a beachfront cottage. Most of the houses around his are summer houses, empty now for the cold winter. A storm is raging on the water, and the waves are pounding over the seawall and lashing the picture windows, like a car wash. The wind rattles the storm windows.

He talks about Komisarjevsky's prison journals, which made their way onto the record in the Hayes trial. In them, Komisarjevsky wrote that Bill's actions on the morning of the murders were despicable in their cowardice. He wrote that Hayley was "a fighter," and that Jennifer deserved credit for leaving the bank because she "left that safety to protect her children and it cost her her life," but that Dr. Petit just sat in the basement until he managed to escape at the last minute. Never mind that he had lost seven pints of blood or that he thought the two able-bodied men upstairs had a loaded gun. He was a "coward," according to the man who killed his family.

You have to play tricks on your own brain to do Jeremiah Donovan's job sometimes. You have to convince yourself that the victims who seek the death penalty are deathmongers, and that their heart-shaped pins are like some kind of lethal force that can brainwash a jury. You have to pretend the murderer is your nephew, because that motivates you. And you, a smart man with three daughters who has seen ghastly photographs of what happened to Bill Petit and his family in 2007, have to try to convince yourself that Dr. Petit could have escaped sooner—could have saved his family, even—because that's what your client needs you to believe.

"We know that he didn't break the bonds, he just slipped out of them," Donovan says. The storm has knocked out the electricity, and he is sitting in the darkness of his kitchen, silhouetted against the tormented sky out the window.

Didn't Petit try desperately to loosen or break the ropes and plastic zip ties over a period of hours?

"I don't think so. If you look at the pictures, they weren't tight enough, and he managed to get his hands out."

So you think it was easy for him to escape?

"I don't know. I don't know. Josh thinks it was."

Sometimes, late at night, when he's lying awake, Donovan walks downstairs and settles into the white wicker couch next to the table of family photos—his three daughters, his wife, his house. The waves outside slosh against the sand in the blackness. And he sometimes remembers that on the night of July 22, 2007, Bill Petit dozed off on the sunroom couch and was awakened by the crush of a baseball bat to his head. And Donovan looks out the big picture windows that frame the black ocean, and he thinks about Joshua Komisarjevsky and the baseball bat, and he pulls a blanket over his body and tries to sleep.

It's a fairytale so tragic
There's no prince to break the spell.
I don't believe in magic
But for you I will.

—Bruce Springsteen,
"Countin' on a Miracle"

MARRIAGE

2012–Present

B ILL KEEPS trying to add bricks and mortar to his new life, a little more every day. Where he was once struggling simply to remain among the living, aiming only to survive each languid day and long, harrowing night, now he can see, maybe, a life in which he might feel happy.

By the end of the second trial, he and Christine were living together, in a small house (572 square feet, Bill likes to note) on Lake Garda, a quiet strip of water about five miles from the Country Club of Farmington. They were only there for a few months, but it was the first place they lived together that neither had lived in before, so it was exciting—the novelty.

The photography business Christine has built has her out shooting all the time. She loves the work, and the hours aren't traditional, so she can make herself free to attend and photograph Petit Family Foundation events. Bill has even served as her assistant at a few weddings on Saturdays, carrying her equipment and providing humor.

Oprah Winfrey asked Bill if he could ever imagine loving anyone again. She had sat in his mother's living room, hands folded in her lap, squinted at him, and said, "Can you see yourself building another family? Can you see yourself loving again?"

"I've imagined it. On good days, yes. On bad days, no."

"What would Jennifer want for you?"

He didn't answer for a few seconds. "She'd probably want me to go back to medicine." Then a pause. He hadn't answered her question, really, because there was no short answer. Winfrey thought he was done and started to ask her next question, but Bill tacked on a joke. "Wives are prejudiced," he said. "She said I was the smartest guy she ever knew. I said, 'You didn't meet enough guys, then.'"

He believes Jennifer—Jenna, as he often called her—would want him to be happy. He no longer wonders whether these feelings he has for Christine are correct. Bill still has that computational mind, still likes statistics, likes knowing who won and who lost and who's averaging better than 80 percent from the free-throw line. Likes knowing that his house is exactly 572 square feet. Can't go to a fundraiser without calculating, out loud on the ride home, how much money they might have raised. *Let's see, tickets were $100 a couple, there were about 150 people there, probably mostly couples, so figure $10,000 plus the 50 singles, so that's . . .* But there is no quantifying this question of moving on with Christine. He knows what some people think, or he can imagine. *She's awfully young, isn't she? They're moving awfully fast, aren't they?* To him, though, it is remarkably uncomplicated. She makes him happy. She seems to be amused by him. They want to be around each other. That's hard to find.

He still wears his wedding ring. He was married for twenty-two years. He takes it off sometimes, puts it back on. Wearing it, not wearing it—both feel right, in a way. Then one day, a friend of Christine's who now lives in Australia—in *Australia*—sees a paparazzi photo of Bill and Christine on the Internet. Her friend texts Christine to politely inquire about the fact that she appears to be dating a guy who wears a wedding ring. This makes Christine laugh hysterically. Bill takes off the ring.

There's a jewelry store in Litchfield, a rural town in the northwest part of Connecticut, that Christine has loved since she was a little girl. They sell estate pieces—antiques, vintage rings and necklaces and bracelets, gorgeous things. The store actually offered Christine a job not too long ago, running the shop, but it was a little too far to drive, and she was worried the hours might have impeded her photography business. But they stopped in sometimes, and she and Bill let the owners know what kind of engagement ring she might like. They said they would keep an eye out for anything like what she wanted and promised to call Bill if they found it.

It was around Christmas when she saw the box on his dresser in the bedroom of the house on Lake Garda. *Oh, Bill,* she thought. She almost laughed out loud. *Really? Right there where I can see it?* The night before New Year's Eve—Bill didn't want to propose on New Year's Eve or Christmas morning or anything like that— Christine went out early in the evening with a few girlfriends for mid-holiday martinis. She and Bill were heading to a party later that night. When she came home from the restaurant, the house was dark. She kicked off her shoes and took off her coat, and there was Bill, lying in bed, dressed for the party but half zonked. He bolted up. She gave him a kiss, told him it was almost time to go.

"Wait," he said.

Eleven Months Later

"You never saw these," Bill says to a visitor as he opens his front door. It's ten o'clock in the morning and he is holding a stack of broken-down cardboard boxes he was supposed to take out to the trash bin. They missed the recycling last week. They're still getting used to the schedule. He and Christine got married three months before, moved into this house a month ago, and she's trying to make it nice. To give it "the feminine touch," as Bill says. And part of the feminine touch is not having recycling stacked by the front door. He scoots out past the pumpkin on the front step, left over from Halloween and half-eaten by squirrels, and gets rid of them before his wife notices.

His hair is damp from the shower, combed back. He wears a beard now, and it is trimmed neat. He wears a checked shirt and jeans. He is a newlywed, for the first time in a long time, and a new homeowner, so his days are full of little interactions with his wife and with his house, the little interactions that make up a life. In the more than five years since the murders, it's these moments that little by little have brought Bill back to life. Back inside, he fiddles with the sliding doors that lead out to the deck. "These sliders don't sit right," he says. "They're not flush. There's huge leakage of air, so when it's twenty degrees, it's not very happy with these sliders." Have to fix that. He jiggles the door shut. The house is a baby-blue prefab sitting on steel beams and cement footings at the end of a residential street along the Farmington River in western Connecticut. Off to one side is a copse of maple trees along the river's edge, some of them felled by the beavers who chew the trunks until the trees topple and land with a deep thud on the bed of brown leaves below. There's a statue of a deer off in the trees, knocked down and forgotten by some previous owner, its head now sticking out of the brush. Scared the heck out of Christine when she first saw it the other week. On the other side of the house, right outside the front door, is a pumping station about the size of a tennis court, with a chain-link fence around it—the town recently put in a sewer system, and a pumping station ended up here in the Petits' front yard. A row of rose of Sharons runs along the fence, between the house and the pumping station, which take your eyes off it somewhat. "The house sags a little bit," Bill says. "Structurally it seems okay so far. We talked to a guy about getting a jack in and jacking it up, but after a while it didn't seem worth it. It's been here for twenty-five years. It sort of was a priority when we were looking at it, but now it's like, ehh, five grand to go up an inch or two?"

The room in the house that's supposed to be the master bedroom faces the pumping station. Bill and Christine instead squeezed their bed into the small room across the hall, which is not much larger than the bed itself, but it faces the river. That's the side of the house they choose to focus on. That's the view they want, the peace they want.

"We painted this, the inside," Bill says, nodding to the white walls of the living room. "This was all dark. All dark. Then she put these funky lights in. Put a new floor in, got rid of some furniture, tried to fit in here. No basement, no attic, no garage, no storage. What you see is what you get."

One of the funky lights is a chandelier that looks like a giant fluffy white dandelion. That's pure Christine. And the benches out on the deck, which the previous owner left behind—she had Bill paint those bright purple.

Christine sings out as she enters the room, "Shangri-la!" She waves her hands around like a hostess on a game show presenting a prize. Then she takes her voice down a notch—still several notches, and a couple of octaves, above Bill's dry New England elocution— and, extending her damp right hand, says of their home, "We like it. It's fun. I just washed my hands. Nice to meet you."

She whirls around the room, putting water on for tea, straightening a blanket on the arm of a chair, sliding an ottoman over in front of Bill so he can put his feet up. "It's peaceful here, you know? It's hard to find that," she says, clanging out mugs and spoons on the counter. "I find the water very calming. And the town here is an artsy kind of place, and there's something about those places that, like—the mind-set is to create new things. Like this lamp. That's the whimsy! Look at the shadows it makes. This is the jewelry, I call it. I'm trying to draw your eye *awaaay* from the bad walls, the bad windows." She flicks her hands at the chandelier and says, "Like, you're not gonna look at *that* because *this* is here!"

She smiles and her eyes wander out the window toward the river. She runs a hand through her curly, beach-blond hair.

"I'll open this door a little," she says to no one. "It's a nice day."

Bill's eyes follow her, and he grins as she buzzes around. "But the house is so small, so it's hard," she says, going on the way she sometimes does, filling the silence. "Like the room that would have been the master but we turned it into a—"

"A whatever room," says Bill.

"You need extra space in this house. Literally, *literally*, you can't walk around the bed in the room we made into our bedroom. But you can see the water! So of course we did it that way. Why would I want to look at that fence?"

"Whose idea was that?" Bill asks.

Christine gives him a glare and a smile.

"Just checking," he says, throwing a droll smile back at her.

She's back in the kitchen now, fixing the tea.

"The thing with such an inexpensive home is, we can do whatever we want and who cares. Like that lamp. Of course, we have no room. No. Room. We buy stuff—like those little things you ordered for—"

"My egg things." Bill shrugs.

"These little things to poach eggs! And I said, 'What? Where are we gonna put those?'"

Bill holds up a glass punch bowl, another recent acquisition that doesn't have a place. "Saint Patrick's Church Bazaar raffle winner."

"Oh yeah, that. What else did it come with?" Christine says.

"Eight margarita glasses!"

"Yeah, like *this* big." She almost hollers with laughter, holding her hands far apart like a lying fisherman. "*And* eight shot glasses. I was like, *Greaaat*."

"It was this little teacup raffle thing—"

"He's a sucker for old ladies."

"So I put most of my tickets on things like the Shop Rite gift card, a pizza a month for a year—but I put *one ticket* in that thing, and that's what I won," Bill says. "It had a bag of chips on top. That's what sucked me in."

In a small room halfway down the hall, Bill has made an office for himself and Christine. On top of a small bookshelf, angled perfectly so that they face each other just slightly, are two framed photographs, one of Michaela and one of Hayley.

In the bathroom, Christine has hung a hand towel with the embroidered words "Keep your face in the sun and your toes in the sand."

Out in the living room, Bill identifies some of the art on the walls. On their honeymoon in Kennebunkport, Maine, they stopped in at an art gallery and Bill immediately walked over to a painting he ended up buying: three birds standing in the grass under a dark blue sky. He printed out the artist's biography and keeps it tucked behind the frame.

"Ellen Welch Granter," he announces, like a docent in a museum. Then he motions to a framed portrait hanging near it, a girl in pigtails wearing a pink dress with blue dots.

"Michaela Petit," he says. "*Self-Portrait.*"

He absently picks up his phone from a side table. His hand brushes a stack of brochures that say "Michaela's Garden," the project Hanna's husband, Dennis, has created for the foundation. Inside each brochure is a small packet of four-o'clock seeds, the flowers Bill and Michaela used to like to plant. Dennis harvests the seeds from the plants he rescued from the house on Sorghum Mill Drive—something like three hundred thousand seeds so far—and the foundation sells them in packets for ten dollars.

Bill pokes his phone with his thumb. "Too many e-mails," he says without looking up. Foundation business, invitations to appear as an honored guest at this function or that, junk mail. "I try to look at the ten worst ones and get rid of them. There's Williams and Sonomas. Somehow Williams and Sonomas—we got a couple of wedding gifts and somehow now they have us on their list for the rest of our lives."

He keeps scrolling.

"That thing at Children's Hospital is next Tuesday at three-fifteen," he calls over to Christine. "Tuesday the eleventh. Meet 'em in the lobby."

She looks up. "What thing?" There are so many things these days, it's hard to keep track. But every "thing" they go to is a reminder of the astonishing success of the foundation. So, no complaints. It's just hard to keep track.

"That lady, Wilma Hoffman, from Bulkeley High School who does the knitting club. They knit stuff for the kids. We gave them a grant, and we're gonna go with them to Children's Hospital."

Christine pulls out her phone. This is what they have to do constantly. Sync.

"The thirteenth?"

"Eleventh. Tuesday the eleventh. Three-fifteen."

"Okay. Children's Hospital. Which one?"

"The one in Hartford," Bill says. He pauses before adding, "The only one."

Christine murmurs a gentle singsong-y reminder: "I don't know that."

They put their coats on. There are the usual errands to do. Bill shoves the storm door closed as he leaves. A gust of wind caught it the other day and busted the bracket that keeps it latched, so you need to really push it to make sure it's shut. Have to fix that.

Lunch first. They'll walk into town, which they like to do. Bill can do things to relax these days. Or at least he can do the kinds of things other people do to relax. He can simulate leisure. At the end of their driveway, an old railroad bridge creaks over the river. On the other side: an antiques barn, a package store, some gift shops, a wine bar, a pub in the old depot, a place to rent kayaks. Cute town.

There's this one sandwich shop where everything's homemade. They do a turkey sandwich with cranberry sauce on pumpernickel that Bill gets almost every time. You just order and grab a seat at one of the mismatched tables. It feels like an old general store. Bill and Christine sit and eat and talk and watch people. No one stares at him here.

Bill sometimes makes jokes that show his age, and Christine's— there are twenty years between them. At the lunch counter, the girl hands Christine a bowl of steaming winter-squash soup. "Danger, Will Robinson," Bill says to his wife as she picks it up, quoting a television show that went off the air nine years before she was born. When she successfully carries it to the table without burning herself or spilling any, he says, "Well done, Grasshopper."

Yeah, well, you gotta make some jokes.

He doesn't talk about it much, his soldiering on or whatever people call it. His courage, his fortitude. It's just how he was brought up, he says. You do what you have to, he says. You just keep going, he says.

No, Christine says. She corrects him: You need to give your-self credit. *You* do what you have to. *You* just keep going. *You* find ways to keep living. Not everyone would, or could. To which Bill scrunches his face into a look that says, If you say so, his fingers absently gathering the fallen leaves from a dying plant into a neat pile on the table.

After that—after you keep going for a while—you yearn for the return of mundane normalcy, if such a thing is even possible, although days like this at the sandwich place suggest it is, if only fleetingly. Your days, like anyone's days, become a mosaic of present and past, each piece as surprising as the next. But in your case, the past is a conflagration, a nightmare. So you go on, and the most im-portant questions in your life, the ones you ask yourself every day and the ones people think but don't say out loud, become: Where, exactly, are you going? Will there ever come a time when you'll be able to salvage what's good and leave the horror behind?

How do you get out of the bed in the morning?

Do you sleep?

"Sorry, dudes. You're out," he says to the Rolling Stones after a couple of verses of "Midnight Rambler," looking at the dash as he punches the buttons. "Oh, crap. Okay, we got about four-tenths of a gallon left. It says we got about ten miles left. Just about get us to Plainville."

"Oh, don't do that," Christine says, half pleading, half joking. "Get gas."

She knows how to poke him like that. He liked that in her from the time they met. Christine knows people worry about her husband, and she knows people miss Jennifer, Hayley, and Michaela. Of course. She also knows she fell in love.

The night after they got engaged was New Year's Eve, and they went over to Ron's house to spend the evening with Ron and his wife, Susan. Susan and Jennifer were friends, seeing each other mostly at countless country-club events, and now Susan has taken a real liking to Christine. The Bucchis live in a fabulous house on a suburban cul-de-sac, a house they designed themselves. When Bill and Christine arrived, Susan and Christine went off to the kitchen. As Ron put away their coats, Bill gave him a nudge and told him, almost in a whisper, that he was going to announce to him and Susan that night that he had asked Christine to marry him.

Act happy even if you're not, Bill said.

Ron clapped him on the back and said, What are you talking about? Of course I'm happy!

It was just that Bill, too, knew people worried about him. Nothing to do with Christine. In fact, Christine is perfect.

She's had her bumps, too—nothing even close to what Bill

endured, but nothing to belittle, either. Life. Fortunately for her, Christine's parents gave her the gift of perspective from a young age. When she was growing up, sometimes her family would invite a member of their church to stay with them for a few days, someone who had nowhere else to go. In doing this they were teaching their daughter compassion. Christine's mother is a psychiatric nurse. She works in hospitals and prisons with tough cases. From her, Christine learned how to listen. How to be present and not say anything. Early on when they were dating, if she saw Bill going to a dark place in his mind, she was quiet, just holding his hand. He used to thank her for that. "For what?" she would say. And he would tell her that a lot of people don't know how to not do anything, which was usually what he needed. Just an easy silence.

The nightmares aren't the toughest part. She comforts him as anyone would comfort a child. The toughest part is looking past his unmoving face and trying to read whether at any particular moment he feels unspeakable pain or feels like going out for a sandwich. Sometimes in the car, on the way to an event, they'll be all dressed up, she's cracking jokes, and suddenly the mood in the car just drops like a rock. Sometimes she tries to lift it back up, and sometimes she knows to let it fall.

Slowly, it's getting easier. He had twenty-two years of marriage before, but it's just the beginning for them, and they're learning. And always, she jokes. "You don't like doing dishes, do you? And how'd that go over with Jennifer?"

And Bill laughs.

They drive on, Bill nixing songs on the radio, searching for something he likes. Unionville Avenue turns into North Washington, and they pass a cemetery.

"This is the cemetery that the girls are buried in," Christine says. "We could probably drive by there on the way back."

Bill doesn't say anything at first.

Vox clamantis in deserto.

"Yeah," he says after driving another hundred yards.

It had to be a hundred degrees the day they put that headstone in.

"Depends what time we get back. Sun goes down around 4:10 now," he says.

It took him a good two years, maybe three, to settle on a design, get it made the way he wanted. The funeral itself happened so quickly—the tragedy took place early on a Monday morning, and the funeral was that Friday, the day before the larger memorial service. But the headstone, that took some time, took until long after the violent anguish of that first week had dissolved into the hideous daily routine of trying to live. Once you plant a rock in the grass with their names chiseled into it, it's set in stone, as they say. Right? It's final. When the task is done, and your mind is unoccupied, the gaping maw of the universe comes to swallow you whole. So Bill took his time, worked and worked on the stone, choosing the right one, getting the design just right, the shape. It's Virginia slate, and the man Bill bought it from said it came from so far deep in the earth that it would last five hundred years.

At the top is a circle divided into four parts, each quadrant etched with an image.

A rose, for Michaela Rose. KK Rosebud.

A rower with a long ponytail, powering a scull through the water—how many times had Bill watched Hayley row? (Watching crew was great, he says. You'd drive to some river somewhere at dawn, wrap yourself in blankets against the cold, and wait for two hours, and then—*zoom!*—a boat would whiz in and out of view in two seconds.)

An angel, with the hint of a smile—that represents all three of them. Jennifer was good to her core. The preacher's daughter, not a mean bone. It wasn't that she always thought the best of people or believed that everyone was good. It was that she gave them the *chance* to be good. That was her gift.

A couple of months after the second trial ended, Bill went to

the cemetery. There had been snow on the ground for weeks. Some-times when it's cold and snowy, or when the spring rains come, there aren't many visitors to the cemetery. When Bill went that day, he didn't see many footprints in the snow. Not a lot of visitors lately. It didn't bother him much—people are busy, and it was a cold winter. But he took a picture of the headstone and tweeted it. "5 years, 7 months and 24 days. We will never forget," he wrote. Numbers matter to Bill.

In the fourth part of the circle, Petit chose the Latin inscription *Vox clamantis in deserto.* From the Old Testament. It's the Dartmouth College motto, and he's known it since he was eighteen. Hayley would have graduated two years ago by now.

It means: A voice crying out in the wilderness.

They've repainted the parking spaces on Whiting Street downtown, and Bill isn't sure he likes it. His practice was across the street for eighteen years, and they never had spaces like this. He used to slide his old car into the same spot every day in the lot behind the small brick building that had his name on it. Now he's backing this big boat of a Mercedes that he bought from Ron, 193,000 miles on it, into an end-to-end spot. "Ever since they put these little cutouts here, it seems like it's harder to park," he says, as if to himself. Then he adds, exhaling as he twists around to see how close he is to the minivan behind him, "Perception and reality." The words come out like a shrug.

The office of the Petit Family Foundation is actually an office within an office, a small room with a desk, leased from a company that no longer needs the space. The foundation has two employees: Rolande Petit, the wife of Bill's cousin Tim, who grew up down the street from him, and Hayley Hovhanessian, the daughter of a guy Bill went to high school with. She met Hayley Petit at basketball camp at Miss Porter's School, and they became friends.

Christine says Hayley is the backbone of the foundation.

"Hey, Hayley-girl," Bill says as he and Christine walk into the office. Hayley is the same age Hayley Petit would be, and wears her long brown hair in a ponytail. She has bright saucer eyes that light up when she smiles.

Hayley-girl.

"Hey!" she says, upbeat, grinning through a stack of papers. Bill looks at the yellow Post-it note on the pile. "Uh-oh," he says. "'Bill to Sign.' Oh, crap." Hayley keeps smiling. She knows he doesn't mind signing these letters. They have a system: Hayley and Rolande enter every donation into a database and generate a letter of thanks to be signed by Bill. He comes in a few times a week and signs and signs. If he knows the recipient personally, he crosses out the formal "Dear Mr. and Mrs." and handwrites their first names.

Bill sometimes writes little notes as he signs. He holds one up for Christine.

"Can you read my handwriting at all, or is it just a mess?"

She tries to read: " 'Thank you for . . . this . . . my'—something."

"Thank you for this very generous gift."

Christine frowns and smiles at the same time. "Show me four letters in that word. Show me two, even. Put the front end on the *v* at least." It is the most loving needling you can imagine.

Bill puts the front end on the *v* and moves to the next letter in the pile. "Here's a guy I went to medical school with. He's an an-esthesiologist in Pennsylvania now." He scratches out some words of gratitude on the bottom. Christine peers over his shoulder and reads.

"Very . . . Christmas."

"That's 'Merry Christmas.' Come on."

Hayley-girl.

It just comes out. That's what he used to call his Hayley. Hayley-girl. It just comes out sometimes when he sees Hayley at the office.

The images fly in and out sometimes, unexpected: chestnut hair, a smile like she knew everything would be all right. Six feet by the time she graduated high school. A force of nature.

One of the letters in the stack on Hayley's desk at the foundation is written in a child's hand.

"Oh, these boys are great," Bill says. There are these three brothers, he explains, and every year at their birthday party, instead of asking for presents, they ask their friends to make a donation to the Petit Family Foundation. And they mail a check with a note.

"Dear Dr. Petit," this one says. "How are you? I just had my 10th birthday party. I invited all my friends and family. We celebrated at my favorite place, the Sports Arena. Like my brothers, I wanted to donate my presents to your foundation. I hope these donations help your awesome foundation to help others who are less fortunate."

Bill knows the girls would be proud of the foundation and its mission, especially Jennifer. The next few years will be interesting. See if the donations keep coming. Self-sustainability remains the goal. For now, the board meets every two months, and Bill drives all over the state drumming up support, handing out big cardboard checks, shaking hands, saying a few words, flashing his best smile. He and Christine go to dinners, they go to balls, they go to galas, they go to silent auctions. And the foundation's gifts are growing. The list of recipients is now in the dozens. The annual gift to Prudence Crandall, the women's shelter, grew from $10,000 to a $100,000 multiyear gift. The board gave $4,300 to Pathways/Senderos, a teen-pregnancy prevention center in New Britain, Connecticut. And they awarded another $100,000 gift, to establish a health center in Jennifer's name at the Channel 3 Kids Camp, a retreat that offers special recreation and leadership programs for children of military parents, children with disabilities, and siblings who have been separated in the foster-care system.

"The fact that the Petits not only give financial support but attend our events signals to our other supporters, and to our potential supporters, that ours is a cause that has merit," says Barbara Damon, the director of the Prudence Crandall Center. "It's a morale booster for all of us. We have forty-three employees. Our budget is two million dollars annually, and we have to raise thirty percent of that. The Petit Foundation support has been an important piece of that patchwork as we try to make sure that our services are able to continue from year to year. We're here for people who have been the victims of domestic violence, but we also want to prevent it in the future."

The foundation has also forged a new relationship with Bay Path University, a small women-only undergraduate school in Massachusetts with a heavy focus on science education. Most of the students are first-generation college students from modest backgrounds for whom the Petit Family Foundation's scholarship is the difference that makes it possible for them to attend. "Many of our students are scraping dimes together," says the school's president, Carol Leary. "They take this scholarship very personally. They are struck by the fact that somebody out there believes in them, and that it's this man, Bill Petit. He has a vision for creating something out of his own pain. He is tireless." The school recently opened a new health science center on an eleven-acre campus, and will plant seeds from Michaela's four-o'clocks on the grounds.

A happy consequence of the foundation's momentum is that Bill's niece Abby has come to embrace it. She had recoiled from it at first, but she thought and thought about it, and she watched the work her family put into it, and she saw the good that came out the other end. And eventually she decided to focus on the good it was doing for her uncle Billy, and for her extended family, and for causes all over the state and now the country. She did this on her own, and it felt good, and now she wears a Petit Family Foundation polo shirt to all kinds of events, smiling, helping, starting to feel good again.

For the first few years, Bill did all those appearances alone. His parents were usually there, sure, and Hanna, and Ron, and his brother Glenn, and his friends. Even Gram Triano, at the Ride for Justice, with all those bikers! But when it came time to step up to the podium or cut the ribbon, it was Bill Petit. Now he has a date, a partner, someone to drive there with and drive home with, and that's no small thing. Now he has a wife. His second wife. Miss Christine, he calls her sometimes. Christine, who hangs funky chandeliers and paints things purple. Funny, vivacious Miss Christine, whose laugh is like an aria and who says what she feels and so be it.

"Bill's so good at going to everything," she says, looking over at him. "Those relationships, the face-to-face. So many people have supported the foundation, and so many of those people have their *own* foundations, and they really like it when he's at their events. I bought more dresses this year than in my whole life. Remember we went to that black tie and you were like, Why don't you have anything you can wear? He thinks it's normal to have all these black-tie outfits. He owns a tuxedo. We come from a little bit different lifestyles. But we're converging, right?"

"What black tie did we go to?"

"New Britain."

"Oh yeah. The museum?"

"Yeah, and you can't wear the same dress you wore to the last one—*hello*, same people. And we have three events in the next week and a half that are all dress-up. And we're going with his best friend's wife to every one of them."

"Ron and Susan. So just call Susan and agree to wear the same dress," Bill says.

Christine glares at him, then lets out a laugh that could power a ship across the ocean.

. . . peaceful, easy feeling, and I know you won't let me down.

"Finally," Bill says, settling on a radio station. The Eagles. Familiar territory. He turns the volume up a tiny bit. They're back in the car now, he and Christine, heading over to a fundraiser for the local food bank in downtown Plainville.

'Cause I'm alllll-ready standing . . . on the ground.

"Do-do-do, do-do-do, do-do-do," Bill sings, doing the instrumental part, tapping the wheel.

Christine enters the Central Café before Bill. He's outside talking to his brother Glenn, who's waiting for somebody. But it's cold, so Christine pushes through the door into the dim warmth of the bar.

The thoughts come and go without warning: Glenn, a champion. Sat with Billy every night in the hospital that first week. Went with Hanna to identify the bodies. Told Billy not to go, to remember them as they were. Told him Jen was unrecognizable.

Tickets are twenty bucks a head tonight, all proceeds going to the Plainville Community Food Pantry. You get two free drink tickets—when Bill finally wanders in, he orders a Bud and Christine gets a Guinness. On one side of the bar, a local sports memorabilia dealer has set up a silent auction, mostly framed photographs of Yankee and Red Sox players, many of them autographed. Bill knows the guy from way back, and they look at the stuff. It's only a few minutes after five, so not many people are here yet—no bidders so far. Over in the back corner is a raffle table, and Bill buys a couple of tickets, stuffs them in the box. He knows the ladies doing the raffle, too, and he chats them up over the music.

The owner of the Central carries out trays of hors d'oeuvres a while later, and Bill parks himself by the tables where the food is. There are these little chicken, bacon, and pineapple skewers that are just delicious, and he downs three of them with another Bud. The memorabilia guy is in here now, jabbering away about how's business, this and that. Hanna shows up, gives Billy a hug, and disappears into a circle of girlfriends. Big Bill and Barbara are over talking to somebody, and every couple of minutes somebody walks by and claps Billy on the back or gives him a peck on the cheek.

Bill is standing next to a tray of raw vegetables and creamy dip when two kids walk in, a boy around eight who looks momentarily stunned to be in a bar full of grown-ups, and a bouncing redheaded girl of five or six. "Here comes trouble," Bill says so the kids can hear him, his eyes going wide. The boy stares, the girl just looks up at him with a little grin. Bill scooches down so he's on their level. He grabs a bunch of grapes and swings them in front of the girl's eyes, but she shakes her head. "What? You don't like grapes?" he asks with mock consternation. He turns back to the table, scans it for something they might want. Baby carrots.

The boy says he doesn't like carrots.

"You don't want a—? Well, that's good because this isn't a carrot," Bill says. "It's French. These are hors d'oeuvres, right? This is a *carrot*." He pronounces the word with a thick French accent: cah-roe. The boy giggles a little bit, and the girl takes him up on it and eats the carrot. He asks them about school, about what they want for Christmas, about anything he can think of. He's squatted talking to these kids for a good five minutes, the roomful of grown-ups swirling around him.

At the beginning, after it happened, Bill could hardly stand to be around kids. Even the ones he loved most—especially the ones he loved most. Abby and Andrew. The two pairs of friends. It was too much. He felt like he made the kids miserable. He felt like an ogre, big, sad Uncle Billy, whom they suddenly didn't know how to act around, or how to talk to.

He told Hanna, who responded by saying, Well, you know what? They make you sad and miserable, too, don't they?

He thought about it.

Yeah, of course. Well, no, they didn't make him miserable. He loved them. But—it was overwhelming to be around kids who knew the girls. All he saw were Hayley and Michaela. It wasn't fair to anyone.

Eventually, the boy and the redheaded girl eating the carrot wander away, and Bill stands up from his crouch, the blood rushing back into to his legs, and exhales. A waiter walks by with more chicken-bacon things.

"These are great," he says, walking over to meet Christine at a table where a representative from Hartford Distributors is offering a beer tasting. Bill immediately starts peppering the guy with questions about hops and brewing processes and alcohol-by-volume. He likes to know the details. Bill tries a taste of the Back East IPA, brewed in Bloomfield, about fifteen minutes away. It's too hoppy for him. Christine loves it.

"That's because her taste buds are still strong, because she's younger," he tells the guy, flashing the quick smile.

After a couple of hours at the Central, Bill and Christine start working their way out of the room. Christine is chatting with someone, and Bill is a few steps behind, finishing his beer, talking to some old classmate or another. Right now he's just a guy at a bar, having a good time.

And then, "Excuse me, Dr. Petit?"

A woman wearing a brown leather coat and hoopy earrings is standing in front of him. She is probably in her forties, with frosted blond hair, warm, forlorn eyes, and a bashful smile. She speaks quietly and politely. "Do you recognize my voice?"

Hoo-boy. This happens sometimes. People approach him, people he met once maybe, who remember him because he's Bill Petit, but who, for him, are part of an endless parade of truly kind, truly nice people whose names are sometimes hard to place. He purses his lips and looks at the floor.

"Okay, talk a little more so I have a chance," he says.

She says her name is Lynn, and that they've talked a lot over the years. Bill is really trying, closing his eyes now as she speaks. He finally opens them and looks at her for help. It turns out she worked at one of the answering services his medical practice used, so she called him probably a hundred times over the years with messages from patients, at all hours.

"Yes!" he says.

Lynn smiles. She doesn't get too close to Bill. "I always wanted to come up to you during one of the road races, but I didn't want to bother you," she says. "I just wanted to say I'm sorry." He gives her a little hug, thanks her, and follows his wife out into the night.

As busy as he was in his medical career, the foundation business keeps him almost as busy now. Today he is standing in the cafeteria of the Connecticut Children's Medical Center at Hartford Hospital, staring at a man made out of Legos. It's a chilly blue December afternoon outside. Inside, the cafeteria is almost empty. The room, all bright colors and happy posters, is at the base of a swirling atrium that rises up six floors. It looks like the bottom of a missile silo decorated by children. Rainbow crepe-paper mobiles bob from the ceiling. Most of the floor tiles are gray, but there are oases of color mixed in—tiles the color of mustard, maroon tiles, royal-blue tiles, tiles the color of pencil erasers. They shine and squeak. The air smells like french fries. Off in a corner, a security guard pays for a Snapple, joking in Spanish with the girl behind the register.

The Petit Family Foundation gave a $500 grant to the knitting club at Bulkeley High School, a fortress of a school in a poor, banged-up part of Hartford. Some of the girls have knit scarves and hats for the sick children in the hospital, and they've come to deliver their gifts. Wilma Hoffman, the lady with orange beauty-parlor hair who runs the club, invited Bill to come. He is always invited to come, and he always shows up. It's important, he thinks, to go. Lets people know he appreciates the good work they do.

The Lego man is life-size, just a few inches shorter than Bill. The statue is holding two Lego crates brimming with Lego vegetables—Lego tomatoes, Lego lettuce, Lego onions—between its muscular

Lego forearms. It stands at the entrance to the food area, knees bent slightly under the imaginary weight of the vegetables, beaming a Lego smile, as if it had just arrived with the day's ingredients. Somebody worked for a long time on this. Bill pauses before the toy man, raises his eyebrows for a second, like a heartbeat on a cardiograph. His wife's camera is around his neck, and he takes a picture.

This is a fun one, the knitting club. The half dozen students here with Wilma don't say much aside from some nudged whispers among one another. An exchange student from Burma speaks not a word as she presents Bill with a knit cap, which he puts on, making a goofy face. Another girl, Cristal, who could be a junior but has the round, bright face of a girl a few years younger, sits on a radiator, knitting. Wilma announces to everyone that Cristal is knitting a hat for her six-month-old baby.

Wilma is great. Some people, you'd give them five hundred bucks and they'd say thanks, see you later. Not Wilma. She sends in every receipt—twelve dollars and forty-five cents for yarn, everything—so that the foundation can see where its money is going. Exactitude. Bill loves it. And Wilma is amusing, the way she leads her girls around the hospital talking about the power of knitting, trying to get them to talk.

It's just—strange. There was a time he would have been in this building wearing a white coat and a beeper on his belt. Now he's here wearing pleated khakis and a cap knit by a girl from Burma, sitting in an empty cafeteria next to a giant man made out of Legos. Cartoons play in closed caption on a flatscreen on the wall. But all he has to do is glance over at Christine and his heart slows down again, feels warm again. Wilma asks Bill if he wants to say anything. The girls stare and fidget. He pauses, then begins: "What you do to help others probably makes you all feel better as well." His voice is soft, and he clips each sentence at the end, letting a beat pass before starting the next. "And while doing those things, you're teaching your classmates about caring for other people. You set off a chain reaction. People say, Huh, they're taking their time and doing this, maybe there's something to it. So it's very nice for you to set the example, especially at your age, help other people with things, and not expecting anything in return."

He pauses, and Wilma talks a little more, makes a spirited but futile effort to get the girls to participate. ("Who wants to say something about why they enjoy knitting?") Then Bill starts speaking again.

"You're quiet leaders," he says. His voice is quieter than before even, the words coming out slowly, just a few at a time. The girls all look up when he says that.

He is looking past the girls now, past Wilma, past this dim, sterile, hot room to another anonymous, institutional room. A small part of his mind is back in Courtroom 6A, New Haven Superior Courthouse.

Hayley went to Sunday school each week and all the teachers wanted her in their class, as she was a natural leader—though quiet.

His impact statement. That phrase, "quiet leader." People used it so many times to describe Hayley after she died. Michaela, too.

I learned many things from Michaela's teachers after she died that I wish they had told me before. One teacher said she always made an effort to go over to someone who was ignored by others in the class.

The impact statement serves no obvious legal purpose—the life-or-death decision has already been made—but, in Bill's mind, it let the record show that when Michaela Rose Petit drew her last breath in her bed, and when Hayley Elizabeth Petit collapsed in the upstairs hall just outside her bedroom, running to try to save her family, and when Jennifer Lynn Hawke-Petit's larynx was crushed by the hands of a stranger—in the horrible few minutes that those three heinous and incomprehensible events transpired, the world became a poorer place, and hell if Bill wasn't going to let the record show it, legal purposes or not.

*I miss Michaela running to the door and yelling "Da-da's home!"
On Friday nights, when she went to Great-grandma's house, she always called my cell phone and wanted to know when I would be
there and what I wanted for dinner. When I arrived, she made a
great show of serving me specially and watching me eat. . . .*

*When you are with someone twenty-six years, it takes a long
time for habits to change. For months, and still on occasion, I start to
think, "I'll just ask Jen" . . .*

*What do I miss? I miss my entire family, my home, everything
we had together as a group. . . .*

"Well, this has been very, very nice." Wilma is thanking Dr.
Petit and the cheery hospital administrators for hosting the girls
from the knitting club. "I'm sure the girls appreciate this."

And Bill stands, folds his knit cap into the pocket of his winter jacket, places his wife's hand in his, and turns up his lips into a
smile.

Christine warms some apple pie and plops a dollop of whipped
cream on it for her husband. Outside the sliding doors, the colored
lights she strung on the deck hang like planets against the black
backdrop of the invisible river beyond.

He sits in his chair, scooping up the pie.

It's getting late, but not for him. He used to take sleep medication after the murders. He didn't sleep more than two hours in a
night for the first three months, but finally he found something to
help him. The problem then was, the more sleep he got, the more
nightmares he had. And the deeper he slept, the greater the chances
that he would wake up in the morning and, for that wonderful, terrible split second, forget.

He doesn't use the pills much anymore. But he gets about five
hours, which isn't bad. He's gotten used to just not sleeping much.
But on a bad night—on a bad night he's lucky to get three hours.

"In the beginning, it was always that night," he says. "In the beginning it was always late at night, since it started to happen at two or three in the morning"—that's when the men broke in—"so I'd be bolt-awake at 3:00 a.m. just like clockwork, no matter what. And then it sorta switched to the mornings. The mornings got bad. It would just always be right in front of me." Those men again, come to end the world. Bill holds his palm, rigid, an inch from his nose. "Right in front of your face."

During Bill's waking hours, Christine is determined to chase away some of the darkness. To remember to be happy, to have some fun. She understands the irony of her position, knows that if all had gone according to plan, Bill never would have married her, because Jennifer would be alive. Which is a strange thing. But she gets that. And she never wants him to forget one minute of that life he built, that life he loved. For eighteen years he lived in the same house, slept in the same bed with the same woman. When he reached over to turn on the light by his bed, his hand knew where to go in the darkness.

She can't replicate that, and she's not trying to.

Life after death requires great effort, and she gets down sometimes, too. But Christine is also warm, and vital, and in life it's just good to have someone to hold you as you sleep. Before they started dating, she saw Bill mostly through her camera lens. Smaller than life, drifting around the frame, his lips moving as he spoke to someone on the other side of the room. "I looked at him and watched him for years at those events, because I had to photograph *him*," she says. "They needed *his* photo. And it was years before I could even get a smile. But then he sorta started to—you could just see things changing. Things were starting to lift just a little. And then there was this humor that was just shocking. When he's in a good mood, forget it. Which was hugely important to me. Because you don't want to be involved with someone who you can't have a normal life with. Who's not going to be fun."

She tucks her feet underneath her on the chair, pulls on the sleeves of her sweater, cups her tea with both hands. Bill is done with his pie. Christine looks over and smiles at him.

"Right?"

Bill sits at a round table in a cavernous and ornate banquet hall that used to be a bank. The building must be a hundred years old. The ceiling climbs up three stories like a golden sky, held aloft by marble columns anchored in limestone and bronze. The place is a relic from the days when people used to have to make a trip into town to do their banking. Now it's a party space, and Bill is sitting in the middle of it wearing a tuxedo, surrounded by hundreds of other men in tuxedos and women wearing their once-a-year gowns. There's a United States senator a few tables away, hasn't touched his wine. Dentists, insurance executives, and lawyers sit at the round tables, a state legislator here and there, picking at the last of their filets of beef, and the risotto with the scallops and some kind of mint sauce, which was pretty good for gala food. Better than at a lot of these things.

Bill takes a bite and makes a face that says, *Not bad.*

Most people in the room are interested in him more than anyone else. They steal looks at him. If they achieve eye contact with him, they offer a quick, knowing smile, the way some people do when they find themselves on an elevator with a celebrity. Even after all this time—it is 2013, and in July it will be six years since the murders—people stare at him from across the buzzing room, shaking their heads a little, almost imperceptibly, dumbstruck.

Tonight Bill is the honorary chairman of this gala, the annual fundraiser for Interval House, a shelter for the victims of domestic violence. The Petit Family Foundation has been a big supporter of Interval House. It's a cause for which he would do just about anything, but tonight all he has to do is let them put his name in the program, wear his tux, shake hands, say a few words at the podium. He is seated at table one, front and center, next to the dance floor, under the swirling balcony and the high, gold dome, pushing around the food on his plate, waving at friends and at people who look like he should know them.

Last night, with a brutal suddenness, sadness swept over his family again. Dennis, Hanna's husband of twenty-three years, Abby and Andrew's dad, Hayley and Michaela's uncle, and Bill's brother-in-law, died unexpectedly in the middle of the night. Hanna is distraught, of course. Bill's instinct is to be there for her, but she told him that of course he should go to the gala. He doesn't need to sit at her house and mourn. Dennis was a kind, gentle man, but strong. He grew up on a farm in Nebraska, understood work, and understood family. He attended the trials every day he could get away from work. And he came up with the idea for Michaela's Garden. He knew about agriculture from his childhood, and he said to Hanna that maybe this could be his contribution. He presented the idea to the foundation's board, they loved it, and it became not only a successful fundraiser but a project that made people feel better about the world. Everyone was supposed to be here tonight—Big Bill and Barbara, Hanna and Dennis. But Bill and Christine are the only Petits here.

Somebody introduces the local sports-talk radio guy, well-known in these parts, been around forever, who will lead the live auction. As the crowd claps, Bill puts down his program, cups one hand around his mouth, and lets out a quick holler.

"Whoo-woooo!"

After almost five years as the president of the foundation, he has learned the routine of these black-tie things, their customs and idiosyncrasies. He has learned how to have a good time.

He leans back in his black party-rental chair and takes a small gulp of chardonnay, finds a place to set the glass down amid the smartphones and smeared plates that clutter the white tablecloth, and looks down at the printed program to see what's up for bid tonight, his bow tie tilting a little under his trimmed pebble-gray beard.

Just then, a hand on his shoulder.

Christine.

Bill looks up and smiles.

She was a couple of tables away, chatting with someone they know vaguely. She is here now, at his side. She folds into her seat, crosses her legs, slides her phone under the lip of a china saucer, brushes a lock of hair behind her ear. She looks fabulous in that dress, he thinks, white geometric shapes floating on bright blue satin. She straightened her wavy blond hair tonight, and it draws attention to her sudden smile.

Always her smile. When she walks into a room she brings a crackling light, like the first half-second a match is lit, that makes everyone sit up and smile and watch her. Whenever she walks into a room, Bill feels a certain peace.

She bought the bow tie for him. It's black, with white stripes *and* white polka dots—both, you ever see that before? She found it at some expensive store, he tells his friend. He likes it. Because she likes it.

You see friends at these things. Also at table one: Hayley Hovhanessian's parents, and another of Bill's old friends from Plainville, who brought his new girlfriend. You have a couple of drinks, and people come up and say nice things. You have to smile a lot, have to give a lot of hugs, and you have to make a lot of small talk, which over three or four hours can be exhausting. You try to remember names. And on plenty of nights, he has to say a few words. But mostly what Bill likes to do at these things is clown around with Christine.

All the other people in this room lead invisible lives, just like most of the people we see every day. We see them, but we have no idea how they came to be who they are—the kids who bullied them and the parents who raised them, the natural intelligence that made everything seem easy or the insecurities that drove them harder. We don't have any clue about their private pains and joys—the new job with double the pay, the favorite uncle who died the day before his birthday, the lump in the breast, the child who made the honor roll. Everyone we see is just a person pushing a shopping cart down the aisle, or driving a car in the next lane, or sitting through the same meeting we are. But not Bill Petit, not anymore. He no longer has the privilege of anonymity. When most people see him, they see a man whose family was tortured and then murdered in their own house—in *his* house—while he sat helpless in the basement, tied up and losing blood. They look at him and they wonder how he does it—how he goes on living. They wonder if they could do it. They wonder what kind of man he is that he can.

"Bill," Christine says, tapping her program. He's chatting with his friend, but he turns to her. She looks up at him, her finger on the program, and he looks down at it.

"Okay, yup," he says. It's the next item up for auction: lunch with the mayor of Hartford. Someone breaks the opening bid of $500.

"A thousand? A thousand dollars," shouts the local sportscaster who's emceeing.

Bill raises his program, which doubles as an auction paddle. The sportscaster points at him.

"Thank you, Dr. Petit! Do I hear fifteen hundred?"

He scans the room, index finger aloft, like some crazed bandleader. "Fifteen hundred? Going once—"

And suddenly a photographer standing in the back of the room—what looks like a skinny twenty-year-old kid, long-lens camera slung around his neck, bulky bag of equipment over his shoulder—raises his program.

"Fifteen hundred! Sold, to the back of the room."

Bill slumps in his chair and pretends to be devastated. "I got beat by the *photographer*?"

People want pictures. All night long, people walk up with their phones out and ask for a picture with Dr. Petit. Friends of friends, friends of friends of friends. He doesn't mind. He's got his smile down—mouth hanging open a little, as if he's mid-chuckle—and he actually looks happy in a lot of shots. In between, he sits back down, eats a little more of whatever they're serving.

"Whoo-wooo!" he hollers when somebody wins dinner with Geno Auriemma, the coach of the University of Connecticut women's basketball team, who's been the coach since Bill first started taking Hayley to games in the early 1990s.

It's getting late. The auction is over, and people are starting to dance to the four-piece soft-shoe band. The drummer looks exactly like Garrison Keillor, a hangdog face bopping vaguely to the beat under a wispy mop of hair. Folded-up programs are strewn across the dinner tables. Bill's lies next to his plate, open to the back page, a full-page ad for the Petit Family Foundation, which shows a black-and-white photo of Bill, Jennifer, Hayley, and Michaela at Hayley's graduation from Miss Porter's.

The servers rush to get the dessert plates down before everybody drifts off into the night. Christine recognizes the Latino waiter pouring coffee—he was passing these ridiculous shrimp tempura during cocktail hour, and she had hounded him. "Hey! No more shrimp?" she hoots at him with that ready smile, as if she's hoping for a great comeback. Christine has the gift of being able to talk to anyone—child, CEO, waiter—with an easy charm. The waiter freezes for a second, not used to joking around with the people he serves, but this woman is beaming at him, sharing a joke, telling him with her eyes and her smile that it's okay, we're all just people in a room.

"No," he says with a shy grin. "Would you like coffee?"

Bill stares at the dessert in front of him. It's a glass slipper made out of chocolate, with tufts of chocolate mousse piped in where the woman's foot would go.

"I don't know how to eat it," he says. He's looking at it the way a child might look who has just been served a whole lobster for the first time. "You just pick it up?"

"Oh, wait, this I have to capture," Christine says, clicking on her iPhone camera. "Hold on."

Bill poses with the shoe in his mouth, holding it there, waiting for her to take the picture.

"Gross," she says finally. "Okay, forget it, this is too weird."

Bill shrugs, chews a bite of the chocolate slipper, wipes his mouth, and drops his napkin on his knee. He draws in a long, deep breath as he looks around the gilded room at the men wearing tuxedoes dancing with their wives, the four-piece band playing "Old Time Rock and Roll" and the chocolate slippers and the local meteorologist holding court and the senator's now-empty chair and the sea of wineglasses reflecting the golden light of the room. Then he looks at his wife next to him, puts his arm around her to pull her close, leans over, and kisses her.

God shall wipe away all tears from their eyes; and there shall be no more death, neither sorrow, nor crying, neither shall there be any more pain: for the former things have passed away.

—Revelation 21:4, tweeted by Bill Petit,
April 2015

A NEW KIND OF DAWN

BILL HAD been here before. A lifetime ago.

When a man walks into the hospital with his wife as she is about to give birth for the first time, he is nowhere else. There is nothing else he can think about, because his purpose in life is suddenly and unbelievably clear, and it doesn't extend beyond the now: He exists to get her from the car to the delivery room and then stand by her bedside for as many hours as it takes. That's it. And after the hospital's automatic sliding doors close behind him, the world outside disappears. The parking lot, the roads and the trees, the wars raging in faraway countries, the mortgage payment due, the darkness or light outside the windows, the rain or the wind, the rattling in the engine, the unreturned calls—it all peels away, totally unimportant. There is no room for any of it. He is nervous and dutiful, alert and yet in a fog. At the bedside, he watches his wife breathe and sweat and endure pain and fatigue worse than any athlete he's ever seen on any field. He has known in the abstract that this was coming for many months, but now that it's here he is worried he will forget something, some responsibility or function that he must perform.

Bill had the advantage of being a doctor, so at least the hospital, odd-smelling and uncomfortably fluorescent to most new fathers, was familiar to him. And it was his hospital, the Hospital of Central Connecticut—the hospital he used to feel sometimes as if he lived in back when he was practicing, all those rounds and early mornings and late nights and unplanned stops on a Saturday afternoon to check on this patient or that. He knew the place, and the people knew him. He also had the advantage of having been a part of something like this, though it was many years before.

This time, it was a crisp night at the end of a cold fall. The ends of the branches on the maple trees along the Farmington River were already brittle. Hanna was there, right in the delivery room. Andrew and Abby were outside, anxious to meet their new cousin. Bill Sr. and Barbara. On Saturday, November 23, 2013, at 2:24 a.m., the darkest part of the night, Christine gave birth to a baby boy, William Arthur Petit III. Six pounds, fourteen ounces, and a long nineteen inches. He was perfect. To a lot of people who knew Bill's story—people around Connecticut, people who read about him in *People* magazine or remembered him from the Oprah show—the baby was a gift from above, a symbol of hope and resurrection, a miracle. Christine and Bill understood that, of course. And even at the hospital, there was an overwhelming emotion in the air, perhaps a sudden realization that yes, the birth of this baby was indeed momentous and heralded the rebirth of his father's soul. Christine and Bill understood this, too. But to them, to his parents, William was a miracle the way every baby is a miracle to every mother and father. He wasn't a prince or a symbol. He was their boy.

Almost from the beginning, the baby was known as Little Bill, and Bill took him everywhere. Down to the office on Whiting Street, where Hayley and Rolande would lean in close and welcome him to the world. Over to Bill's parents' house on Red Stone Hill, of course—all the time. To UConn basketball games—he was born at the beginning of the season, and before he was six months old, both the men's and the women's teams won the national championship, a rare occurrence in the world of college athletics. Bill and Christine took Little Bill to his first fundraising gala when he was four months old, an event for Jane Doe No More, an organization that helps victims of sexual assault to which the Petit Family Foundation recently gave a $13,000 gift. (Part of the gift will help Jane Doe No More offer free self-defense classes to women and girls across

Connecticut. So far more than 3,000 people have taken part. "We are so grateful," says Donna Palomba, who founded the organization after she was raped by an intruder in her home. "It's amazing how Bill hasn't given up, like so many people would have.")

To the gala Bill wore a houndstooth blazer and a pink shirt, Christine wore a stunning white dress with black stripes, and Little Bill wore a onesie that had a pocket square. They took him to the golf tournament, where Christine photographed him in the warm sunlight, crawling around, studying the manicured grass, wearing madras pants and a baby bowler hat over his sandy curls. Bill went to Little Bill's pediatrician appointments, took him to meetings, and took him to a local TV station when he was filming a commercial for the foundation.

Hanna expected, or hoped, anyway, that the baby would be a jolt for Bill, but even she was shocked by the energy Bill suddenly had. Ron, for his part, wasn't sure he would ever see his friend this happy again, and yet here he was. Christine and Little Bill—LB, to friends and family—had given Bill not only happiness but purpose. A lot of new fathers feel something like this, a new and permanent sense of duty that comes with being responsible for a person's life, health, and happiness. They see that this tiny person they've created can't live without them, and suddenly their days at work have a clearer goal, and their weekends and early mornings become sacred for a new reason. They are dimly aware that every man they know also has kids, and that those men's children are the center of their universe, but all that really matters is their own child. For Bill, however, the new sense of purpose was a little different. More than six years ago, he had been well along in the process of raising a family, and the job of raising Hayley and Michaela was more important to him than being a doctor or a son or even a husband. The job had been ripped from him, not by illness or accident or any of the usual tragedies, but by torture and excruciating cruelty. By evil. When the girls, all three of them, were gone, and when he had not been able to save them, what possible reason could there be for him to continue to draw breath?

His life, unequivocally, had been over. And now, impossibly, this.

In the months before Little Bill was born, Christine had found a studio and office space for her photography business, Le Petit Studio. The work was picking up, and she was shooting everything from weddings and headshots to baby pictures and family portraits. She had worked as a newspaper reporter early in her career, and credited that experience with teaching her to find the moments that matter.

Just as Christine was opening her studio, Bill was being recruited hard by the Connecticut Republican party to run for Congress. Through his ordeal, he had become known as both a steadfast champion of his family's memory and also as a staunch advocate for capital punishment. He took the appeals to run for office seriously, saying in the fall of 2013 that he was "50-50" on the proposition. Of course, he had other things to consider as well. "Just married a year, a new baby due in eight weeks," he said. In the end, the other considerations won out, and Bill decided against mounting a campaign. He, too, has learned a great deal about the moments that matter.

Abby babysits Little Bill a lot. Her office is in the same suite as the Petit Family Foundation's—she sells airtime to advertisers for a local radio network—so she sees Bill and Christine and the baby all the time. Before, when she was growing up with Hayley, she always wanted to impress her uncle Bill. She saved her smartest questions for him, always tried to show him what she knew. He brought that out in people. Now it's different. If you sit back and try to hold on to what was, she says, you'll never be able to understand this new happiness, this new blessing. She has always loved her uncle, but now, on a lot of days, she feels even closer to him than she did before, back when she would wake up in his house on all those weekend mornings, lolling around in Hayley's sun-filled room or bouncing on the trampoline while Uncle Billy worked on his flowers and his lawn. Now that he has a wonderful new wife and a beautiful new baby, Abby feels like herself again around him. He's funny, and he's fun—that's what Christine and Little Bill have done for him. Abby couldn't imagine a better partner for Bill than Christine, and she can't wait to tell Little Bill all about Hayley and Michaela when he gets older. And seeing her grandparents, Bill Sr. and Barbara, with the baby—they're in their eighties but they act like kids around him, and Abby just smiles at the bittersweetness of it all, at the gift of this child. New life doesn't make everything better, and it doesn't bring anyone back. But it restores hope to life, and hope is the difference between living and merely existing. For years after the murders, Abby didn't cry at all. She was never happy, and never really sad. She felt nothing. And now when Bill lumbers into the room with Little Bill in his arms, smiling, making funny faces and silly noises, a diaper bag over his shoulder and the creases of an exhausted smile fanning from the corners of his eyes—when that happens, Abby feels a happiness she had forgotten was possible.

Of course it was just yesterday that Bill was holding baby Hayley in his arms, or hoisting Michaela through his office showing her off. How he loved to nuzzle his tiny girls, the depth of feeling almost incomprehensible to him, his emotions beyond words. And beyond words is where Bill is at this moment, a different man in the same body as he hoists Little Bill through the office of the foundation he has made to remember the boy's sisters and their selfless mother. Look at the man's silent face, a picture of peace and pleasure as he holds on to the life he has made.

Bill never slept all that much to begin with. Even before, when his daughters were growing up and he was seeing patients until all hours and giving lectures all over the place and going to their games and Hayley's races and growing his flowers and writing a book and being everything to everybody, his sleep patterns were not patterns at all but rather Bill just closing his eyes when he had no other choice. And then after it happened, there were the years when he simply did not sleep, the delirium stretching for months at a time. Life, it seemed, would forever be one long sleepless night. Those were the days when if he could will himself to stay positive for a few consecutive minutes, it was a big deal. Then Christine came and filled the dark corners of his mind with light when he needed her to, and let them hide in blackness when he needed that, too. And now with the baby, Bill's boy, that hole in his heart seems a little smaller. The dark days still come, and maybe they always will. Sometimes he still gets pensive, and lost in thought, and he might turn to you over a beer at the bar down the street from his house, an old blues musician up on the stage wailing away on the harmonica, grab your shoulder, and say, seemingly out of nowhere, "Spend time with your kids," a piece of advice you have heard before but that, coming from this man, knocks you in the stomach, and that you will think of on Saturday mornings when your children wake you up and ask you to play, and that you will never, ever forget.

But now, instead of minutes, Bill Petit is able to string together stretches of good hours, entire portions of a day when he feels good. Absolutely, unapologetically, and completely *good*. The long night has given way to a new kind of dawn, filled with the sunshine of a little boy's smile.

Bill changes diapers in the middle of the night. Feeds the boy, walks him around bouncing him, calms him if he's crying. He's fifty-seven years old and has an eight-month-old baby, but he feels healthy, all things considered. If he's tired, he's no more tired than he's ever been. And while he loves whisking his boy all over the place, because it's never too early to see what the world is like, some of the best times are at home, in the little house by the river, his wife there, her knees tucked under her in the chair by the big window, the water rushing by outside, water boiling for tea on the electric stove, when Bill settles his hulking frame onto the couch, the afghan blanket under his head, and he can feel the pressure dissipate from his body as his bones settle, and Little Bill lies on his chest, and the two of them slowly close their eyes, the baby rising and falling gently with his father's breath, his tiny pink fingers twitching a little as he learns how to dream, and for a peaceful, perfect hour together, they sleep.

AUTHOR'S NOTE

I GREW UP in Connecticut, about a twenty-five-minute drive from Cheshire, where Bill Petit and his family lived the night they were attacked. My town was a lot like Cheshire: suburban, peaceful, and possessive of a strong sense of community. Safe. A good place to raise a family. I remember thinking when it happened that it could have been my house, on my street, in my town.

Three years later I was living in New York City and working as an editor at *Esquire* when, visiting my parents back in Connecticut for the weekend, I heard Bill Petit's voice on the radio. He was welcoming the public to attend the annual 5K road race that would benefit the foundation he had set up in memory of his wife and daughters. His voice sounded strong and healthy, and it was shocking. I felt compelled to find out more about this person and how he had found a way to live his life. I asked the editor in chief of *Esquire*, David Granger, if I could do the story. I told him that it struck me as a story of survival and redemption, and I hoped it was. Knowing next to nothing about Petit, judging mostly by the sound of his voice, I thought that the fact that Bill Petit was still alive enough to even have a voice might be inspiring to people.

For the next few months, I was in New Haven almost every day, attending the proceedings in *State of Connecticut v. Steven Hayes.* I soon learned that most of the several dozen other reporters in the courtroom every day also wanted to interview Bill Petit, but that

Bill Petit didn't give interviews. I eventually called Rick Healey, a lawyer and Petit family friend who acted as a sort of liaison with the media, who confirmed as much. After the trial, I began making calls to whomever I could think of outside of Petit's family and close friends: a woman with whom he had coauthored a reference book on diabetes, college classmates, reporters who had covered the actual crime. Few people would talk to me without Petit's permission. A few days later I received a call from Healey, who had heard about some of my inquiries and asked if I was actually going ahead with a story. I told him I was. Healey said that in that case, he had spoken with Bill, and I was hereby authorized to interview some of those closest to him: his sister, Hanna; his father, Bill Sr.; his oldest friend, Ron Bucchi; and a former close medical colleague, Steve Hanks.

In addition to the access Petit (through Healey) granted, I continued to seek out and interview people outside his inner circle and to conduct independent research. I attended the trials of Steven Hayes and Joshua Komisarjevsky almost in their entirety.

Eventually Bill married again, to the former Christine Paluf, and I wanted to write a second story for *Esquire.* For this I would need access to Bill himself. I called Ron Bucchi and explained my desire to write another story that would show readers that it was possible to embrace life even after such unspeakable evil. Ron arranged a dinner with himself, Bill, and me at a restaurant Bill liked. This was the first time I ever met Bill. I told him that after the first story was published, I had heard from many people who said they felt inspired by him, and that they thought about him often as they dealt with whatever troubles their own lives brought. I told him I wanted to write another story so that as many people as possible could know about him and, maybe, feel inspired, too.

I ended up interviewing Bill and Christine extensively, at their home, at foundation events, and over meals, and I will be forever grateful for their generosity, hospitality, and candor. I also once again found value in seeking information independent of Bill to make sure the story was as complete as possible. The same was true in writing this book. I am indebted to everyone who spoke to me, many of whom revisited painful memories in their efforts to help me fully understand the story.

A list of all those interviewed, in addition to Bill and Christine Petit, is as follows:

Hanna Petit-Chapman, who was unfailingly patient, honest, and kind during our interviews, and I thank her for every minute of them;

Ron Bucchi, who offered not only stories and insights about his friend's life but advice and guidance whenever I needed it, often accompanied by a glass of good whiskey;

Bill's parents, Bill Sr. and Barbara Petit, who were generous with their time and their thoughts, and I truly appreciate their support;

Cynthia Renn, Jennifer's sister, who spent many hours on the phone telling me about Jennifer's life before and after meeting Bill Petit;

the late Dennis Chapman, Hanna's husband, a kind and thoughtful man who spoke eloquently about his brother-in-law and about Jennifer, Hayley, and Michaela;

Abby and Andrew Chapman, Dennis and Hanna's two extraordinary children;

Patty Poisson and her remarkable children, Otis and Mairi;

Jeremiah Donovan, who spoke with me patiently and at length about his own life and the unique nature of his work;

and others who shared essential remembrances, insights, and bits of information: Steve Hanks, Susan Bucchi, the Reverend Stephen Volpe, Herb Graham, Sue Haigh, Todd Bussert, Terry Donovan, Jerry Kristafer, and Hayley Hovhanessian. Additional sources include the Plainville Public Library and the Rauner Special Collections Library at Dartmouth College.

ACKNOWLEDGMENTS

WITHOUT THE generous and trusting participation of Bill Petit and his wife, Christine, when I was reporting two feature stories for *Esquire*, this book would not have been possible. They spent many long hours answering every question I had with care and thoughtfulness, and I will be forever grateful for their openness, their time, and their trust. Bill also facilitated interviews with members of his family and his close friends, which was invaluable.

Hanna Petit-Chapman, Ron Bucchi, and Bill Sr. and Barbara Petit were incredibly kind and open to talking with me, and my interviews with them are a large part of the foundation of this book. (The names and contributions of other people I interviewed can be found in the Author's Note.)

I owe an insurmountable debt to David Granger, the editor in chief of *Esquire*, for his encouragement and support. I have learned more from him, about a great many things, than he could know.

Mark Warren, my editor at *Esquire*, was a guiding force from the day I set out to write about Bill Petit. He is a tireless teacher who cares deeply about stories and their power. I leaned on him at every turn.

My agent, Richard Pine, is as cool as they come, and his wise words kept me on track more than once. I want also to thank Rick Horgan, the editor who acquired this book for Crown and was its early champion, and Kevin Doughten, who edited it with compassion, reason, and clarity. And a thank-you to Claire Potter at Crown for making sure it all happened something close to on time.

I first knew Rick Healey, a member of the Petit Family Foundation who served as the family's liaison with reporters, as a stranger on the other end of the phone, but in time he became a friendly sounding board. As the man wedged between the media and the Petit family, he showed nothing but wisdom and grace.

Several fellow reporters offered selfless assistance to me, a novice courtroom reporter, during the trials: Robert Goulston of WFSB showed me the ropes and has become a good friend, as has Bill Glaberson of the *New York Times*, whose wit and experience heightened the quality of my own work. Helen Ubinas of the *Hartford Courant* and Erin Cox of WTNH shared freely their veteran advice, and Randall Beach of the *New Haven Register* helped me with his recollections and insights.

My sister Elizabeth Carpenter and her husband, Joe, opened their house to me during long stints reporting in New Haven, and I always felt at home and well fed. My father-in-law, John Moran, did the same while I was writing, providing a quiet retreat on the shores of the Chesapeake. I also spent a week in my childhood bedroom writing without being interrupted except for perfect dinners with my parents, evenings I will never forget. Yvonne Fisher, my mother-in-law, helped immensely throughout the project.

I was extremely lucky to have a handful of highly intelligent people to read this book at various stages and offer much-needed critiques: Kendall Hamilton, Jon Gluck, Peter Heimbold, Robert Goulston, my mother, Sheila D'Agostino, and my brother Michael, who stayed up all night—twice—so I could read it to him. Each of them made the book better.

Thanks also to John Kenney, peerless copy editor, for his careful reading of this story over the course of several years, and for his many words of wisdom. And to João Canziani, for his amazing photographs.

In the Connecticut Judicial Branch: head marshal Thomas Bouley, public affairs officers Rhonda Hebert and Melissa Farley, and court reporter Jean Kindley are all true professionals who were always willing to help.

Thank you also to Andy Ward, Lindsay and Rett Coluccio, Eloise Bune D'Agostino, Margo Estrada, Susan and Richard Romanski, Chris Jones, Tom Junod, Tom Chiarella, Cal Fussman, Francine Maroukian, Katie Heimbold, Margaret Felice, Peter Griffin, Ross McCammon, Rich Dorment, Tyler Cabot, Peter Martin, Michael Norseng, Lisa Hintelmann, Ellen Levine, Lucy Kaylin, Gayle King, Alexandra Carlin, and David Curcurito, all of whom helped me in significant ways.

The three people to whom I owe the most are my sons and my wise and loving wife, Sarah, who was unflinching with her support from beginning to end, listening to me every night and encouraging me every day. Her strength, her patience, and her capacity for love astonish and inspire me constantly.

I look forward to the day when our two boys are old enough to read this book, so that they, too, can be inspired by the man at its center.

ABOUT THE AUTHOR

Ryan D'Agostino is the editor in chief of *Popular Mechanics* magazine. Previously, he was an editor at *Esquire*, and he has written for *The New Yorker, Ski,* and other publications. He lives in New York with his family.

To learn more about or donate to the Petit Family Foundation, visit petitfamilyfoundation.org. (The Petit Family Foundation is not affiliated with this book nor did it participate in the writing or publication of this book in any way.)